Religious Conscience, the State, and the Law

KNIGHT-CAPRON LIBRARY
LYNCHBURG COLLEGE
LYNCHBURG, VIRGINIA 24501

SUNY Series in Religious Studies
Harold Coward, Editor

Religious Conscience, the State, and the Law

Historical Contexts and Contemporary Significance

John McLaren and Harold Coward,
Editors

KNIGHT-CAPRON LIBRARY
LYNCHBURG COLLEGE
LYNCHBURG, VIRGINIA 24501

State University of New York Press

Published by
State University of New York Press, Albany

© 1999 State University of New York

All rights reserved

Printed in the United States of America

No part of this book may be used or reproduced
in any manner whatsoever without written permission.
No part of this book may be stored in a retrieval system
or transmitted in any form or by any means including
electronic, electrostatic, magnetic tape, mechanical,
photocopying, recording, or otherwise without the
prior permission in writing of the publisher.

For information, address State University of New York
Press, State University Plaza, Albany, NY, 12246

Production by E. Moore
Marketing by Patrick Durocher

Library of Congress Cataloging-in-Publication Data

Religious conscience, the state, and the law : historical contexts and
contemporary significance / John McLaren and Harold Coward, editors.
      p.   cm. — (SUNY series in religious studies)
      Includes index.
  ISBN 0-7914-4001-X (alk. paper). — ISBN 0-7914-4002-8 (pbk. :
      alk. paper)
  1. Freedom of religion—United States. 2. Freedom of religion–
–Canada. I. McLaren, John, 1940– . II. Coward, Harold G.
      III. Series
      BV741.R428   1998
323.44′2′09—dc21   97-52270
                                       CIP

10 9 8 7 6 5 4 3 2 1

Contents

KNIGHT-CAPRON LIBRARY
LYNCHBURG COLLEGE
LYNCHBURG, VIRGINIA 24501

v

Acknowledgments

This volume is the result of a team interdisciplinary research project of the Centre for Studies in Religion and Society, University of Victoria, Victoria, B.C., Canada. Historians, scholars of law, and scholars of religion gathered at the Centre from the United Kingdom, Canada, and the United States to contribute their wisdom to the problem of the clash between religious conscience, the state, and the law. After an extended seminar devoted to the critiquing individual presentations, the chapters were thoroughly revised. The project's intellectual leadership was provided by John McLaren holder of the Lansdowne Chair of Law, University of Victoria.

Funding for the project was provided by the faculty of law and the vice-president Academic University of Victoria, The Vancouver Foundation and the Law Foundation of British Colombia. June Bull, the Centre's Secretary, handled the project logistics and Ludgard De Decker, the Centre's administrator, together with Tiffany Tsang, prepared the manuscript for the Press.

Thanks are due to the staff at SUNY Press and especially Nancy Ellegate, editor, for their fine work in the publication of this volume.

HAROLD COWARD

Chapter 1

Introduction

Harold Coward and John McLaren

What are we to do if the dictates of our religious conscience bring us into conflict with the state and its laws? Or, conversely, what are politicians and governments to do if religious people, by following the teachings of their own tradition, seem to endanger others or to threaten the underlying stability of the state? The tension between state or civil authorities and religious belief is as new as today's news from India and as old as the conflict between the Hebrew prophets and the rulers of ancient Israel. Indeed, it is from the prophets and their clashes with the rulers of their day that the term "the prophetic tradition" has arisen—a tradition embodying religious and ethical critiques of secular and majority policy and action, and providing a basis for moral dissent within political communities.[1] Throughout history repression of religion has often occurred when faith communities have not shared the belief of the rulers or the majority of the population, or worse, have been viewed as "infidels" or "heathens" by adhering to an "alien" or "other" religion. Early Christians were viewed this way by the Roman State and subjected to persecution,[2] Jews were treated badly throughout medieval Christendom and in modern Europe.[3] In both western and eastern Europe, Albigensi, Lollards, Hussites, Mennonites, Hutterites, Quakers, and Doukhobors, by virtue of preaching a more personal relationship with God, rejection of materialism, and the primacy of conscience in matters of faith, were branded as heretics by religious and secular authorities.[4] During the colonial period there was the subjugation and attempted destruction of native spirituality around the world.[5]

Of course, there have also been examples of tolerance in history such as in the Iberian Caliphate, the Ottoman Empire, and the Mughal Empire in which Muslim rulers allowed Christian, Jewish, Hindu, or Buddhist communities to practice their own religions.[6] In India, Akbar (1556–1605), the greatest of the Mughal emperors, engaged Hindus in his senior administration, removed the hated *jizya* or poll tax on non-Muslims and welcomed Christian, Parsi, Buddhist, Hindu, and Muslim scholars to dialogue on equal terms in his court.[7] However, even in India, with its reputation for religious tolerance, an example such as Akbar is more the exception than the rule.

In Europe the beginnings of the movement toward toleration based on religious conscience are found in the Reformation and in the Enlightenment thought. In announcing his break with Rome, Martin Luther's proclamation "Here I stand, I can do no other" is the clarion call of an individual religious conscience before the civil authority of the state.[8] However, the Lutheran Church that he occasioned, and the other more institutional reformers such as Calvin in Geneva soon instituted civil rule just as repressive of individual differences as the old Roman orthodoxy. Intolerance was directed to Roman Catholics, to other reformers who had taken different roads, and to non-Christians who were seen as being entirely outside the bounds of tolerance.[9] And as the following chapters will show, this pattern is all too common. Religious groups who have been victims of repression by the state and orthodox religion have not been free of intolerance themselves—when they achieve a role in civic governance or when they face theological challenge from within. Hutterite, Doukhobor, and Mormon history all provide examples of this phenomenon.

Luther's appeal to the individual conscience was significantly strengthened by the Enlightenment movements of the sixteenth and seventeenth centuries. Martin Fitzpatrick in chapter 4 shows how religious toleration came to be viewed in a positive light in the Enlightenment, and how claims of religious conscience came to be accepted. The old approach had been based on the idea that church and state were intertwined, that the King had a divine mission to fulfill on earth, and that it was desirable that all subjects belong to one tradition. In the Enlightenment approach, however, the church was seen as separate from but subordinate to the state and as especially useful in helping preserve social and moral order. Conscience was democratized and seen as the "natural law" present within each person—a moral parallel to the Enlightenment ideas of universal, natural laws in the world of nature. Such a conscience was freed from its Christian dress and could appear within any religion—as indeed it should. The way was thus opened for the kind of cultural and religious pluralism we experience today.

Fitzpatrick shows that the philosophers of the day played a major role in the development of thinking regarding religious liberty and freedom of conscience. Pierre Bayle combined biblical, rational, and skeptical arguments to the effect that individuals were bound by conscience to stand by truth as they understood it, and not to yield to persecution. Such liberty of conscience was a "right" possessed by all persons by virtue of being rational. John Locke agreed with Bayle that individuals should have the right of conscience, the freedom to worship as they pleased but added the safeguard—so long as they did not espouse doctrines harmful to civil authority and society. Thus one should not tolerate those who were intolerant, who owed allegiance to a foreign authority, who did not believe in the moral order, and who could be absolved by their religion of moral and political crimes. Locke's ideas provide a framework within which both religious groups and states could reach a compromise. As Fitzpatrick puts it, religious minorities would try to show that their adherents were loyal citizens and so worthy of toleration, and politicians and civil authorities for their part would see the utilitarian value of allowing religious minorities a measure of toleration. While individuals should have the right to worship as they pleased, in secular affairs religions need to be subordinated to the state. Voltaire, Shaftesbury, and Bishop Butler added to the development of the Enlightenment conception of conscience as the universal moral "inner voice" of human nature. This movement culminates in Rousseau and Kant who, as Fitzpatrick puts it, eliminate both the elements of special grace and expert advice from conscience. With them the inner voice of conscience possesses illumination, conviction, rational persuasion, and has been universalized and democratized. The rights of conscience have become natural rights and the purpose of government is to preserve them. Yet these Enlightenment thinkers still saw an intimate connection between the religious and the natural moral dimensions of conscience. They realized, says Fitzpatrick, that the obligation to follow conscience ultimately arose from a religious duty. Religious toleration would allow all the freedom to actualize that duty and thus result in a flourishing of moral conscience and good order in society. Behind this, of course, is the Enlightenment assumption, currently being put to the test, that the actualization of the natural moral law present in each person, even if done by the means of different religions, would result in a common set of core values on which polity, law, and society can be grounded.

Modern liberal, secular democratic societies have adopted this Enlightenment assumption and seek to implement it in varying degrees. One difficulty is that in present-day Europe and North America, increasing numbers of people no longer see the actualization of the moral conscience within as a "religious duty." Yet for the Enlightenment thinkers the practicing of "religious duty" was seen as essential for the development of core values on which society is to be founded. In the content of our increasing pluralism and multiculturalism, religious cultivation and duty is often down played because of the conflict between groups that sometimes results (e.g., Protestant versus Catholics in Ireland, Muslims versus Hindus in India, and Khalsa versus non-Khalsa Sikhs in Canada). A knee-jerk response is to banish all expressions of religion from the public sphere and to foster a strictly secular society. But what will replace the role of religion that the Enlightenment thinkers saw as crucial for the development of the moral conscience and the unifying value on which to ground a liberal, democratic state?

In a fine article that grapples with this dilemma, Paul Horwitz concludes that, in Canada at least, courts today are too much favoring the goals of the state over the obligations of religion.[10] Religion, he notes, has been treated as nothing more than one of a number of choices that an individual can make. This attitude betrays the state's tendency to treat religion as a "hobby" rather than as a total worldview that conditions all of the individual's decisions. Because it is only one among many mere choices, religion must give way to the administrative encroachment of the liberal state. From the state's perspective, religion is relegated to the sphere of private action. The liberal worldview, on which Canada as a state operates, focuses on "the autonomous individual, on the maximization of individual conceptions of the good, and tends to give it in practice an emphasis on freedom over tradition, will over obligation, and individual over community."[11] A liberal state seeks to maximize happiness among a diverse number of groups and understands this concept of the common good in rational terms that are grounded in rational argument—a direct conflict with religious faiths that usually transcend rational argument in their ultimate assumptions. Contrary to its self-perception then, the liberal state is not a value-neutral safe haven where all religions can meet, for its rational conception of the good is in fact discriminatory against religion—as is its privileging of the individual over the collective in the decision-making of the religious citizen. Charles Taylor has made it clear that liberalism, as it stands, is not a possible meeting ground for all cultures and religions.[12] It is the political expression of one range of cultures and as such is often incompatible with others.

It is not surprising then that in the history of religion-state relations in Canada, religious discrimination has often occurred. Jews, Jehovah's Witnesses, Hutterites, Sikhs, Japanese Buddhists, and Aboriginals have all been victims. The guarantees of freedom to practice one's own religion, although given in law, have not been granted. The problem has been "a tendency to treat rationalism and liberalism as a bedrock epistemology, a mode of thinking that tolerates other modes of experience but ultimately asserts its superiority over them."[13] It is not rationalism only that is the problem but also liberalism's other touchstones of empiricism, skepticism, individualism, and autonomy—which often run counter to the basic assumptions of religious ethnic communities. While liberalism is willing to value religion as one choice among many for the autonomous individual, it fails (because of its presuppositions) to recognize that for many, religion is much more than a mere choice on the part of an individual. Rather, says Horwitz, it is "a radically different but equally valid mode of experiencing reality"—and one that Canada's constitution suggests it protects. In court cases, however, the liberal rational worldview has a profound effect on what the courts decide. Horwitz concludes, "It leads to the courts according a lesser weight to religious considerations when it makes decisions balancing state and religious goals"[14]

Horwitz thinks that Canada's approach to date has been unfair to religious and ethnic groups and is blind to the value of religion as a social force. Liberal democracy, he says, devalues religion and religious freedom. "It does so by viewing religion through the lens of the unbeliever and treating it as a mysterious and threatening force that cannot be understood by rational, secular reasoning and so must give way to the state's rational goals."[15] However, Horwitz thinks that there is one aspect in the thinking of liberal democracies that would give a different result, namely, the awareness that beyond the language of individual rights, society is made up of groups or communities to which individuals may belong. From within a religious or ethnic community, one's identity may well come from being a part of the larger group rather than from one's own individuality. "Though to the outsider such communities may seem less significant than the individuals that comprise them, to the participant the community as a whole might be more real and more important than his or her part in it."[16] Therefore, it is the community that acts as the intermediary between those in the group and citizens outside the group. Canada has given particular recognition and value to the intermediary communities in the principle of multiculturalism that is embedded within the Charter of Rights and Freedoms. The charter states, "This Charter shall be interpreted in a manner consistent with the preservation and enhancement of the multicultural heritage of Canada."[17] With this protection, religious and ethnic communities are in a position to make a positive contribution to Canada's liberal democracy as groups. Religious groups have been and continue to be powerful forces to resist or provoke social change. The political impact of Rev. Martin Luther King, in his call for civil disobedience against state laws that did not square with moral justice or the law of God, is an example of how a religious community can be a powerful force for good in a liberal democracy. Religious communities, said De Tocqueville, "provide a valuable moral restraint on the state by informing the moral consciences of the governors and the governed."[18] In Canada, the Sikh and Muslim communities have challenged practices within public institutions that unfairly discriminated against their members. Aboriginal communities have brought to the fore the havoc created by discriminatory policies such as residential schools and antipotlatch laws.

Of course, it must also be recognized that a religious community can be a disruptive force in the public realm if it attempts to force the views of its members on the whole of society. Rather than safeguarding freedom, a religion might attempt to outlaw from society secularism or groups with differing religious views. But, concludes Horwitz, none of these worries equals the value of religion as a positive social and political force in society. Religious groups in liberal democracies (such as Canada) that recognize the value of pluralism and multiculturalism "are less likely to resort to homogenization when seeking social change."[19] Because religious or ethnic communities operate from different worldviews that deny the absolute authority of the state and its views, these communities exert a constant check on the abuse of power and morality by the state and its institutions. These groups can function as the conscience of a liberal democracy. Further, religious and ethnic communities may enrich secular liberal democracies by bringing ideas from outside of its sphere of common concepts and practices. In this way, political debate may be enlivened and valuable social change fostered within a liberal democracy that might otherwise grow stale and self-justifying.

The chapters in this book are in many ways case studies of religious conscience and its function in various states and societies. Justin Champion in chapter 2 shows that in seventeenth-century England, the transformation from a confessional state with an established religion to one in which religious diversity was respected was a very gradual one. Roman Catholics and more radical Protestant sects suffered persecution at the hands of the law. Champion shows that "conscience" was then a very loaded term, invoked both to buttress the institutions and demands of the state, as well as the claims of the dissenters to follow their own beliefs. Even among Puritan apologists, arguments for freedom of conscience were often limited to their own faith communities and denied to other confessions. In the end, England's governors made partial peace with the Protestants dissenters by giving up active persecution of them and allowing them to worship in private, yet maintaining many of their civil disabilities. This modest compromise was embodied in the Act of Tolerance of 1689.

In chapter 3, Cornelia Dayton examines religious orthodoxy in colonial New Haven under the challenge of the religious conscience of Anne Eaton, the governor's wife. Even in the American colonies to which European victims of religious oppression had fled, the thrust of religious orthodoxy in the absence of an established church maintained considerable force. Liberty of conscience was narrowly defined by the Congregationalist Puritans of New Haven to justify their own freedom but used as a weapon against anyone who would challenge their conceptions of the "true gospel." So Anne Eaton was excommunicated because of her own Baptist beliefs, but allowed to remain in the community and suffered no civil disabilities for her apostasy. This action, suggests Dayton, prefigures the politics of tolerance for religious diversity which, by the end of the seventeenth century, was largely accepted within the American Puritan community. Freedom of religion and conscience were limited intellectual and legal conceptions at the end of the seventeenth century, reflecting the grudging concessions of freedom of religious association and worship in England and America.

These initial advances were fostered by the eighteenth-century Enlightenment thinkers discussed earlier, and put into law, most dramatically, in the American Bill of Rights with its embodiment of freedom of religion and no establishment of religion as basic constitutional values. Elizabeth Clark in chapter 5 shows how one group in nineteenth-century America, the Unitarians of New England, sought to embody these beliefs in a form of civil religion based on personal prayer and free inquiry. With a strong rationalist belief in the power of individual conscience and a commitment to democratic principles, this group became actively involved in the movement against slavery in the *antebellum* period. Clark argues that the beliefs and practices of the Unitarians of New England had their roots in the strong dissenting tradition of liberal Protestantism. For this group, the "inner life of the spirit" required the release and actualization of the innate religious conscience as individuals within society engaged in a common moral quest. In this group, we see the translation of the protesting power of religious conscience engaged in the antislavery campaign and the endeavor to secure public opinion in its support.

Attempts to protect religious rights have not been limited to Christian libertarians. Irwin Cotler, in chapter 6, engages in a comparative study of Jewish nongovernmental organizations (NGOs) in Canada and the United States as advocates of freedom of religion and conscience. Working in the fields of civil liberties and human rights, these organizations have adopted diametrically-opposed views on several issues, reflecting in part the different politicolegal cultures in which they operate. While Jewish NGOs in the United States have actively opposed the display of religious symbols in public places because of perceived opportunities for interference by the state with religious values and observance, their Canadian counterparts have supported the bringing of religion into public life in order to enhance its role. A difference is also seen between the two countries on the issue of hate messages directed against ethnic and religious minorities. In Canada, Jewish NGOs have led the campaigns to pass and enforce legislation that invokes state power to outlaw hate propaganda. In the United States, by contrast, Jewish NGOs have constantly used the courts to vigorously protect freedom of speech (including hate speech) in order to prevent the state from intruding into the preserve of individualism and democratic discourse.

Despite a greater respect for religious rights in contemporary North America, the law experienced difficulty in dealing with the claims and inner stresses of more radical Christian communities. Alvin Esau, in chapter 7, analyzes the litigation over division and schism in the Manitoba Lakeside

Hutterite Colony. He shows that secular assumptions of law, which make civil courts reluctant to become involved in internal religious disputes, can still produce questionable results. The Supreme Court of Canada, in this case when the Hutterite authorities sought to expel the Hofer brothers and other dissenters from the colony, refused to interfere with the internal rules of the sect relating to discipline and property rights. However, it did fault the colony authorities for failure to observe the rules of natural justice, quashing the expulsion decision and restoring the dissidents to membership in the colony—but without rights to their property and without real participation. In the second round of litigation, the Manitoba courts upheld the position that the colony leadership must treat all property within the colony, even that of the dissenters, as communal and sent the latter packing, empty handed. No attempt was made, as it might have been, to treat the dispute in the light of which group had the better claim to represent the faith tradition in question.

John McLaren, in chapter 8, charts a more positive outcome in the ongoing negotiation between the government of British Colombia and the Sons of Freedom Communal Doukhobors (SFCD). Here, negotiations rather than litigation have been employed to resolve tensions between SFCD religious beliefs and the demands of the dominant legal system. This seems to have forced government to recognize that even within its own legal heritage and tradition, these are mechanisms for accommodating groups that, because of their faith, reject the individual ownership of land. This is a far cry from the marginalization which has so often been, and sometimes continues to be, the experience of religious minorities which put duty to God before duty to state.

In chapter 9, Carol Weisbrod examines the Mormon experience in the United States for what it tells us about the price of religious intolerance and the modes of interaction between the state, law, and the accommodation of minority religious beliefs more generally. This group, which suffered persecution from the date of its emergence as a definable sect and sought to detach itself from the broader society to find its own space in which to practice its own theology, found there was no escape, and that it had to compromise to avoid harassment by the federal authorities. The major bone of contention was the Mormon belief in and practice of polygamy or plural marriages. Despite attempts by group leaders to secure exemptions from federal laws prohibiting this practice, the bid failed and prosecutions of Mormon men for polygamy continued as members of the sect found themselves up against the full might of the U.S. legislative and judicial arms. For decades, this conflict stood in the way of the statehood for the Utah territory. Only in 1890, when the church disavowed polygamy, did the way open for a constitutional accommodation. The price paid for peace was high, namely, a significant reordering of social and family relationships and a substantial loss of internal autonomy for the group. In modern times, this faith community, with its emphasis on family values, developed great respectability, combining religious dominance and influence in its homestate, and strong minority advocacy outside on issues which concern it.

Despite enlightenment and modern development toward religious tolerance of mainstream and respectable Christian dominations, non-Christian faiths continued to experience pressure for conformism or assimiliation. Anti-semitism and the growth of rights consciousness in Western Europe and North America are studied by Phyllis Senese in chapter 10. She suggests that in Britain and France, Jews became acceptable as citizens *if* they merged into the social fabric of communities that continued to reflect Christian tradition, values, and assumptions. When Jews arrived in the British North American colonies, anti-semitism was more subtle but no less malign. Jews witnessed the break-up of traditional, tightly-built communities that had enabled them to survive centuries of persecution as they adjusted to the individualistic forces of the Enlightenment. Even then they were faced with a new force for hostility—nationalism. As the history of the nineteenth and twentieth centuries so tragically shows, even assimilated Jews did not fit the vision of a national identity and were again persecuted. The resulting fragmentation of community and tradition is seen by Senese in the North American Jewish community and evidenced in the different positions taken by liberal and conservative Jews on issues of civil liberties.

In chapter 11, Youngblood Henderson examines the struggle to preserve Aboriginal Spiritual Teaching in the face of Christian colonization and the liberal Enlightenment. As Youngblood Henderson shows, the impact of these "universalizing" forces was devastating on aboriginal communities. Despite the romantic identification by some Enlightenment thinkers of the "noble savage," the pragmatic dictates of colonial policy, together with a strong sense of religious and cultural superiority, fostered policies of subjugation, enforced assimilation, and, in some instances, physical genocide. Aboriginals in North America, it was thought, would either be absorbed into the superior European religion, culture, and population or simply waste away. White society sought to strip them of their land, language, and belief system under which they had flourished for countless generations. In the face of the loss of their language, cultural knowledge, and self-respect, freedom of religion and conscience are really meaningless terms in the case of the Aboriginal peoples. In Canada, as the chapter notes, the most destructive results were achieved by the regime of residential schools paid for by the federal government but run by the churches. To these schools, thousands of Aboriginal children were sent, cut off from family, language, and spiritual roots, to be "Canadianized." Youngblood Henderson calls for a new spirit of respect for Aboriginal religions and spirituality in Canada to match and support the legal protections of the new constitutional order.

In chapter 12, we cast our eyes beyond Europe and North America to India where Robert Baird looks at how these forces have played out in India's transition from a traditional society to a modern secular state. The establishment of India as a secular state, embodying in its constitution the sometimes inconsistent values of equality as well as freedom of religion and conscience, has produced a complex result. As Baird shows, the courts progressively constrained religion in India in a number of ways. They have extended state involvement in religious affairs by marking off secular matters, even in temple administration. Concerns over morality, public order, and health have been balanced against the demands of religious devotion. Limits have been placed on the evocation of Hindu ritual by the state or its representatives, and further limits have been placed on the practice of proselytization and conversion by the missionary religions of Christianity and Islam. Under the democratizing impulse, the state has ordered holy places open to all Hindus regardless of caste, thus challenging strongly the traditional purity prescriptions of orthodox Brahmanical religions. However, where the secular intentions of the framers of the constitution have been thwarted most is in the failure of parliament to secure a uniform civil code. Instead, the Hindu law code has been "rationalized" over loud protest, but traditional Muslim law has remained untouched.

Although far less complex than in India, Elizabeth Shilton shows that tensions between religious belief and the secular state have been a problem in public education in Canada. As Shilton observes in chapter 13, the historic accord on the protection of religious rights in matters of education contained in the British North America Act of 1867 continues to qualify and override the commitment to freedom of religion and conscience in section 2(a) of the Canadian Charter. In Canada, the extent to which special constitutional rights should be accorded to particular religious groups is still very much a live issue in matters of education. The Supreme Court has confirmed that the separate Roman Catholic school system in Ontario is entitled to full funding by the province, in accord with the undertaking in section 93 of the Constitutional Act. There is also an older authority, which is likely still persuasive, stating that provinces may extend public funding to minority religious schools, Christian and non-Christian, not contemplated in 1867. Some provinces have done just that. None of this would be possible in the United States. Where lower courts in Canada have drawn the line is in denying that members of religious minorities can claim as a constitutional right state support for religious education.

In the final chapter, Azim Nanji examines the way the Muslims in modern western countries have dealt with the dual challenges of existing in an individualistic culture that can be insensitive to the communal and extended family base of reference which is their heritage, and of representing a faith tradition that is viewed with suspicion in certain quarters in the host societies because of its attributed association with international terrorism, fundamentalism, and anti-Western feelings. Muslims in North America have dealt with instances of demonization as "Others" that other non-Christian groups, especially the Jews, have encountered in the past. In several instances that Nanji outlines, barriers have been erected against free pursuit of their religion by the invocation of the law or the exercise of political pressure against the construction of places of worship. Moreover, because the Islamic population of North America is spread out, Muslims have lacked the support systems and sense of local community that would allow them to press publicly for greater recognition of their culture and traditions. Compromises, Nanji argues, have been made in the areas of traditional Islamic family law and custom, elements of which, such as polygamy, are not acceptable in the West, and others of which do not fit easily into the dominant legal system. The results have been liberating for some, especially women, but also subversive of a shared sense of community and family cohesiveness. He argues persuasively that both law and administration as they relate to family and education need to be more sensitive to and accommodating of the cultural realities of religious minorities.

These chapters show that the struggle for free expression of religious conscience within the state that began with Martin Luther and the Enlightenment thinkers continues to challenge us today. The global spread of the modern secular state, together with the increasing migration of religious minority groups around the world, makes the issues examined in this book as timely today as they were in the sixteenth and seventeenth centuries. Only today their scale and complexity is much larger than was contemplated by John Locke or Emanuel Kant. While giving us very real advances, their solutions have been overtaken by the changed nature of our contemporary world in which secularization threatens to further marginalize religion as a source of critique of state and community, as well as individual actions and motives. As many of the case studies presented in these chapters show, new answers are being demanded and new sensitivities required of religious leaders, lawyers, judges, and frames of public policy at all levels of society. This book is a beginning contribution in that direction.

Notes

1. See Wheeler Robinson, *Inspiration and Revelation in the Old Testament* (London: Oxford University Press, 1946).

2. Herbert B. Workman, *Persecution in the Early Church* (Oxford: Oxford University Press, 1986).

3. Jeffrey Richards, *Sex, Dissidence and Damnation: Minority Groups in the Middle Ages* (London: Routledge, 1994), pp. 88–115.

4. See R. I. Moore, *The Formation of a Persecuting Society* (New York: Basil Blackwell, 1987).

5. For the Americas, see Thomas R. Berger, *A Long and Terrible Shadow* (Vancouver: Douglas and McIntyre, 1991).

6. See, for example, Bernard Lewis, *The Middle East: 2000 Years of History* (London: Weidenfeld and Nicholson, 1995), pp. 269–270.

7. Stanley Wolpert, *A New History of India* (New York: Oxford University Press, 1959), p. 310.

8. Williston Walker, *A History of the Christian Church* (New York: Charles Scribner's Sons, 1959), p. 310.

9. Mark U. Edwards, *Luther's Last Battle: Politics and Polemics, 1531–46* (Ithaca, NY: Cornell University Press, 1983).

10. Paul Horwitz, "The Source and Limits of Freedom of Religion in a Liberal Democracy: Section 2(a) and Beyond," *University of Toronto Faculty of Law Review*, vol 54, Winter 1996, pp. 1–64.

11. Ibid, p. 14.

12. Charles Taylor, *Philosophical Arguments* (Cambridge, MA: Harvard University Press, 1995), p. 249.

13. Horwitz, op. cit., p. 22.

14. Ibid., p. 25.

15. Ibid., p. 47.

16. Ibid., p. 48.

17. Ibid. (as quoted in Horwitz).

18. Ibid., p. 50 (as quoted by Horwitz).

19. Ibid., p. 51.

Chapter 2

Willing to Suffer: Law and Religious Conscience in Seventeenth-Century England

Justin A. I. Champion

In 1662 John Audland and John Wilkinson were imprisoned at Bristol, having been arrested at a Quaker Meeting house and committed to jail for refusing to subscribe to the oath of allegiance.[1] In this by no means singular example, the conflict between law and private conscience in the early modern period is starkly manifest. Audland and Wilkinson were examined by the civic authorities in the persons of the Mayor and two Aldermen and an attendant audience: conscience and legal authority confronted each other head-on. While the Magistrates invoked the language of obligation, the two men petitioned both the court and the attendant audience with an alternative discourse of tender conscience and passive sufferance. For the magistrates the court was not a place of debate and discussion but one of enforcement: "we have a law." Disobedience, refusal, evasion, and defiance of this law could only be characterized, from the magisterial perspective, as an act of sedition; consequently the accused were "dangerous persons," attempting to seduce the people from their true obligation to the King. On the contrary, to Wilkinson and Audland the court procedure was a testing ground for their conscience, an opportunity to proclaim their suffering and witness their convictions. That the demeanor of Wilkinson and Audland was less than passive is clear from their combination of evasion and challenge in response to the magistrates' inquiries. Recalling that, as the transcript said, there were "many people present," the threat that their behavior presented to the public dignity of the court is perhaps best exemplified by the actions of the clerk who hurriedly snatched the Bible away from the defendants before they could turn the injunctions of scripture against the authority of the procedure. Rather than submitting to the indictment, the defendants proclaimed their righteousness in suffering under the unjust and ungodly persecutions of latter-day Pharisees. Ultimately the two men were punished for the "Testimony of a good conscience" with imprisonment.

Importantly and unhappily, the fate of Wilkinson and Audland was not unique. Historians of Quakerism, using the martyrological accounts, have written with great detail about the savage and brutal persecution experienced from the mid-1650s. Especially after the restoration of political and religious authority, in 1660 radical sectarians like the Quakers, the Fifth Monarchists, and Baptists experienced a systematic and intense oppression that has very often been marginalized by historians of the period. The persistence of radical conspiracy and political plotting in the early years of the Restoration riveted the connection between religious and political dissidence: the disastrous rising of Fifth Monarchists in London, in early 1661, encouraged this culture of intolerance and legal proscription. Carefully contrived and ensnaring systems of statutes were established with the ambition of eradicating the more radical forms of dissent. Indeed, as many historians have argued, it was only the gap between enactment and enforcement that meant that religious minorities like the Quakers survived. It only requires the most superficial examination of the state papers, quarter sessions records, and cases of sufferings to gain a flavor of the extent and savagery of this persecution. Justified by the argument from authority, as the Mayor of Bristol put it in 1661 "that the laws of England [are] the Supreme Conscience of England," men and women, young and old were arrested, molested, abused, harassed, and murdered for a series of activities such as failure to attend the parish Church, refusing payment of tithes, and nonswearing of oaths. Hundreds of men and women died in close, unhealthy, and filthy prisons, at the mercy of ignorant and malicious guards.[2] Those who suffered did so, as a group of men in West Chester stated in 1660, "out of pure Conscience, not obstinacy or Disaffection to the Government."[3]

In the early summer of 1689, after much parliamentary wrangling and debate, chapter 18 of the statutes of the first year of William and Mary's reign took away many of the legal restraints against religious conscience.[4] Commonly called the "Toleration" Act, the statutory repeal of penalties against Protestant dissidents has very often been linked with the intellectual defense of the liberty of conscience articulated famously by John Locke. There was a distinction between a defense of the rights of conscience, and the mere taking away of certain penalties against religious worship. The 1689 Act did not break the link between civic liberties and religious identity. So, for example, while Quakers were no longer in danger of eradication by persecution (as long as they registered as nonconformists), they were still exempt from holding local, civic, or national offices that continued to be protected by statutory tests of conscience.[5] The "Toleration" Act gave no liberties to non-

Protestant confessions.[6] Although the act of 1689 established some measure of relief to private conscience, battles over the legitimacy of the impositions of religious tests and oaths raged throughout the eighteenth century.

The current historiographical impression, however, is still that, in some sense, 1689 marks a watershed in the history of the confrontation between law and the conscience. Traditionally the history of the relationship between conscience and authority has been written from the perspective of the denominational minorities. The achievement of liberty of conscience was forged by the theoretical defenses articulated by those religious cleavages who suffered at the hands of persecuting authority: thus, in some sense, the arguments advanced by John Locke in defense of sincere Christian liberty of thought and worship had their origins in sectarian justifications of dissidence from the established order. Thus, the classical histories of toleration trace the origins of such ideologies back to the puritan writings of the sixteenth and early seventeenth century.[7] To characterize the meta-arguments of this historiography, rights of conscience were born in the struggle of Godly minorities against the tyrannical and unjust imposition of the state. The progressive victory of liberty of conscience over a persecuting political authority was teleologically linked to the rise of rationalism, modernity, and democracy. More recently, these Whiggish narratives have been challenged and exposed: the connections between liberty and conscience were determined more by confessional imperatives than any teleological commitment to pluralistic modernity. When "puritan" pamphleteers and polemicists wrote in defense of tender consciences they, in the very act of defending their liberty, proscribed the same "rights" to other confessions.[8]

One of the topoi of studies of the history of toleration is the construction of a simple opposition between arguments for authority and arguments in defense of conscience. The history is ordinarily written from the perspective of conscience as if theoreticians of authority had no other intellectual ambition than unjust imposition. Those who imposed tests, penalties, and shackles on private conscience did so, not just in the name of political order, but in the name of God: they had sincere and conscientious motives for persecution. Conscience then was not a concept simply monopolized by the dissidents but lay at the very heart of the operations and understandings of state power. Conscience was an instrument of order and government. Roger L'Estrange writing in response to nonconformist pleas for liberty in the 1660s declared that "to ask that ye may govern yourselves by your own consciences is the same thing with asking to be no longer governed by the King's Laws." Dissent was "no longer a plea of conscience but a direct conspiracy against the government." Samuel Parker, echoed L'Estrange's position: "If tenderness of conscience be a sufficient excuse for disobedience, it is a destruction of the force of laws, giving every man liberty to exempt himself." "Public conscience" had "command and determination" over individual liberty.[9] By default, debates about the rights and limits of conscience were debates about the authority and power of the state. Discussions were not simply about the rights of conscience against the state, but ultimately about how the state functioned: in order to think clearly about the place of conscience in the period it is important then to explore not only how conscience came into conflict with authority, but also how conscience constituted authority.

The social power of the English state was built on an infrastructure of confessional identity and allegiance: it was a Protestant State both in "idea" and "system."[10] In both of these senses the core identity of the functional power of the state was constituted by the construction of a particular confessionalism. Key discourses of order, authority, and religion, were structured around consensual understandings of the truth of the Protestant faith. These languages of government were not simply ideological fictions but were reified into institutions, disciplines, and practices. The origins of the Protestant "Church-state" were in the breach with Rome in the 1520s and 1530s: central to the ideological justification of the jurisdictional separation from Papal authority was the notion of the Imperial monarchy and the National Church. Onto this jurisdictional construction was grafted a theological indictment of Roman Catholic theology and faith: the monarchy and the church became not only National but Protestant too. The understanding of the Royal Supremacy was built on the foundations of conscience. Apologists for the Henrician and Edwardian "Church-State" developed arguments that promoted a Protestant order embodied in the person of the monarch as a "nursing father" to the realm.[11] The keystone of state power was thus represented as a figure of order, but also a figure of conscience: in effect a Protestant political theology had been established as the device of true government. The structure of power authorized in this theory was hierarchical with the monarchy enshrined in jurisdictional omnicompetance at the apex: it was also inherently unstable given its symbiotic relationship with the Protestant confession.

As Quentin Skinner has elegantly shown, radical Protestant theorists, when confronted with Roman Catholic state authority, asserted that Godly conscience had a duty to resist spiritually corrupt sovereignty: God rather than man must be obeyed. The resistance theories of the Marian exiles set the tone for the hostile reception of claims of conscience in later contexts.[12] However, while the claims of authority and conscience were united in the person of a Protestant sovereign the martyrology of suffering was successfully reoriented and reintegrated to support the authoritative claims of the Protestant 'Church-state' against the incipient threat of Roman Catholic subversion. Marian resistance theories were constructed to legitimate the withdrawal of conscience from the Roman antichrist: as they enfranchised this disobedience they also reinforced the duties of the Godly conscience toward justly constituted authority. The point was, however, that it was part of the Protestant ideological infrastructure that conscience had a role authorization of legitimate power, and that also in certain extreme situations it might disengage that allegiance. Determining when, and to what degree, and by whom that disengagement might occur was the crux of the history of conscience and authority from the 1560s to the 1700s.

Conscience also functioned as a key instrument in the practice of government. Much has been written about the material history of the early modern state. The lineages of the absolutist state combined a centralization and bureaucratization of the processes of coercion, administration, and law, with the ideological defense of power.[13] The theme of much of this work is of the development of structures and process of power that were central, national, and increasingly penetrated into civil society. Combining these insights of historical sociology with an intimate understanding of social history, Braddick has developed a more decentered, negotiated, and pragmatic understanding of how government worked in early modern England: "The early modern state depended upon participation."[14] The early modern state did not function by the centralized imposition of law and values: these concepts were mediated into local society by the participation of individuals and officeholders: "self government by the King's command" as G. A. Aylmer put it most succinctly.[15] Government was a process undertaken by a complex hierarchy of officeholders ranging from the great offices of state, the county magistrates, down to sheriffs, justices of the peace, petty constables, headboroughs, bailiffs, churchwardens, pinders, swineherds, haywards, and neatherds. Each of these officeholders both acted as agents of the state but also had a role in the local communities: as enactment became enforcement it was mediated by the rival social and religious injunctions of neighborliness and conscience.[16]

The English state was elastic and diffuse: conscience was one means of giving it some rigidity. This functioned in two broad ways. First, most of the web of offices mentioned above could only be held by men (very rarely women) who acknowledged allegiance to the established "Church-State." Conditional on service, duty and conscience was sworn to uphold the law and religion of the land: conscience reinforced the authority of the state in the locality. It is clear how doubts about the godliness of government or particular statutes might compromise the effectiveness of state power; it is also clear how conscience might exclude the Godly from accepting any of these offices. So in some respects conscience acted as a means of ensuring a disciplined and dutiful magistracy. The role of conscience was not, however, just restricted to those who held state, civic, or ecclesiastical office. Conscience was frequently and consistently used as a badge of political obedience throughout the early modern period. Keith Thomas has gone so far as to term the early modern period as "an age of conscience." Political casuistry was one of the main ways central government was authorized: oaths of allegiance, oaths *ex officio*, and oaths of association, were tendered to the adult male population at moments of crisis and as commonplace reaffirmations of obligation. Oaths were not only employed in judicial procedure, but crucially to structure loyalty and obligation. Daniel Featly summarized their importance in 1646, "Oaths are necessary for the execution of the magistrate's office and the preservation of human society. For without such oaths the commonwealth hath no surety upon public officers and ministers: nor Kings upon their subjects."[17] The act of subscription and confirmation of these state oaths invoked careful consideration: a conscience compromised and perjured implied eternal damnation. As periodic subversion threatened the stability of the state oaths were tendered to the nation: the Oath of Allegiance controversy in the early years of James I reign was calculated to neutralize the danger of Roman Catholic conspiracy.[18] In 1640s and 1650s there were successive attempts to construct covenants, and engagements, to draw the population to conscientious obligation. The 1660s, 1680s, and 1690s again saw successive regimes reinforce their authority by these means. Continental Roman Catholic casuistry was notoriously flexible in recommending strategies for accommodation to imposed oaths.[19] Protestant casuistry denied the morality of such devices as equivocation and mental reservation: popular Protestant authors of all theological hues argued that falsehood could never be accommodated with conscience.[20] These works of moral guidance were supplemented by oral advice: curates held weekly surgeries and meetings where matters of conscience might be talked through.[21] Ultimately casuistry would be supplanted by political theory.[22] Conscience was then not just the vocation of dissident minorities but constitutive of the consensus of political culture.

The authority of the confessional state suffered a virtually unremediable rupture during the English Revolution. In the twenty years between the outbreak of the first Civil War in 1642 and the reconstruction of the monarchical polity in 1660 conscience was unhinged from authority. As John Morrill has shown the social power of the Church of England was taken away in the Parliamentary legislation of the 1640s. England moved from a profoundly stable, ordered, and hierarchical society to a situation where the religious infrastructure of Bishops, Churches, and ecclesiastical courts had been dissolved, dismantled, and destroyed and the King had been defeated, imprisoned, and finally executed. Although it is tempting to overestimate the radicalism and social revolution of the period, there is some general consensus that in practical terms a liberty of worship was de facto established. It is clear that there was a proliferation of confessions. The National Church was disestablished and conscience was given a practical liberty.[23]

The battle over the preservation or destruction of this practical freedom for tender consciences provided the dynamic for what has been called the politics of religion from the restoration of the monarchy in 1660 to the "Toleration Act" of 1689. Between 1660 and 1665 the legal infrastructure of persecution discussed at the start of this chapter was enacted. The Clarendon Code established a uniformity of doctrine and discipline; it established compulsory attendance at parish Churches under the rubric of the Book of Common Prayer; it outlawed private conventicles and meetings; it ejected nonconformists from civil and ecclesiastical office. Parading the blasphemy and subversion of the interregnum the Anglican Church reimposed discipline on licentious conscience. From the early 1660s the dissidents conducted a diverse polemical campaign in defense of Christian conscience. Many nonconformists acknowledged duties to the supreme magistrate but called for a relaxation of the severe penalties against private worship. Others argued for a broadening of the ecclesiastical settlement that might accommodate or comprehend their scruples. One group appealed to the sovereign to establish on his ecclesiastical supremacy an indulgence for Protestant dissidents. Arguments were proposed that claimed it was in the economic interests of the nation (since the Dissenters were so industrious) to encourage liberty. A more radical cleavage asserted that liberty of conscience was part of the freeborn Englishman's birthright.[24] In essence there were two types of argument: the first, an argument to authority, appealed to the Crown to establish liberty; the second, an argument from conscience, suggested that imposition was unjust and ungodly. Ultimately neither of these strategies were to be the determinant of the final achievement of the reduced measure of liberty established in 1689. By exploring the career and arguments of one of the more radical Restoration dissidents it will be possible to illuminate the parameters, limitations, possibilities, and indeed contradictions of the demands and arguments for the liberty of conscience.

The conundrum in the career of Henry Care (1646–1688) is that he earned his radical reputation by the pungency of his pamphleteering campaign against the succession of the Roman Catholic, James Duke of York between 1679 and 1683. When James came to the throne in 1685, Care was to be at the forefront of the campaign to defend the King's policy of establishing a *de facto* liberty of conscience between 1686 and 1688. It has been commonplace to dismiss Care as a turncoat: a man who wrote for money rather than principle. Care's radical credentials were excellent: a member of the semirepublican Green Ribbon Club, his weekly *Pacquet of Advice* was prohibited temporarily by the state for its virulence against "popery" and for "writing too sharply against the government" in 1680.[25] The Green Ribbon Club raised a subscription to pay for his defense when he was put on trial.[26]

By 1687 Care was writing with equal vigor in defence of James II's policy of indulgence: again a weekly newsletter *Public Occurrences Truly Stated*, advertised the benign qualities of the Jacobean regime, and asserting axioms such as "no man (keeping within the bounds of the law morall) ought to suffer in his civil rights for his opinions in matters of religion."[27] This weekly contribution was supplemented by a number of pamphlets addressing themselves to the legality of James II's policy of dispensing with the penal laws against all dissidents (Roman Catholic as well as Protestant). The theme that links these two apparently incompatible positions was Care's commitment to tolerationist arguments. The mistaken accusation of time-serving hypocrisy originates in a misunderstanding of the relationship between authority and conscience in his polemic. Care's primary conviction was in the liberty of religious expression: his opposition to the succession of James, Duke of York was motivated by the (understandable, given Protestant understandings of the Marian precedent) belief that the new king would establish a persecuting regime. Care's indictment of "popish" authority was not because it was theologically insupportable (although he undoubtedly thought Roman Catholic theology was corrupt and mistaken), but because it imposed on tender conscience. Indeed from a close reading of Care's publications between 1679–1683, it is possible to argue that his hostility toward "popery" was directed, not just at the Roman Catholic Church, but also at the intolerance of the Church of England. As discussed above the restored order in 1660 reinvigorated and reinforced the authority of a uniform Anglican establishment: a panoply of statutes and penal laws were directed against both Catholic and Protestant dissent. After the defeat of Charles II's court-led attempt to suspend these laws in the early 1670s, the government had turned the harsh edge of the laws against Protestant dissent, very often using statutes designed to trap Catholic recusants against Protestants. It was against precisely these abuses of the law that Care complained: the prelacy and persecution conducted by the Church of England was as "popish" as Roman Catholicism. Any who claimed the legitimacy of establishing "an unlawful hierarchy over the consciences of their brethren" were corrupt.[28] In works like *Utrum Horum* (1682), Care argued that the difference between the Church of England and the Protestant dissenters was not one of theological substance, but that the former imposed their understandings in matters indifferent and ceremonial on the latter: it was a question of ecclesiastical ambition.

The keystone of Care's belief in the legitimacy of liberty of conscience was a profound epistemological skepticism. As he wrote "all mortals are full of mistakes, especially in the business of religion, and since there is no such thing as infallibility on earth, why all this bitterness and persecution?"[29] Since no authority could be confident that it understood the form of true religion, so each conscience must have an equal ability to find its own beliefs. To punish conscience for sincere belief was unjust, irrational, and ungodly. This ethical defense of liberty of conscience was advanced consistently from the period of radical opposition between 1678 and 1683 through the period of collaboration from 1686 to 1688: rather than cut his cloth according to the times, Care persisted in his support of the principle of liberty regardless of the political context. Care's contribution was not merely one that proposed a theoretical defense of the rights of conscience: importantly, he also represents a more practical response to the problem of persecution by law. It was ultimately this pragmatic advice that was to be more effectual. Drawing from his ethical condemnation of intolerance, Care had argued from the early 1680s that the penal statutes were unjust, when James II issued his Declarations of Indulgence in 1687; again in 1688, suspending the penalties and establishing a *de facto* toleration, Care defended the morality and indeed legality of the sovereign's actions. Put simply, he argued that the rights of sovereignty in ecclesiastical affairs legitimated the suspensions. In effect he turned the Royal Supremacy against the advocates of persecution. Once again authority was used to reinforce rather than destroy rights of conscience. Similarly Care defended the exercise of regal jurisdiction in the creation of legal commissions to investigate the actions of the clerical persecutors.[30] Care's attitude to the relationship between the law and conscience also took a far more precise and pragmatic turn: again this was a concern and strategy for defending conscience that was persistently advanced from the early to the late 1680s.

This chapter started with a discussion of how two dissidents behaved and confronted their persecutors. It was this nexus that interested Care. Attention has been paid in historical writings to the strategies that radical sectarians like the Quakers contrived, but the example of Care's popular writings of the 1680s suggests that such forms of engagements with the processes and procedures of the law were far more mainstream. The three key texts are *English Liberties: or, the Freeborn Subjects Inheritance* (1682), *A Perfect Guide for Protestant Dissenters in case of prosecution upon any of the penal statutes* (1682) and *The Laws of England: or a True Guide for all persons concerned in Ecclesiastical Courts* (n.d. ca 1680–82). Little scholarly attention has been paid to any of these texts, although the first, *English Liberties*, was perennially popular and reprinted later in the seventeenth and eighteenth century. Although it would be anachronistic to say it, the most accurate description of these works is as handbooks for civil and religious liberties. Written for the "reader's information," these books were intended to give practical advice on how dissidents might react to the legal charges and judicial procedures that they suffered. *English Liberties* was composed to defend the "lives, liberties and estates" of the nation. Much of the first half of the book involved reprinting "magna charta, the petition of right, the habeas

corpus act; and divers other most useful statutes": constitutive of the argument
was that the law and correct judicial procedure were the preservatives of
liberty. Care went into detail about the functioning of important processes
such as habeas corpus.[31] In the second part of the text he presented similar
legal advice on how to construct legal defenses against the many ecclesiastical laws that compromised conscience: to facilitate familiarity with the statutes
against dissent he reprinted them, distinguishing carefully between penalties
established against sedition, papists, and Protestants. Specific counsel was
given on the powers and procedures of ecclesiastical courts: in particular "a
discourse of the nature of excommunication, and how to prevent or take off
the writ de excommunicato capiendo."[32] Care cast doubt on the jurisdictional
competence of most ecclesiastical courts, but still thought it important to
"inform our reader of the course of their practice, as it is used at this day, and
his best course to defend himself."[33] Pro forma writs and responses were
printed: lists of costs for diverse actions and materials were displayed. The
advice was that every part of the charge and writ was to be examined; any
deviation from established protocol should negate the presentations. Care
insisted that the accused should challenge the authority of the courts especially if charged under Canon law.[34] The last thrust of the work was straight-
forward: "We may conclude, It is an abuse, and utterly illegal, to prosecute
Protestants on such laws as were made solely and wholly against Papists."[35]
In a series of complex and closely argued passages Care asserted that many
of the Elizabethan antirecusancy laws that had been turned against Protestant
dissenters were "not now in force."[36] In the two other works, one of them
printed in populist black-letter, Care exposed the "pretended jurisdictions" of
the ecclesiastical courts, and gave again a very detailed handbook on the
procedure of citations and their remedies: "of the ways, means, and causes to
overthrow, frustrate, or avoid."[37] In the *Laws of England: or a true Guide for
all persons concerned in Ecclesiastical Courts* Care extended the range to
cover defenses against the tendering of oaths and the payment of tithes. He
also added brief instructions to Churchwardens and sidesmen of how they
might avoid compromising their own consciences by the nonenforcement of
penalties. In the pamphlet *A Perfect Guide for Protestant Dissenters* (1682),
which reproduced some of the material from the other works, Care reprinted
yet more statutes to indict "Protestant Persecution." He exposed the illegal
activities of informers and suggested legal methods for retaliating. The themes
of this work, to be echoed in the later defenses of James II, were erastian:
Church courts and jurisdiction were popish usurpation, any legal suit that
occurred without Royal Commission in the ecclesiastical courts was liable to
prosecution by praemunire.[38]

In these works Care developed a strategy for how the conscientious
dissident might engage and oppose the threat of legal persecution by knowl-

edge about the function of the law. He was not alone, especially in targeting the ecclesiastical courts. There is evidence that the ecclesiastical courts had been reinvigorated by the Anglican interests as an effective way of punishing dissidents: certainly the procedure of excommunication followed up by a writ *de excommunicato capiendo* was a feared and debilitating process. Imprisonment under the writ was not subject to the usual counter pleas of habeas corpus: the imprisoned could be incarcerated until they submitted to the ecclesiastical authorities.[39] In the crisis years of 1679–1682 some attempt had been made to alleviate Protestant dissent from some of the penal statutes in Parliament but in the chaos of the debates about the succession this had failed. In the internecine battle fought between Tories and Whigs, Anglicans and Dissenters, especially in the urban parishes of London, Bristol, and Norwich, the ecclesiastical courts became one instrument of disabling dissidents. Between 1681 and 1683, when the parliamentary crisis was at its height, there was a flurry of handbooks exposing the corruption of the Church courts and especially the practice of excommunication. *The Admonisher Admonished* (1683) rehearsed the case of James Jones who had been excommunicated in the court of Thomas Pinfold, official to the archdeacon of London. Again very much like Care's work, the pamphlet, in giving a narrative of Jones dealings with Pinfold and a young George Jefferies provided a method for "keeping of a good conscience." Jones challenged the authority of the court, issued counter writs and affidavits.[40] An anonymous pamphlet *The Case and Cure of Persons Excommunicated* (1682), which has close textual parallels with Care's publications, gave detailed advice on how to "slip or untie" the knot of excommunication, providing the Latin pro formas for "exceptions" and appeals.[41] An earlier tract, *Excommunication Excommunicated, or legal evidence that the Ecclesiastical Courts have no power to excommunicate any person whatsoever for not coming to his parish church* (1680), complained bitterly that the spiritual courts were being used to disable freeholders from voting in elections. Excommunication could only ever be a "spiritual weapon" and should not be turned against "civil rights." Given the fierce battles being fought out over election to parliament and other civil offices, the connection between religious and civil tyranny was underscored. Care redeployed the same tactic of publishing the statutes and the procedural remedies wherein he acted as publicist for James II. His *Draconia: or an abstract of all the penal laws touching matters of religion* (1688) justified the monarch's indulgence because it took away the need for the costly and difficult defenses. James II's indulgence freed conscience from the powers of "an angry priest, or a peevish justice, or a malicious neighbour, or a beggarly informer." The coercive statutes were both "useless and ineffectual": they were not good foundations for government and stability.[42] However, the "universal liberty" that James had established was rejected in the autumn and winter of 1688.[43] Even this minimal level of toleration, the mere withdrawal of penal severity against Protestant Trinitarian dissent, was only achieved in the face of stern clerical opposition trumpeting uniformity over liberty. The compromise of the 1689 toleration was a successful attempt to stave off the threat of James II's alternative of a much more radical liberty of conscience. Christian consciences of a Unitarian or Catholic commitment would have to wait until the early decades of the nineteenth century to gain full rights of citizenship.[44]

The failure of James II's attempts at establishing a unique and radical measure of toleration is one of those great historical ironies and is ample testimony to the limits of political and cultural possibility in the period: the language of conscience was a resolutely Protestant idiom. James's sincere commitment to religious pluralism was perceived by Protestant contemporaries as advancing the dual standards of the Papal antichrist and political tyranny: the fact that religious radicals such as Quakers supported the indulgence merely reinforced the dangers to social order.[45] The failure of toleration in 1686–1688 underscores the confessional nature of the state. Even the most radical theorists were limited by their Christian identity. John Locke defended the liberty of conscience on ethical and epistemological grounds. Whereas for the Anglican apologists true belief was the product of a shared confessional community, for Locke conviction was only attainable and indeed authenticated by individual effort, consequently the imposition of others' opinions was both illegitimate and pointless. For Locke there were limits to tolerable opinion. Atheism and popery were beyond the pale. Such beliefs were the result of willful ignorance: because such people could be held to have no conscience they were to be thought of, and treated, as threats to social order. Importantly, Locke specifically thought atheists were a danger to society because they could not be bound by promises or oaths (that were sanctioned by the threat of divine retribution). So even for Locke, still studied as a founder of modern liberalism, the defense of conscience was ultimately rooted in a conception of the duty to pious conviction, rather than the logical rights of free expression: that is, what Locke enfranchised was the free expression of a Christian conscience, rather that the rights of free expression.[46]

The relationship between conscience and political order was so firmly riveted in the period that even those writers and polemicists who opposed the Anglican establishment—the Freethinkers, Deists, and Republicans like John Toland, the Third Earl of Shaftesbury, and Charles Blount—although they upheld extensive rights of religious expression, still insisted on the value of a national church establishment.[47] Men like John Toland attempted to deconstruct the power and authority not only of the clerical caste but also of Christian revelation: there is little doubt that he did not believe in an orthodox conception of a Judaeo-Christian God. In a number of political pamphlets he still defended the existence of a national church, alongside provisions for the liberty of conscience. Although men of reason might be allowed to pursue the logic of their inquiries, Toland (and writers of his ilk) saw that a civil religion was crucial to the maintenance of a community of moral value and social order. Religious conformity or discipline then, even for those who devalued the sanctity of any particular religious confession, was still considered as a key part of the infrastructure of cultural and social power. The language of conscience, because it was still a central element of political discourse, remained delimited by confessional imperatives.[48] The achievements that did alleviate the suffering of dissidents were not the product of the victory of rationalism, but the result of practical and hard-fought civil disobedience. Henry Care's advice books on civil liberties had more effect than Locke's writings on toleration. Religious dissidents by withdrawing their obedience to constituted authority exposed the limitations of state power. Increasingly, as the agency of government became more concerned about the necessity of religious uniformity, the possibilities for enforcing such a conformity in the face of conscientious objection became less easy. Ultimately, as the "Toleration" Act indicated, the ambition of uniformity was sacrificed in order to preserve the principle of the confessional premises of citizenship.

Notes

1. *An Abstract of the Sufferings of the People Called Quakers for the Testimony of a Good Conscience, 1660–1666,* vol. 2 (London, J. Sowle, 1738), pp. 335–38.

2. Craig W. Horle, *The Quakers and the English Legal System, 1660–1688* (Philadelphia: University of Pennsylvania Press, 1988), p. 102.

3. See *An Abstract of the Sufferings,* pp. 48, 137, 85.

4. See Henry Horowitz, *Parliament, Policy and Politics in the Reign of William III* (Manchester: Manchester University Press, 1977).

5. See David L. Wyckes, "Friends, Parliament and the Toleration Act," *Journal of Ecclesiastical History* 45 (1994): pp. 42–63.

6. See E. N. Williams (ed.), *The Eighteenth Century Constitution, 1688–1815* (Cambridge: Cambridge University Press, 1970), pp. 42–46.

7. See Wilbur K. Jordan, *The Development of Religious Toleration in England* (London: Allen and Unwin, 1938), 4 volumes; J. Lecler, *Histoire de la Tolerance au siecle de la reforme* (Paris: PUF, 1954), 2 volumes.

8. See Blair Worden, "Toleration and the Cromwellian Protectorate" in *Persecution and Toleration,* William Sheils, (ed.), *Studies in Church History* 21 (Basil Blackwell: The Ecclesiastical History Society, 1984), pp. 199–233 at p. 200.

9. Cited in A. A. Seaton, *The Theory of Toleration Under the Later Stuarts* (Cambridge, 1911), pp. 117–19, 163–64.

10. P. Abrams, "Notes on the Difficulty of Studying the State" *Journal of Historical Sociology* 1 (1988): pp. 59–81.

11. See John Guy, "The Henrician Age," in J. G. A. Pocock (ed.), *The Varieties of British Political Thought 1500–1800* (Cambridge: Cambridge University Press, 1993), pp. 13–47.

12. Quentin Skinner, *The Foundations of Modern Political Thought* (Cambridge: Cambridge University Press, 1978), 2 volumes.

13. See Perry Anderson, *Lineages of the Absolutist State* (London: Verso, 1974); Michael Mann, *The Sources of Social Power* (Cambridge: Cambridge University Press, 1986), vol. I; John Brewer, *The Sinews of Power* (London: Hyman, 1989).

14. See Mike Braddick, "The Early Modern English State and the Question of Differentiation, 1550–1700," *Comparative Studies in Society and History* 38 (1996): pp. 92–111.

15. See G. A. Aylmer, "The Peculiarities of the English State," *Journal of Historical Sociology* 3 (1990): p. 99.

16. See Keith Wrightson, "Two Concepts of Order," in John Brewer and John Styles (eds.), *An Ungovernable People?* (London: Hutchinson, 1980).

17. Cited in Christopher Hill, "From Oaths to Interest," in *Society and Puritanism in Pre-Revolutionary England* (London: Secker and Warburg, 1966), pp. 382–419 at p. 383; Keith Thomas, "Cases of Conscience in Seventeenth Century England," in John Morrill, Paul Slack, and Daniel Woolf (eds.), *Public Duty and Private Conscience in Seventeenth Century England* (Oxford: Clarendon Press, 1993), pp. 29–56.

18. See Johann P. Sommerville, *Politics and Ideology in England, 1603–1640* (London: Longman, 1986).

19. See Peter Holmes, *Resistance and Compromise: The Political Thought of the Elizabethan Catholics* (Cambridge: Cambridge University Press, 1982).

20. See Perez Zagorin, *Ways of Lying: Dissimulation, Persecution and Conformity in Early Modern Europe* (Cambridge, Mass.: Harvard University Press, 1990), pp. 221–55.

21. See Keith Thomas, "Cases of Conscience in England," pp. 39–40.

22. See Edmund Leites (ed.), *Conscience and Casuistry in Early Modern Europe* (Cambridge: Cambridge University Press, 1988), pp. 72–118.

23. See John Morrill, *The Nature of the English Revolution* (London: Longman, 1993), pp. 31–175; Christopher Hill, *The World Turned Upside Down: Radical Ideas During the English Revolution* (London: Penguin, 1972).

24. See John Spurr, *The Restoration Church of England, 1646–1689* (New Haven: Yale University Press, 1991), and Gary de Krey "Rethinking the Restoration: Dissenting Cases for Conscience, 1667–1672," *The Historical Journal* 38 (1995): pp. 53–83.

25. *State Trials,* vol. 7, col. 1,119.

26. Magdalane College, Cambridge, *Pepys Miscellanies,* vol. 7, no. 2,595.

27. Henry Care, *Public Occurrances Truly Stated,* no. 8, April 10, 1688.

28. Henry Care, *A Perfect Guide to Protestant Dissenters* (1682), Preface.

29. Henry Care, *A Weekly Pacquet of Advice,* vol. 5, no. 8, October 13, 1682, p. 64.

30. See, Mark Goldie, "James II and the Dissenters' Revenge: The Commission of Enquiry of 1688," *Historical Research: The Bulletin of the Institute of Historical Research* 66 (1993): pp. 55–88.

31. *English Liberties* on habeas corpus, pp. 117–128.

32. *English Liberties,* pp. 154 and following.

33. *English Liberties,* p. 157.

34. *English Liberties,* p. 161.

35. *English Liberties,* p. 177.

36. *English Liberties,* pp. 178–83 at p. 180.

37. Henry Care, *The Laws of England: Or a True Guide for All Persons Concerned in Ecclesiastical Courts,* p. 65.

38. Henry Care, *A Perfect Guide* (1682), postscript p. 19.

39. See Fredrich Makower, *The Constitutional History and Constitution of the Church of England* (London: NP, 1895). See also Christopher Hill, *Society and Puritanism in Pre-Revolutionary England* (London: Secker and Warburg, 1964), pp. 354–82.

40. Anon, *The Admonisher Admonished,* p. 18 and passim.

41. Compare pp. 29–33, pp. 42–43 with *English Liberties.*

42. Henry Care, *Draconia* (1688), p. 18, pp. 26–27, pp. 33–34.

43. For accounts of the Glorious Revolution, see William Speck, *Reluctant Revolutionaries: Englishmen and the Revolution of 1688* (Oxford: Oxford University Press, 1988); on the specific question of religious toleration, see Gordon Schochet, "John Locke and Religious Toleration," in Lois Schwoerer (ed.), *The Revolution of 1688–1689: Changing Perspectives* (Cambridge: Cambridge University Press, 1992),

pp. 147–64; Mark Goldie, "The Political Thought of the Anglican Revolution," in Robert Beddard (ed.), *The Revolution of 1688* (Oxford: Clarendon Press, 1991), pp. 102–36, is an important study that reorientates much historical thinking on the period. See also James R. Jones (ed.), *Liberty Secured? Britain Before and After 1688* (Palo Alto, CA: Stanford University Press, 1992), especially Gordon Schochet, "From Persecution to 'Toleration'," pp. 122–57.

44. See J. D. C. Clark, *English Society, 1688–1832* (Cambridge: Cambridge University Press, 1985) and for the Anglo-North American perspective idem, *The Language of Liberty, 1660–1832* (Cambridge: Cambridge University Press, 1994); see also R. K. Webb, "From Toleration to Religious Liberty," in James R. Jones (ed.), *Liberty Secured?*, pp. 158–98.

45. See Mark Goldie, "John Locke's Circle and James II," *The Historical Journal* 35 (1992): pp. 557–86.

46. See John Dunn, "The Claim to the Freedom of Conscience: Freedom of Speech, Freedom of Thought, Freedom of Worship," in Ole Grell, Nicholas Tyacke, and Jonathan Israel (eds.), *From Persecution to Toleration: The Glorious Revolution and Religion in England* (Oxford: Clarendon Press, 1991).

47. See Justin A. I. Champion, *The Pillars of Priestcraft Shaken: The Church of England and Its Enemies, 1660–1730* (Cambridge: Cambridge University Press, 1992), pp. 170–96. See also, in general, Roger Lund (ed.), *The Margins of Orthodoxy: Heterodox Writing and Cultural Response, 1660–1750* (Cambridge, Cambridge University Press, 1995).

48. See J. G. A. Pocock, "Religious Freedom and the Desacralisation of Politics: From the English Civil Wars to the Virginia Statute," in Merrill D. Petersen and Robert C. Vaughan (eds.), *The Virginia Statute for Religious Freedom* (Cambridge: Cambridge University Press, 1988), pp. 43–73.

Chapter 3

Excommunicating the Governor's Wife: Religious Dissent in the Puritan Colonies before the Era of Rights Consciousness

Cornelia Hughes Dayton

In 1644 Roger Williams, the famous dissenter from the New England Way and founder of Rhode Island, declared it a "monstrous paradox" that in the Puritan colonies "Gods children should persecute Gods children."[1] Although the founders of the three most Puritan colonies, Massachusetts Bay, Connecticut, and New Haven, protested that there was no established religion in their jurisdictions, their statutes and practices made clear that anyone who publicly challenged the reigning congregational orthodoxy would be either reclaimed or banished. New England's earliest leaders believed that the only sure path for their societies lay in achieving and enforcing consensus among inhabitants on matters of doctrine and worship. Each congregational church had the right to excommunicate a member for persistently defending religious ideas that departed from the fundamental tenets of "true religion" as expounded by the pastor and his cleric and magistrate colleagues. Furthermore, the lawbooks of all three colonies contained statutes authorizing secular magistrates to mete out penalties (fines, reprimands, whipping, banishment, death) for crimes of religious belief.[2] The *Body of Liberties* adopted in Massachusetts in 1641 and influential for all Puritan colonies perfectly expressed the blinkered view of the founders on the concept of liberty. As an interpretation of the eleven "Liberties the Lord Jesus hath given to the churches," the code extended not only "full liberty" to godly persons to gather themselves into churches but also freedom to exercise all the ordinances of God, "according to the rules of scripture." This last phrase betrays how central the reformist, communitarian impulse was to Puritan leaders; the right to worship freely would extend only to those who cleaved to the ministers' and magistrates' conception of godly, scriptural rules.[3]

Nathaniel Ward encapsulated the founders' approach to dissenters when he wrote that the success of New England's bold experiment depended on maintaining the policy that radical sectarians such as "Anabaptists . . . shall have free liberty to *keepe away* from us."[4] With respect to this clear message that anyone who did not subscribe to the New England Way should simply depart, Puritan leaders were arguably tested most sorely by the dissenting group they had the most in common with: Antipedobaptists, or those among them who adhered to Calvinist beliefs but rejected the validity of infant baptism. Puritans rarely looked at an individual Baptist for his or her proclaimed beliefs, but instead saw someone who was inevitably headed down the slippery slope toward far more extreme forms of dissent—familism, ranterism, and Quakerism. Thus part of their motivation in excluding Antipedobaptists stemmed from the fear that to tolerate Baptists would be to open the floodgates for truly radical dissenters to enter. Moreover, the Puritans felt righteous in their policy of intolerance because they were sure that, if the Baptists (or any other sect) became the majority, adherents to Puritanism would in turn be persecuted.[5]

Here we have arrived at the heart of the tortured logic of religious liberty held by most seventeenth-century nonconformist groups. Amid all the religious ferment of the seventeenth century, few voices joined Roger Williams in defining religious liberty as a vision of many faiths coexisting in peaceful harmony.[6] Instead, each group saw itself as the only true vanguard of the revolution begun by Luther and Calvin. In William McLoughlin's words, "They argued not in terms of denominationalism, but in terms of which of them had the clearer insight into the revealed will of God." The goal of the great majority of dissenters both in England and New England was to convince as many Christians as possible that there was only one true gospel way, thereby "unchurching" multitudes, gathering them into one great fold, and fulfilling their group's destiny as the saving remnant of Protestantism. We can say, then, that pleas for liberty to worship on the basis of religious conscience were made out of concern for the group's *own* salvation: they struggled for freedom to worship so that their members would not be corrupted by papist or unscriptural practices. Claims for religious liberty in the pre-1680 Anglo-American world neither were made in the interest of pluralism nor did they often resort to the language of rights.[7]

The purpose of this chapter is to highlight how Puritans, once they took the reins of government in seventeenth-century New England, confronted the problem of dissenters who claimed to belong to the Puritan fold. As we shall see, despite its origins as a protest movement, New England's Congregational system could not, at least in its infancy, shelter a multiplicity of prophets while maintaining the vision that its New World churches embodied the saving arm of the Church of England. In order to look closely at the rituals of interrogation and negotiation that characterized heresy trials, the chapter focuses on the excommunication of Anne Eaton, wife of Theophilus Eaton, the much-respected, pious governor of New Haven Colony. Somewhat neglected in the chronicles of New England dissenters, the Eaton case helps us to perceive the internal and external factors that led orthodox leaders to move from seemingly utter rejection of modest dissenters in the 1640s to grudging toleration in the 1680s.[8]

The Case as Narrative

Anne Eaton had many more identities than that of wife to Theophilus Eaton, the governor and presiding magistrate whom Cotton Mather called "the Moses" of New Haven and a "Terror" to "Evil Doers." She doubtless imbibed a strong appreciation for religious learning and a heightened sense of her rank when growing up in the walled city of Chester as the daughter of the bishop, George Lloyd. When her first marriage to Thomas Yale ended with his early death, her reputation as "a Prudent and Pious widow" recommended her to Theophilus Eaton, who was also widowed. When they married in the mid-1620s, Eaton, then in his mid-forties, had just returned to a settled life in London from Denmark, having completed several terms as a diplomat and trade negotiator—a career built on the strength of his abilities as a merchant in the Baltic trade. The merged household of Anne Lloyd Yale and Theophilus Eaton was complex; she brought three minor children from her first marriage, and he still had the care of his unmarried daughter Mary. Before the Eatons emigrated to the New World, three more children were born.[9]

Anne and Theophilus were matched in ways that extended beyond their widowed states. First, they shared strong Puritan convictions and attended together the Coleman Street parish whose vicar was John Davenport, with whom they would emigrate. Second, they each by midlife were accustomed to a high standard of living. Anne brought substantial resources to the marital property, and Theophilus had amassed such an impressive fortune that he was accounted a "Merchant of great Credit and Fashion."[10] Later, in New Haven, the Eatons would build one of the grandest houses ever known in the early English settlements, a two-story mansion filled with the sort of opulent goods that ordinary settlers could only dream about.[11]

The Eatons, their vicar John Davenport, and many of the Puritan allies belonging to their London parish, emigrated to Massachusetts Bay in 1637, but moved on in 1638 to found the colony of New Haven along Long Island Sound. Davenport and Eaton were the two great leaders of the colony, and the sustained nature of their leadership (Eaton's lasting until his death in 1658 and Davenport's until 1667) goes far to explain why Perry Miller and others have pointed to New Haven as the most Puritan of the New England colonies, the "laboratory" where the Puritan program of reform received its most "rigorous working out."[12] In the realm of church governance, full church membership (which brought the privileges of communion, of having one's children baptized, and of voting in church affairs) was open only to those who passed a rigorous test of their faith. And as in Massachusetts, only men who were full church members could vote for civil magistrates or hold office. Such virtuous voters were entrusted to return to the bench men of "ungainsayable" probity, piety, and majesty—men like Theophilus Eaton whose skills as an interrogator allowed him to cajole almost every miscreant who appeared before him into truth telling and repentance. Since juries had been dispensed with because they were viewed as unscriptural, New Haven's legal system partook more of the continental inquisitorial approach than the incipient adversarial mode of English common law. The overriding purpose of the system was to root out all sin, punish it, and seek repentance from the malefactor so as to prevent the ever-watchful God from venting his wrath on the community. The colony's inhabitants apparently supported the broad powers of the magistrates to ferret out ungodliness: they continued Eaton in the governorship for twenty years until his death, they showed up without being forced or trying to flee when charged with crimes, and they broke down under magisterial grilling to confess in 85 percent of all criminal cases.[13]

As far as the records reveal, Anne Eaton's reputation for Puritan godliness was as yet unsullied during her first years in New Haven. She became one of the earliest full members of the church, delivering a public confession of her faith that passed John Davenport's approval.[14] It was in 1643, five years after arriving, that Anne embraced Baptist views. The precipitating event was Anne's receiving a book from her friend Lady Deborah Moody that denounced the "vanity of childish baptism." Moody, a wealthy widow who had much in common with Anne, had been admonished both in the Salem church and in the secular court for renouncing infant baptism. Before a trial could be held, Lady Moody left the Bay Colony on her own accord. On her way to settle on Long Island under the Dutch, Moody stopped in New Haven where her visit with Anne Eaton must have confirmed the latter in her Baptist beliefs.[15]

Soon Anne began to manifest her dissatisfaction with Davenport's orthodox position on baptism by publicly "departing from" the worship service whenever a child was baptized, by walking out of some services just before the sermon, and by absenting herself from communion or even from the entire worship service. For the governor's wife, who occupied a seat in the first row of the meetinghouse on the women's side of the aisle, to make her displeasure so dramatically visible, demanded an immediate reaction. At a church meeting held three days after the first incident, Mistress Eaton told fellow church members about the book that had dissuaded her from the conventional Puritan interpretation that "baptism had come in the room of circumscision [*sic*] and therefore might lawfully be administered unto infants." Davenport obtained her assent that he should examine the book, a tract by an English Baptist, Henry Denne, and prepare an answer.[16]

On the next sabbath, Davenport preached from Cor. 2:11–12 to prove the validity of infant baptism, anticipating that with this set of sermons he would persuade Anne back to the "truth" and save others in the congregation from error. On seeing that Anne would not "yield to the truth," the minister took an extraordinary step: he wrote out in full his sermons on baptism and arranged to have them copied "in a fair hand" and delivered to Anne through her husband. This was the start of a pattern stretching over the next twelve months, in which oral debates would alternate with written exchanges in the negotiations to win Anne Eaton back to the Puritan fold. At the outset of the process, Davenport's stance was rather patronizing: he wondered if Anne was suffering from problems of understanding, or listening, or memory, perhaps due to some sort of mental illness that prevented her from hearing her minister. Showing himself to be a deft strategist in the crisis, Davenport arranged for three men—Anne's husband, an elder of the church, and finally, William Hooke, Davenport's assistant and the clergyman Anne trusted most at this moment—to read aloud Denne's book *and* Davenport's sermonic replies in stages to Anne, "that she might understand what was read and have liberty to object . . . while things were in her mind." Anne responded in the classic fashion of an obstinate dissenter: she was silent and contemptuous. At the end of the exercise, the men left her with the written copies of both sides of the debate. This constituted Davenport's second means to win her over: to test if on "her own private reading" there would be "any better success." When Davenport next visited Mistress Eaton he was shocked that she adhered to her rejection of infant baptism and lacked the humility even to "propound . . . question[s]" to him, as any parishioner laboring under doubt should do.[17]

At this juncture, the next step would have been a disciplinary hearing before all church members over whether Anne should be censured or excommunicated. But other issues intervened to complicate the charges. This evidence arose from rumors that described great turmoil under the roof of the Eaton mansion and pointed to Anne Eaton as the chief instigator. From this point on, these charges threatened to overwhelm the theological issues in the dispute. But, as we shall see, the domestic turmoil was undoubtedly deeply bound up with Anne's strong religious beliefs.

Servants and members of the extended Eaton family testified to what were written up as seventeen counts against Anne: allegedly she had slapped and reviled her husband's mother; struck her unmarried stepdaughter, Mary, and accused Mary of being pregnant; abused servants physically and verbally; charged members of the household with "working with the devil"; argued with her husband when the church elders were present, and stated the desire to live apart from him. She was also accused of lying about her own actions, spreading false accusations, and speaking "very rashly." To New Haveners, these were shocking indications that the governor's wife, a middle-aged gentlewoman, was grossly mismanaging that aspect of household governance for which she was responsible—namely maintaining orderly relations among the women of different generations and statuses who inhabited the Eaton mansion.[18] The one account we have of the case was written by John Davenport; nothing remains of Anne's many replies to the charges. But we can guess that much of her outrage and frustration in the early months of 1644 stemmed from her doctrinal change of heart and her subsequent conviction that those she shared living spaces with and had responsibility for—kin, spouse, servants, enslaved Africans—were corrupting influences and damned souls because of their endorsement of infant baptism. Anne's bitter statements, her rash violence, and her insistence on sleeping apart from her husband must have arisen from her misery, her fear for her own soul and the souls of those around her, and her sense of the Christian duty to speak out and testify against those whom *she* saw as holding to untruths.[19]

Hoping to deal with these "evils" "in a private way," Davenport once again offered Mistress Eaton opportunities through both verbal and written exchanges to clear herself or repent. These overtures failed to solicit anything but "her hardness of heart and impenitency." Indeed, Anne indicated her impatience that the church had not yet proceeded with a full hearing. A date of August 14, 1644, was set, but the elders denied Anne her demand for a debate format in which critics of the procedures against her could speak freely.[20] At the meeting, after the charges were read aloud, Anne refused to object or plead. By a show of hands, the "brethren" voted, first, that the charges were sufficiently proved, and second, on Davenport's urging, that Mistress Eaton for now be admonished rather than cast out. The admonition offered Anne a period of reflection on the several rules of godly walking that she had been found to have broken. She was expected in the coming weeks to mend her "scandalous walking" and repent. Repentance would mean a public acknowledgment before the church that she had transgressed the Third, Fifth, Sixth, and Ninth Commandments and other biblical "rules" by her disrespect to her mother-in-law, her lies and reproaching, her rejection of infant baptism, and her failure to defer to her husband, pastor, and the church elders over theological matters.[21]

But the troubles in the Eaton household continued. By this time Anne was sleeping in a separate room from her husband and the elder Mrs. Eaton had temporarily removed to another house. Besides persisting in her "offensive . . . carriage in her family," Anne evidently was not prepared to abandon her Baptist principles. In this phase of the negotations, Anne became the initiator in attempting to set the terms for her reconciliation with her church. By twice sending "writing[s]" to the elders, presumably spelling out her positions on infant baptism and on the religious concerns that had so disturbed the Eaton household, Anne turned herself into an author of a "tract," thus putting herself on a par with the learned Davenport who had used written interventions to instruct her.[22] The elders, finding the missives to fall short of adequate repentence, tried to shift the negotiations back to the plane of visitation and verbal persuasion.

Nine months had gone by without progress following the church's admonition of Mistress Eaton. By late spring 1645 the lengthy string of visits that church officials had paid to the haughty and recalcitrant Anne at the Eaton mansion may have begun to look to many like an unseemly inversion of the civil court hearings that were presided over by Theophilus and held in the very same rooms. That the authorities appeared to be waiting on Mistress Eaton, both literally and figuratively, began to tarnish the reputation of New Haven Colony among New Englanders. Rebuked in private correspondence, Davenport named a day in May 1645 for hearings on the issue of excommunication. After two days of testimony and listening to Mistress Eaton express her views "without any show of remorse and . . . with an ostentation of empty words which fell short" of repentance, the church members "with much grief of heart, and many tears" voted unanimously to excommunicate the governor's wife.[23]

What was Anne's position throughout these proceedings? Without surviving accounts of what she wrote and declared to her church, we are forced to speculate and infer. Was she arguing in the end that she and Davenport did not differ significantly on theological points and therefore she had no need to apologize? Or did she, like some other New England Baptists, stipulate the conditions on which she would come to the Lord's table, including an insistence that the New Haven church abolish infant baptism? A third scenario seems the most likely. We know that Anne professed not wanting to lose her church membership and that her goal was not to establish a separate church. When she submitted a written defense of her theological views to the elders, she could very well have been arguing for the right to hold her different view of baptism while continuing to be a full member of Davenport's church. This advocacy of open or mixed communion was the position of many Congregationalists in England by the mid-seventeenth century, and it was the compromise position taken by Thomas Gould in the mid-1650s before he established the first Baptist church in Boston. Gould did not wish to leave the Puritan church of which he was a member and his message to Massachusetts authorities was in essence that Puritans should be able to differ on the issue of infant baptism and still remain in church fellowship.[24] Ten years earlier, Anne Eaton *may* have made the same claim. If so, she was arguing that a heterogeneity of believers could exist within the Puritan fold, as long as all church members accepted Calvinist tenets. In a broad sense, such a position on Anne's part would have constituted a foreshadowing of the settlement on limited toleration that was achieved in Massachusetts in the 1680s. And if Anne's position was not the radical one that denounced all New England churches as invalid, her moderate stance as a dissenter must have contributed to the aura of quiet, even of forgetfulness, that eventually enveloped her reputation.

Coda: Aftermath

Anne Eaton never rejoined the New Haven church. Yet she also did not go down the paths chosen by some of her compatriot dissenters: she did not abandon her family or her husband's colony; she did not move to set up a Baptist church; she did not become a Quaker. Neither did the civil courts in New Haven choose to prosecute her as was done in a cluster of mid-1640s prosecutions of Baptists in Salem, Massachusetts. Of course, perhaps this lapse in New Haven was due to the fact that no one dared deepen the misery of the presiding magistrate, Anne's husband. However, in June 1646, a year after Anne's excommunication, the New Haven civil magistrates, including Eaton, showed that they were willing to prosecute religious dissenters.

The 1646 trials of three defiant, female critics of Davenport's church serve as a coda to the Eaton case, for the women had maintained close relations with Anne Eaton over the past year and they raised the specter of a possible "party" of dissidents stirred up by Anne. It emerged during the testimony, however, that Anne's theological complaints were at odds with those of her friends. None of them presented herself as a Baptist, and one of their criticisms—that taking up contributions in church was a papist invention—was disputed by Anne. The defendants were Lucy Brewster, an extremely wealthy widow, and two recent migrants to New Haven, the mistresses Moore and Leach, neither of whom were church members. They were brought to trial because they had—"against the rule"—mingled with excommunicate Eaton, satirized and critiqued the elders' practices in interrogating dissidents in church discipline cases, meddled in ongoing disputes (thus usurping the authorities' role), and spread other blasphemous ideas that were more radical than those raised in Anne's case. Unsatisfied with the women's responses in court, the authorities still did not take the ultimate step of banishing the trio:

Brewster was slapped with the largest fine ever heard of and the other two were roundly reprimanded. Besides warning assertive women against the vanity of believing they were capable of envisioning a purer church than the colony's leaders, the trials gave Governor Eaton the chance to show that he was as capable as any ordained clergyman at lecturing unorthodox thinkers on the correct exegesis of critical biblical passages.[25]

Why Eaton's vaunted powers of persuasion failed in the case of his wife remains a mystery to us. Equally surprising is the failure of Davenport and other elites to chastize Eaton for his inability or refusal to control his wife's outrageous behavior. Theophilus seems to have adopted, and been accorded, a Job-like stance toward Anne's spiritual turmoil and the resulting domestic disturbances. Perhaps his quiet resignation came from an intimation either that Anne's estrangements (from their kinfolk, from his bed, from her earlier religious convictions) would be temporary or that she deserved unusual forbearance because she could be suffering from an episodic madness similar to that of her daughter by her first marriage, Ann Hopkins.[26]

From the late 1640s on, the atmosphere in the Eaton household probably became less charged. The unmarried stepdaughter whom Anne had picked on married and moved away, and Theophilus's mother died, so that intergenerational conflict inevitably lessened. Signs crop up in the sparse records we have of the Eatons' family life that Anne and Theophilus effected some sort of reconciliation. When the governor wrote to his friend John Winthrop, Jr., in January 1655/56, he noted: "My self, wife, and daughter remember our due respects to your self, Mrs. Winthropp [*sic*], and all yours, desiring much to see you here."[27] Eaton was either adeptly keeping up outward proprieties or obliquely revealing an affectionate marital partnership that survived the crisis of Anne's excommunication. Under English rules of inheritance, Theophilus had the chance to show any disapproval of his wife when he wrote his last will. Instead, the 1656 document carefully spelled out that, "in token of my love," Anne was to receive 50 pounds "over and above her thirds." He also signaled his trust in her managerial good sense by naming her as one of his two executors. By Theophilus's death in 1658, the New Haven town authorities also were ready to extend a "token of . . . respect to Mistress Eaton": learning that Anne had decided to return to England, they agreed that the town should pay for an escort to attend her to Boston where she would board a ship. This was a gesture more befitting the respected widow of the colony's honored governor rather than a social outcast. Anne returned to her dower lands outside of Chester and died there in 1659. Writing in eulogy of Theophilus Eaton, Cotton Mather chose to leave the magistrate's memory unsullied by Anne's discretions. Not only did Mather omit any reference to Anne's excommunication, but he also made the claim (laughable when applied to events of 1644–1646) that Eaton had had no peer in ensuring that "the Government of his Family" was "ordered with . . . Wisdom!" Thus did one of early New England's most famous chroniclers conspire to render the apostasy of the governor's wife's invisible.[28]

The Case as a Window on New England Dissent

A facile interpretation of the Eaton case would hold that the long drawn-out negotiations with Anne and the absence of further punishments beyond excommunication stemmed from her high status and from the authorities' fear of endangering the respect that Governor Eaton commanded among colony residents. But while Anne's marital and social status may have ultimately protected her from more precipitous, civil proceedings, it also *enabled* her public dissent. Well-connected in networks of correspondence with educated elites across colony lines, secure in her knowledge that she could support herself if a break with her husband became irrevocable, and long accustomed to receiving deference from those around her, Mistress Eaton was the type of seventeenth-century woman who could risk the act of delivering an ultimatum to church authorities: accept me on your terms or cast me out. For women *more* than men, the privileges of status were a chief determining element in one's willingness to take a defiant public stand against the authorities. A strikingly high number of women who faced down heresy charges or excommunication in seventeenth-century New England shared the wealthy background of Anne Eaton, even if they were not governors' wives.[29]

Anne's case was not unusual in a second respect. The decision by Davenport and the elders to proceed in phases, and very gradually, is typical of other well-documented New England excommunication cases. Church officials and members alike harbored extreme, heart-felt reluctance to cast out someone who had once been accepted as a saint. They shaped the disciplinary process after the model of the exchange of teaching, albeit a one-sided exchange in which they confidently expected the dissenter to "receive [the] light" and "truth" of God, to "fall under" the rule of obedience to better interpreters, and to be reclaimed to the church fellowship.[30]

Third, along with other New England Baptists, Anne's difference with her church rested on her claim to be reaching for an even purer church—one that had stripped away all papist and unscriptural accretions so that it resembled the earliest Christian churches. If denied the freedom to espouse her rejection of infant baptism, she could claim "spiritual coercion" just as Davenport and other Puritan ministers in England had done under Archbishop Laud. Believing firmly that the Bible contained no model for infant baptism, Anne's resistance to being disciplined most likely stemmed from the fact that she thought there was no "rule of Christ that [she] had broken."[31] By attempting to stay within the Puritan fold, Anne, like most other New England Baptists, was arguing for a very limited notion of religious liberty. Nowhere do we overhear her asserting that there should be a multiplicity of denominations in New Haven, that the laws requiring all residents to attend church should be abolished, or that a tax system by which everyone paid to support the orthodox churches abrogated natural rights.[32]

In her struggle against New Haven's strict notion of orthodoxy, Anne Eaton deployed one weapon frequently resorted to by seventeenth-century dissenters: mockery. Mockery was a flag thrown down between the contending parties that, on the one hand, announced that all involved knew how the debate would end (excommunication, banishment, censure) and, on the other hand, allowed the institutional loser, the dissident, to vent a complex melange of emotions (pride, contempt, frustration, grief, vindictiveness) and perhaps even to hint at the absurdity of the parties' shared rituals. Anne Eaton did this by allowing the elders to think that she was close to acknowledging the charges against her, and then casuistrically announcing that she could not repent as they wished because she did not perceive "her husband's Mother to be her Mother" and therefore, how could she have breached the Fifth Commandment. John Farnam did it on the day of his excommunication by laughing when the minister read the sentence, then announcing, "This place is too hot for me," and walking out. Anne Hutchinson is just the most famous of many dissidents who used mockery to prick holes in the Puritans' inflated notion of their own, exclusive righteousness.[33]

The Eaton case also reminds us of the limited consequences of excommunication in Puritan New England. As David C. Brown has pointed out, since the New Englanders recognized only two sacraments (commmunion and baptism), excommunicates were not barred from marrying, from proper burial (since there was no concept of consecrated ground), or (except in New Haven) from attending worship services. John Davenport was harder than his fellow ministers on those cast out: if Anne wished to hear the service at any point after 1646, she was forced to stand "at the doore, [even] in frost, snow, and raine."[34] Moreover, New England clergymen agreed that, unlike the situation in England, excommunication would be properly interpreted as "a spiritual punishment" and would not interfere with one's civil and property rights or make one liable to imprisonment. In addition, Puritans let lapse the Church of England practice of punishing those who socialized with excommunicates. Full church members were warned not to be familiar with the likes of Anne Eaton, but such shunning seems not to have been rigorously enforced.[35]

It is clear that in 1646, Puritans in neither New Haven nor the Bay Colony were ready to see any virtue in the possibility of allowing Anti-pedobaptists to worship with them or in sanctioned churches. And yet the ways in which the case of Anne Eaton was argued and negotiated foreshadowed the compromise that was reached between Baptists and Congregationalists forty years later. By allowing debate, by letting dissidents publicly air their views, by encouraging the give-and-take among minister, elders, congregants, and the unorthodox, New England's leaders doomed their own policy of intolerance. For as the colonies' population grew, the myth of consensus became ever more impractical to enforce and uphold. By 1668, when Thomas Gould and other Boston-area Baptists were allowed two days to offer their viewpoints to the public, open debate began to create popular support for a limited degree of toleration. Thirteen years later, Massachusetts authorities gave up on harrassing Gould and his followers, effectively sanctioning their worship services in a church they had secretly erected. The key ingredients of the compromise were: (1) that Gould and his adherents had established themselves as respectable, propertied, God-fearing neighbors before they turned to Baptist beliefs; (2) that these Baptists presented themselves as Calvinists who did not deny the validity of the orthodox Puritan churches; and (3) that they were committed in an unspoken pledge to refrain from disturbing the peace or openly proselytizing in the name of their beliefs. Anne Eaton shared these qualities of respectability, prior Calvinist credentials, moderation in attacking her church's ways, and restraint after sentencing.[36] But she lived in a place and decade in which the laity were not yet ready to challenge their ministers' insistence on total conformity.

Edmund S. Morgan has characterized the New England Puritans as tribalistic—in other words, inward-looking, concerned for their own salvation, and little interested in saving others.[37] This attribute goes far in explaining their reluctance to move against insiders like Anne Eaton and Thomas Gould. We can see the crucial shift of the 1680s as a moment when the laity embraced a slightly expanded notion of tribe whereas nearly all clergy remained bitterly opposed to the language of individual rights and the formal policy of toleration that was imposed on them by the king and parliament in the wake of the Glorious Revolution. Cotton Mather wrote in his diary in 1692 that, despite the new Massachusetts charter's promise of "liberty of conscience" to all Christians except Papists, he believed himself to be "the only minister living in the land that have testifyed against the supression of heresy by persecution." According to Perry Miller, Mather had declared: "For every man to worship God according to his conviction is an essential right of human nature." Yet Puritan ministers after the settlement of the 1680s treated Baptists, Quakers, and Anglicans with as much contempt as they could muster.[38]

Even as Puritan principles faded as the organizing values for New England society, the "unresolved conflict" named by A. S. P. Woodhouse as central to Puritanism—that between a "passionate concern" for liberty of conscience and a "passionate zeal" for achieving earthly reform—would cast a long shadow over believers of all stripes. Disestablishment would not occur in Massachusetts until 1815, and religious tests for office-holding would persist in the United States long after the passage of Thomas Jefferson's landmark 1786 Act for Establishing Religious Freedom.[39] Although the dueling passions of Protestantism suffused American culture long after Anne Eaton's excommunication, the epistemological skepticism advanced by Enlightenment thinkers and the American revolutionaries' embrace of a "constitution of aspirations"[40] created new legal and ideological terrains for negotiations over religious liberty.

Notes

1. Quoted in Philip F. Gura, *A Glimpse of Sion's Glory: Puritan Radicalism in New England, 1620–1660* (Middletown, CT: Wesleyan University Press, 1984), p. 15.

2. Such statutory crimes included failing to attend sabbath worship services, interrupting a minister during preaching, schismatically gathering a church that only "pretended" to follow the "Orthodox" way, uttering blasphemies, and "seduc[ing] others" into heresies. See Emil Oberholzer, Jr., *Delinquent Saints: Disciplinary Action in the Early Congregational Churches of Massachusetts* (New York: Columbia University Press, 1956), pp. 79, 95; Charles J. Hoadly (ed.), *Records of the Colony and Plantation of New Haven, from 1638 to 1649* (Hartford, CT: Case, Tiffany & Co., 1857) [hereafter *NHCR*], II, pp. 576, 587–88, 599.

3. Quoted in David D. Hall, *The Faithful Shepherd: A History of the New England Ministry in the Seventeenth Century* (Chapel Hill, NC: University of North Carolina Press, 1972), p. 124.

4. Quoted in Gura, *Glimpse of Sion's Glory*, p. 20 (emphasis added).

5. William G. McLoughlin, *New England Dissent, 1630–1833: The Baptists and the Separation of Church and State*, 2 vols. (Cambridge, MA: Harvard University Press, 1971), I, pp. 4, 6. For thorough analyses of the doctrinal debate over infant baptism, see ibid., pp. 26–48, and Gura, *Glimpse of Sion's Glory*, pp. 93–125.

6. On the marginal status of such thinkers in England, see Champion's chapter above, at [p. 5].

7. McLoughlin, *New England Dissent*, I, pp. 4, 6. Note the absence of religion in the civil liberties enumerated in the early New England codes, codes that remained in the books until the Revolution. For New Haven Colony's 1656 Code, see *NHCR*, II, pp. 571–72.

8. For brief references to the Eaton case, see Stephen Foster, "New England and the Challenge of Heresy, 1630 to 1660: The Puritan Crisis in Transatlantic Perspective," *William and Mary Quarterly*, 3d ser., 38 (1981): p. 642, and Mary Maples Dunn, "Saints and Sisters: Congregational and Quaker Women in the Early Colonial

Period," *American Quarterly*, 30 (1978): p. 587. Grudging toleration is McLoughlin's phrase (*New England Dissent*, I).

9. "Moses" and "pious widow": Cotton Mather, *Magnalia Christi Americana, Books I and II*, ed., Kenneth Murdock (Cambridge, MA: Harvard University Press, 1977), p. 257. On the Eatons, see Elizabeth Tucker Van Beek, "Piety and Profit: English Puritans and the Shaping of a Godly Marketplace in the New Haven Colony" (Ph.D. diss., University of Virginia, 1993), pp. 78–116, and Donald Lines Jacobus, (comp.), *Families of Ancient New Haven*, 3 vols. (originally published in 1922–1932; reprint, Baltimore, MD: Genealogical Publishing Co., 1981), pp. 591, 2030. Sources vary on whether Anne's first husband was David or Thomas Yale.

10. Mather, *Magnalia*, p. 256; Lilian Handlin, "Dissent in a Small Community," *New England Quarterly*, 58 (1985): p. 198. There is no evidence that the widow Yale signed a prenuptial agreement with Eaton before their marriage.

11. For Eaton's inventory, see Van Beek, "Piety and Profit," pp. 449–59. Eaton was listed in 1643 with assets of L3000 (*NHCR*, I, pp. 91–93).

12. Perry Miller, Review of *The New Haven Colony*, by Isabel M. Calder, *New England Quarterly*, 8 (1935): pp. 583–84; Gail Sussman Marcus, " 'Due Execution of the Generall Rules of Righteousness': Criminal Procedure in New Haven Town and Colony, 1638–1358," in David D. Hall et al. (eds.), *Saints and Revolutionaries: Essays on Early American History* (New York: W. W. Norton, 1984), p. 101; Cornelia Hughes Dayton, *Women Before the Bar: Gender, Law, and Society in Connecticut, 1639–1789* (Chapel Hill, NC: University of North Carolina Press, 1995), pp. 22–34, 66–67, 173–81, 290–300.

13. Mather, *Magnalia*, p. 257; Marcus, "Due Execution," pp. 99–105, 110, 132–33.

14. Franklin Bowditch Dexter (comp.), *Historical Catalogue of the Members of the First Church of Christ in New Haven, . . . 1639–1914* (New Haven, CT: [s.n.], 1914), p. 2; Handlin, "Dissent," p. 198.

15. Linda Briggs Biemer, *Women and Property in Colonial New York: The Transition from Dutch to English Law, 1643–1727* (Ann Arbor, MI: UMI Research Press, 1983), pp. 11–32. Moody, the widow of a baronet and grandaughter of a radical English bishop, had settled on a grand estate in Lynn; excommunication was passed on her only after her departure from Massachusetts. By not persisting in outspoken dissent as a resident of the Bay Colony, Moody preserved her friendship with the Winthrops. By promising to hold Baptist services in private houses and to refrain from proselytizing, she won a unique grant of "free libertie of conscience" from the Dutch government, which otherwise enforced conformity to the Reformed Church (ibid., pp. 20, 29–30).

16. Newman Smyth (ed.), "Mrs. Eaton's Trial (in 1644) as It Appears upon the Records of the First Church of New Haven," *Papers of the New Haven Colony Historical Society*, 5 (1894): p. 135.

17. Ibid., p. 136; Handlin, "Dissent," p. 199.

18. For women's primary responsibility for recruiting and supervising female workers in the household economy, see Laurel Thatcher Ulrich, "Housewife and Gadder: Themes of Self-Sufficiency and Community in Eighteenth-Century New England," in Carol Groneman and Mary Beth Norton (eds.), *"To Toil the Livelong Day": America's Women at Work, 1780–1980* (Ithaca, NY: Cornell University Press, 1987), pp. 21–34.

19. Smyth, "Mrs. Eaton's Trial," pp. 138–44. Anne's words echo those of the Salem Baptist William Witter who believed "that they who stayed [in church] while a childe was baptized doe worshipp the dyvill" (McLoughlin, *New England Dissent*, I, p. 18).

20. This aspect of the dispute was revealed in the later excommunication trial of one of Anne supporters: "The Trial of Ezekiel Cheever," *Collections of the Connecticut Historical Society*, 1 (1860): pp. 44–45.

21. Smyth, "Mrs. Eaton's Trial," pp. 136–138, 144–45. For the correct dates, see Isabel MacBeath Calder, *The New Haven Colony* (New Haven, CT: Yale University Press, 1934), p. 93n. We do not know if female church members were allowed to vote. The votes were unanimous, meaning that Theophilus Eaton felt compelled to vote against his wife. Only after the votes did Anne choose to stand up and speak; Davenport dismissed her request "that at that time there might be no censure passed upon her."

22. Smyth, "Mrs. Eaton's Trial," pp. 145–47. On Anne and Theophilus sleeping apart, see *NHCR*, I, pp. 268–70. When dissenter Anne Hibbens of Boston offered to express herself to her church in writing so as to ensure clarity and accuracy, minister John Cotton found the practice threatening; he denounced it as unprecedented, dilatory, and "uncouth" (John Demos [ed.], *Remarkable Providences, 1600–1760* [New York: George Braziller, 1972], pp. 226–27).

23. Smyth, "Mrs. Eaton's Trial," pp. 146–48. On the governor's examinations of criminals, see Marcus, "Due Execution," pp. 102–03, 121–27.

24. For stipulating conditions, see John Farnam's case as summarized in Oberholzer, *Delinquent Saints*, p. 92. For Gould, see McLoughlin, *New England Dissent*, I, pp. 22, 54. This interpretation accords with the claim Anne made several times that she had answered or acknowledged some of the charges against her "but not to the churches satisfaction" (*NHCR*, I, p. 243; Smyth, "Mrs. Eaton's Trial," pp. 146–48).

25. "Party": Smyth, "Mrs. Eaton's Trial," p. 135. For the 1646 trials, see *NHCR*, I, pp. 242–57; Handlin, "Dissent," pp. 203–12; and Mary Beth Norton, *Founding Mothers and Fathers: Gendered Power and the Forming of American Society* (New York: Knopf, 1996), pp. 174–79. The evidence on whether Lucy Brewster was a full church member is contradictory.

26. As Mary Beth Norton points out (*Founding Mothers*, p. 441), a eulogistic poem penned for Eaton chose the analogy of Job for the verse in which the governor's

patience, wisdom, and love in his family life and marriage were lauded (Abraham Pierson, "Lines on the Death of Theophilus Eaton," *Collections of the Massachusetts Historical Society*, 4th ser., 7 [1865]: p. 479 [hereafter *MHS Colls.*]). Mental instability as an explanation of Anne Eaton's rash behavior in 1644–1646 has been suggested by Newman Smyth ("Mrs. Eaton's Trial," p. 133) and Edward E. Atwater (*History of the Colony of New Haven to Its Absorption into Connecticut* [New Haven, CT: Printed for the author by Rand, Avery, & Co., 1881], p. 234n). Genevieve L. Davis uses the term "a nervous condition" and notes that Anne often cared for her mentally troubled daughter in the Eaton's New Haven household (*Theophilus Eaton, "New England's Glory," 1637–1657*, typescript, New England Historical and Genealogical Society, 1977, pp. 23, 115). Insanity was largely perceived as an episodic visitation, rather than a permanent condition, in the colonial period.

27. *MHS Colls.*, 4th ser., VII (1865): pp. 476–77.

28. Mather, *Magnalia*, p. 257. Will: Leonard Bacon, *Thirteen Historical Discourses on . . . the First Church in New Haven* (New Haven, CT: Durrie & Peck, 1839), pp. 354–55. Escort: Franklin Bowditch Dexter (ed.), *New Haven Town Records, 1649–1662* (New Haven, CT: New Haven Colony Historical Society, 1917), p. 357.

29. During the discipline process, Anne was charged with having once said to her husband "I can get my bread and cost you nothing" (Smyth, "Mrs. Eaton's Trial," p. 143). Wealthy, high-status women who were close to those in power before their trials include: Anne Hutchinson, Lady Deborah Moody, Anne Hibbens, and Lucy Brewster.

Note that under other circumstances, Anne might have been accused of witchcraft. Women with this profile of independence and outspokenness were disportionately accused as witches (Carol F. Karlsen, *The Devil in the Shape of a Woman: Witchcraft in Colonial New England* [New York: W. W. Norton, 1987], espec. Chaps. 3, 5).

30. Quoted phrases: Smyth, "Mrs. Eaton's Trial," pp. 137, 146. In general, see McLouglin, *New England Dissent*, I, pp. 26–27.

31. "Coercion": an English Puritan manifesto quoted in David C. Brown, "The Keys of the Kingdom: Excommunication in Colonial Massachusetts," *New England Quarterly*, 57 (1994): p. 539. "No rule of Christ . . .": This was the statement that Baptist Thomas Gould made to his Puritan minister in 1655 (McLoughlin, *New England Dissent*, I, p. 53).

32. For similar points on the nonradical positions of Gould and other Baptists, see ibid., pp. 60, 62–63, 68n.

33. Smyth, "Mrs. Eaton's Trial," p. 147; Oberholzer, *Delinquent Saints*, p. 92; Jane Neill Kamensky, "Governing the Tongue: Speech and Society in Early New England" (Ph.D. diss., Yale University, 1993), pp. 425–26.

34. Thomas Lechford, *Plain Dealing: Or, Newes from New-England* (London, 1642), printed in *MHS Colls.*, 3d ser., 3 (1833): p. 73.

35. *NHCR*, I, p. 249; Brown, "Keys of the Kingdom," pp. 540, 552–55. But note that known Baptists were not allowed to vote or hold secular office (McLoughlin, *New England Dissent*, I, p. 15).

36. McLoughlin, *New England Dissent*, I, pp. 62–72 (on Gould), 75, 77, 79–90, 107. Evidence presented in the Brewster trial indicated that Anne Eaton had not attempted to acquaint other discontented women with her Baptist beliefs (*NHCR*, I, p. 246).

37. *The Puritan Family: Religion and Domestic Relations in Seventeenth-Century New England*, rev. ed. (New York: Harper & Row, 1966), espec. Chap. 7.

38. McLoughlin, *New England Dissent*, I, pp. 108–09.

39. Woodhouse (ed.), *Puritanism and Liberty, Being the Army Debates (1647–9)* . . . , (Chicago: University of Chicago Press, 1951), Intro., p. 53; McLoughlin, *New England Dissent*, I and II; Merrill D. Peterson and Robert Vaughn (eds.), *The Virginia Statute for Religious Freedom: Its Evolution and Consequences in American History* (New York: Cambridge University Press, 1988).

40. Hendrik Hartog, "The Constitution of Aspiration and 'The Rights That Belong to Us All,' " *Journal of American History*, 74 (1987): pp. 1013–1034.

Chapter 4

Enlightenment and Conscience

Martin Fitzpatrick

In this chapter I shall discuss changing attitudes, to conscience and rights in the period from the late seventeenth to the late eighteenth century, as expressed by some leading writers, At the beginning of this period, the idea of toleration was profoundly contested and rarely implemented. At best it was granted as a privilege rather than as a right. By the end of the period, many minority religions in Europe had been granted some degree of toleration and the foundation had been laid for what has been described as "a culture of rights."

During the Enlightenment there occurred what has been regarded as the democratization of conscience[1] and the concomitant development of natural rights demands for toleration and liberty of conscience. The democratization of conscience was the moral and spiritual counterpart of Enlightenment ideas about the world of nature, which, as Sir Isaiah Berlin has noted, rested on, "a secular version of the old natural law doctrine according to which the nature of things possessed a permanent, unalterable structure, differences and changes in the world being subject to universal and immutable laws."[2] One consequence of this trend was to focus attention on the moral as opposed to the religious dimensions of conscience. Also universalization of conscience in a religious sense tended to de-Christianize it, to emphasize the natural religionist content, and to free it of some of its cultural constraints,[3] a tendency resented by critics of the Enlightenment.[4]

Although it is not possible to provide a detailed context for this discussion of Enlightenment ideas of conscience, it may be useful to take note of some of the broad changes in Enlightenment theory and eighteenth-century practice. *Ancien Régime* states were confessional states, that is, they were based on the belief that church and state were intertwined, that kings had a divine mission to fulfil on earth, that it was a matter of vital concern to statesmen to exercise religious as well as social control over subjects and that it was highly desirable that all subjects should belong to one confession. Such ideas were weakening in the eighteenth century when contractarian notions of the state found favor: religion was seen to be useful to the state in preserving the social and moral order, but was regulated by state needs and demands. Church should be subordinated to state. This was also in accord with enlightened jurisprudential ideas in which religious matters were seen as an inappropriate area of concern for the criminal law. The rational and the useful came to be the favored criteria for thinking about law. Laws were codified to provide consistency of application, and this was often accompanied by the incorporation of natural law ideas into court judgements. Law reform was closely connected with the campaign for religious toleration, since so many legal abominations were still being committed on the basis of laws outlawing religious diversity. Reform was demanded on humanitarian grounds and as a means of creating a more enlightened citizenry and polity.[5] The growing tendency to see the state as a moralizing agency did not mean that questions relating to freedom of conscience were not still important. Indeed the development of a culture of rights can been seen as a response to this newly found mission of states; civil liberties needed to be protected and ideas concerning freedom of conscience in matters relating to religious belief extended. Yet it remains important to distinguish between religious and civil liberty and so before discussing conscience as it relates to earthly duties, it will be necessary to say something about religious liberty.

Although most cases of intolerance in the early modern world were against religious communities, and those who suffered did so for their adherence to a proscribed church or sect, the arguments put forward in favor of toleration centered on individual religious liberty. Indeed, the Reformation began with Martin Luther's conscientious stand.[6] As his example shows, religious liberty begins with interior conviction that no amount of coercion can change, but it also demands the right to witness one's faith through worship and deed. Although related to the civil liberty of freedom of speech and expression, it is not identical, for its demands stem from the conscientious relationship between God and man.

The Reformation caused an immense amount of confessional and civil strife, and the dominant view in early modern Europe was that religious peace could only be ensured by uniformity of religion within a given territory. Toleration, it was believed, only brought conflict. There seemed to be an impasse between positive and negative views of toleration. However, in the late seventeenth century the situation was beginning to change. The revocation in 1685 of the Edict of Nantes (1598), which had afforded some measure of toleration to French Protestants, created a situation far worse than the existing one of limited toleration. In contrast, in England and Wales in 1689, a compromise was worked out that allowed a degree of freedom of conscience on terms that might set an example to other states. At the same time the issue of toleration was debated more vigorously than at any period since the Reformation. Contributors included philosophers of major importance, notably Pierre Bayle and John Locke.

Pierre Bayle's views on toleration drew on a tradition going back to the Renaissance, which combined biblical, rational, and skeptical arguments. This stressed the difficulty and the unwisdom of persecuting erroneous or heretical consciences. Individuals, it was argued, were bound by conscience to stand by the truth as they understood it, and not to yield to persecution. Liberty of conscience should be regarded as a "right that men have everywhere merely by virtue of being rational creatures."[7] In this tradition, talk about the rights of conscience arose not from abstract argument about such rights, rather it arose from a religious duty to obey conscience and hard thinking about the consequences of that duty. Bayle's own thinking was informed by knowledge of the tragedy of persecution, including the loss of his own brother. Stressing the obligation to obey one's conscience led him to argue for toleration in the widest sense to include even atheists.

Bayle was profoundly influential in the Enlightenment. He forged powerful weapons of destructive criticism. However, his ironic style tended to obscure his own position; he was viewed alternatively as an atheist, pyrrhonist, and a fideist. Moreover, although he was very much in touch with the latest thinking, his instinct was to compartmentalize, to keep matters concerning morals apart from those concerning faith, natural philosophy apart from those concerning theology, religious toleration apart from those concerning political philosophy. He parted company with currents of thought leading into the Enlightenment that represented a concern to construct a sound philosophical basis for relating ideas to action, beliefs to behavior, and which sought to retain an intimate relationship between religion and morality by reducing faith to essentials and subjecting morality to rational simplicities. Bayle agreed with the ethical dimension of the enterprise, but not the religious, for it led, he believed, in the direction of Socinianism. He did not share the growing confidence instilled by the achievements of natural philosophers, which encouraged the belief that a unified body of truth could be constructed through reason and experience.[8]

The confidence inspired by the achievements of the scientific revolution would have general implication for Enlightenment ideas of conscience, but it could only grow by stages. John Locke, dubbed by D'Alembert as "the Newton of the moral world," in providing a more guarded case for religious toleration than Bayle allayed some of the political and moral fears aroused by conceding the rights of conscience. He addressed the concern that following one's conscience could lead to antisocial and politically subversive behavior by suggesting that individuals should have the right to worship as they pleased providing they did not espouse doctrines harmful to civil authority and to society. Thus one should not tolerate the intolerant, those who owed allegiance to a foreign authority, those who could be absolved by their religion of moral and political crimes, and those who did not believe in the moral order. On these grounds, Locke was opposed to toleration for Roman Catholics and atheists. His ideas on toleration were accompanied by a contractarian account of political authority and a view of churches as voluntary organizations that exercised only religious authority. Although regarded by some as dangerously radical, he did put forward a positive notion of toleration within criteria that could be adapted to different states and circumstances. In secular affairs, churches needed to be subordinate to states, and his preference was for the separation of church and state. In effect he subordinated conscience to *raison d'état* provided that that *raison* was reasonable in enlightened terms.

Lockeian style ideas provided a framework of thought within which dissenters *and* states could adjust their demands and some form of compromise be reached. Religious minorities would try to show that their adherents were good and loyal citizens and so worthy of toleration. Statesmen for their part saw the utilitarian value of allowing dissenters some measure of toleration, of mitigating the intolerance of established churches, and of posing as champions of enlightened ideas. Frederick the Great of Prussia was the first of such exemplars of enlightened kingship. He declared that he was the "first servant of the state" and wrote proudly of religious toleration that existed in his kingdom.[9] One of his subjects, Immanuel Kant, did not swallow entirely his propaganda. He lived in Königsberg in East Prussia where the dominant Lutherans coexisted with Quakers, Mennonites, Socinians, Herrnhuters, German Swiss Calvinists, and Huguenots. In his famous discussion of "What Is Enlightenment?," Kant wrote:

> As things are at present, we still have a long way to go before men as a whole can be in a position (or can even be put in a position) of using their own understanding confidently and well in religious matters, without outside guidance. But we do have distinct indications that the way is now being cleared for them to work freely in this direction, and that the obstacles to universal enlightenment, to man's emergence from his self-incurred immaturity, are gradually becoming fewer. In this respect our age is the age of enlightenment, or the century of *Frederick*.[10]

Kant reflects the growing optimism in the mid to late eighteenth century in the power of enlightenment in its own right, and its ability to make toleration safe. This feeling owed much to Frederick the Great's old friend, Voltaire, who became in the evening of his life the Enlightenment's greatest champion of religious toleration. His *Traité sur la Tolérance* (1763) demonstrated that his lifelong fears of enthusiasm and of the *canaille* were conquered by his contemplation of the prospect of enlightening mankind. He came to believe that the progress of reason was inexorable, that it should be viewed in a positive light, that reason should be cultivated, the population educated, and government adjusted to enlightened precepts.[11] It is no coincidence that in such matters Voltaire believed that he was following English ideas and practice. Although it was the wrongful execution in 1761 of the Huguenot Jean Calas on the charge of murdering his son that led him to campaign actively for toleration and to fight superstition, his years in England between 1726–1729 were crucial in forming his ideas. He saw there a tolerant society, a liberal government and a culture that expressed and absorbed the latest ideas. He was the first Frenchman to appreciate Locke's many-faceted achievement and understood that his contribution to thinking about toleration provided new ways of looking at man and society as well as specific criteria for allowing toleration. His *Lettres Philosophiques/Letters Concerning the English Nation* (1733/1734) provided powerful propaganda for the creation of tolerant open societies.[12] By relating English tolerance to English culture, Voltaire generalized thinking about toleration. Religion no longer need be a source of strife, it could be a source of general happiness and individuals could unite on the basis of a limited number of central truths. Dogmatism could be banished, confessional strife eliminated, and religion become a beneficent force.[13] Conscience need no longer be feared; it could be regarded, in the words of the Marquis de Mirabeau as the "coadhérence universelle des intérêts humains."[14] Mirabeau proposed the term *humanisme* (or *humanitisme*) as synonymous with the love of humanity. Earlier Abbé Saint Pierre coined the neologism *bienfaisance* as indicative of a secular virtue free of the overtones of ecclesiastical language. Thus *"bienfaisance annonce une morale, selon laquelle l'ici-bas se suffit à lui-même, en dehors de toute référence à la justice transcendante."*[15]

Such views indicate important trends in Enlightenment attitudes toward conscience. Enlightenment attitudes did not arise solely from the recognition of the power of the case for conceding the right of conscience in religion They arose from the parallel concern to find ways of preventing the concession of such rights from causing strife. Enlightenment thinkers worried about persecution *and* the consequences of tolerating enthusiasts. These worries were not assuaged solely by creating Lockeian style parameters for tolerating religions, or by optimism about enlightening religious beliefs and practices. They were allayed in part by the displacement of the religious dimensions of conscience from its core. Instead the Enlightenment's focus was on the moral conscience.

The growing focus in the Enlightenment on the moral conscience was an intimate part of the Enlightenment project to moralize man. Although the desire to civilize the conscience was an important aspect of Enlightenment ideas on tolerance, this theme developed more strongly in relation to moral than to religious liberty. Thus we find that Locke in his political philosophy tended to take the conscience as given, an inner voice of truth, or a divine, inner legislator.[16] Yet in his *Essay Concerning Human Understanding* he made explicit his departure from intuitionist notions of conscience. Conscience, he agreed, does indeed judge the morality of our actions, but conscience was not given, it was learned or imbibed, it came from education and environment. Reason had now become the divine legislator and natural law was the law of reason.[17] If in his political philosophy, the claims of conscience had to be conceded, subject to certain reservations; in his moral philosophy, conscience was something that could be enlightened.

There already existed grounds for thinking about conscience in this way in the work of one of the natural law theorists whom Locke himself recommended, namely Pufendorf.[18] Natural law theorists in the early modern period were particularly anxious to circumvent confessional strife and to found "a new morality able to gain the consent of all Europeans."[19] Thus Pufendorf taught his students to assent to truth only through rational persuasion, to "avoid all dogmas which tend to disturb civil society" and to believe that "all human knowledge which is not useful for human and civil life is worthless."[20] Indeed, conscience properly understood might well provide the clue for the renewal of civil society, as it did for Rousseau, a reader of Pufendorf. Pufendorf, however, was more cautious.

In his influential work, *On the Duty of Man and Citizen According to Natural Law* (1673) Pufendorf embodied potentially conflicting concepts in a way that was fruitful for the development of enlightened ideas of conscience. On the one hand, the laws of nature were essentially simple and so accessible to mankind; on the other, conscience could be informed and enlightened.[21] This left the prospect of an increasing number of those who would be enabled to act on the basis of right conscience.[22] One important feature of Pufendorf's application of conscience to morality is that he made a sharp distinction between theology and reason.[23] His moral conscience needed neither grace nor revelation to gain its sense of rightness. This trend for the separation of theology and morality was greatly strengthened by Deist thought in the early eighteenth century, and never more so than in the work of John Locke's pupil, the third Earl of Shaftesbury. The latter's *An Inquiry Concerning Virtue, or Merit* was profoundly influential in the first half of eighteenth-century. As a Deist, Shaftesbury was able to set aside traditional Christian concerns such as original sin, grace, and salvation. He treated conscience both religiously and morally as two aspects of man's relationship with God, but in such a way as to give priority to the moral, for it is through our moral sense of right and wrong that the religious conscience is developed. Through the moral conscience we approve or disapprove of our actions. The religious conscience, which was derived from the moral conscience, is fearful of God's disapproval of our actions and hopes for his approval of good behavior. It was not, however, the main motivating or regulating force. Our prime concern is to do good for its own sake for, although fear of divine retribution is an element of the religious conscience, that fear itself is derived from an evaluation of conduct by the moral or natural conscience. Shaftesbury presented a reassuring view of mankind, and made conscience central but benign. He believed that the public and private affections are not in competition with each other, but essentially in harmony. Properly understood they favored the public good, the pursuit of which brought personal happiness as well as furthering social well-being. Conscience, which owed its power to its ability to apprehend "the moral deformity and odiousness of any act," played a crucial role in the promotion of virtue and hence of the general good.[24] No wonder Leibniz recognized a kindred spirit in Shaftesbury.[25] In concluding that "VIRTUE *is the good*, and VICE *the ill* of every one" he encapsulated the optimistic spirit of the early Enlightenment.[26]

Deistic thinking placed secular morality at the heart of conscientious concern; it set aside fears of future rewards or punishments as the basis for conscientious action, for to act on such a basis would imply a loss of moral freedom, involving doing the right thing for the wrong reasons. Shaftesbury's God was a loving God; his enthusiasm a rational enthusiasm, which if consistently attained would lead to a harmony between man and nature. Such a harmony implied a tolerant society in which conscience would be able to take its own decisions about the public good; a society in which there was a healthy public arena in which one could openly pursue truth and submit one's ideas to the test of public opinion. Whereas Locke had placed checks on liberty of conscience because of the tendency of sectarian consciences to undermine social and political stability,[27] Shaftesbury's views, in which conscience properly understood would enhance public well-being, implied the relaxation of restraints. As Stanley Grean has noted, Anthony Collins carried through the logic of Shaftesbury's views in his *Discourse of Free-thinking* (1713), in which he argued for complete freedom of expression.[28] Thus optimism, the belief in a beneficent God, and in the power of truth, had potentially radical implications, ones that were easier to embrace by *philosophes* than specific arguments about liberty of conscience.[29] The notion of a liberal public sphere in which ideas could be discussed and truth could be cultivated was broadly attractive in the eighteenth century. That still left open the question of how extensive that public sphere should be, and how equal the participants in it might be. Although the Deist argument from freedom of conscience to free thought marked an important stage in the expansion of ideas about toleration, and in the development of a strategy for Enlightenment, the precise articulation of the demand for a more open society would be related to a sense of conscientious priorities as well as to specific circumstances.

Shaftesbury's views on conscience were a fertile source for the development of moral thinking. One trend was increasingly to emphasize utilitarian dimensions of conscience in the service of the public good. This was a particularly strong theme in the Scottish Enlightenment. Francis Hutcheson argued that "in all . . . sects there are the same motives to all social virtues from a belief in moral providence . . ."[30] On this basis religions could be encouraged, but their claims to liberty of conscience needed to be scrupulously examined. Many *philosophes* would have preferred the world to have been peopled by Shaftesbury-like Deists. In David Hume's *Dialogues Concerning Natural Religion*, the Deist, Cleanthes, expresses the view that "The proper office of religion is to regulate the heart of men, humanize their conduct, infuse the spirit of temperance, order and obedience."[31] Scottish philosophers were indeed suspicious of traditional notions of conscience in which it would exercise its sovereign sway without reference to circumstance. Adam Smith's impartial spectator can be seen as an alternative to the conscience, and one in which one's sympathy and understanding had to be engaged if one were to take correct decisions.

Not all who read Shaftesbury would interpret conscience in such a way as to ensure that it would be disciplined by social circumstance. Some who were influenced by him thought that he had weakened the authority of conscience by "stressing moral taste at the expense of duty."[32] Such a critic was Bishop Butler who preferred to emphasize the authenticity of the voice of conscience:[33]

> There is a superior principle of reflection or conscience in every man, which distinguishes between the internal principles of his heart, as well as his external actions: which passes judgement upon himself and them; pronounces determinately some actions to be in themselves just, right, good; others to be in themselves evil, wrong, unjust: which, without being consulted, without being advised with, magisterially exerts itself, and approves or condemns him, the doer of them, accordingly . . . [34]

To argue with or question the immediate intuitions of one's conscience "in all common ordinary cases" was to behave dishonestly.[35]

Butler was out of tune with the Enlightenment tendency to see the pursuit of *all* knowledge as virtuous. But, despite his insistence on the direct intuitive nature of conscience, he favored the cultivation of moral knowledge.[36] There were other elements to his thinking about conscience that would find resonances in later Enlightenment thought. Conscience could be viewed in both rational and sentimental terms. It was democratic in that it belonged to the constitution of all human beings; it did not depend on revelation, on any special grace or sophisticated knowledge or abilities.[37] The assertion of the infallibility of conscience chimed in with the growing feeling that the old world of *ancien régime* Europe was corrupt and that it could be reformed by the assertion of the natural rights of conscience. From the midcentury there was a powerful trend within the Enlightenment to trust the "inner voice."[38] The leading exponents of such views were Rousseau and, following him, Kant. It is not that they did not share affinities with those who were suspicious of the infallible conscience, for the crucial feature of their thinking is that enlightened moral rather than traditional religious concerns were at the center of their thoughts. Essentially they were presenting a late Enlightenment version of natural law thinking, infused as it was with confidence in man's reason and right instinct. Rousseau dispensed with all external authority believing that "only one's 'reason enlightened by feeling' can have access to the legitimate law."[39] In *Émile,* he asserted the autonomy of the individual conscience: "What God will have a man do, He does not leave to the words of another man, He speaks himself; His own words are written in the secret heart."[40] Here Rousseau prefigured Kant's philosophy of the autonomy of practical reason.[41] The power of this view was that moral authority came from the restoration of individual autonomy, man reclaimed his essential nature, yet he needed to be enlightened to do so. In order for that to occur one needed an open public sphere. Both Rousseau and Kant suffered from public censorship and so had special reasons for recommending openness and the free exchange of opinion. Kant in the *Conflict of the Faculties* argued that the people "want to be led" and to adhere to doctrines that involve the least use of reason and so freedom of expression for philosophers needed to be protected in order that the government itself was properly informed of its own interests.[42] Although Kant believed that the ordinary people would not understand scholarly debate, the implication was that the government would learn that the "lower faculty" of philosophy would prove a better guide than that of the authoritarian higher faculties of theology, law and medicine. Moreover, since the precepts of living by reason were relatively simple and natural, perhaps, if governments learned to be counseled by philosophy, so too might the people by reason.[43] In many ways Kant was elaborating on his argument in "What Is Enlightenment?" (1784) in which he argued for the free "*public use* of one's reason" as the means of bringing about enlightenment and rather more optimistically suggested that it was "man's inclination and vocation to *think freely.'"*[44] Although open discussion was important, freed from the domination of authority, the people would respond to the verities within.[45]

Comparing Rousseau and Kant with their intellectual forebears it is noteworthy that they eliminate both the elements of special grace and of expert advice from conscience. Special illumination, interior conviction, and rational persuasion have been universalized and democratized. The rights of conscience had been transformed into natural rights and the end of government was to preserve them. But if we wish to understand fully why the free communication of opinions was regarded as "un des droit les plus précieux de l'homme"[46] one needs to understand why candid free inquiry was regarded as precious in its own right. In moral and conscientious terms, that case was best made by Richard Price.

Richard Price, an influential figure in the late Enlightenment world, combined the deep devotion of a Dissenter to liberty of conscience with an enlightened awareness of the dangers of regarding conscience as infallible. D. O. Thomas has pointed out that the Kantian interpretation of conscientious action as autonomy obviates the need for interpersonal consultation and advice. As far as moral judgment is concerned, all rational men are equal in capacity. Free public inquiry was a crucial element in an enlightened community, but its role was essentially secondary; its purpose was to teach the autonomous authority of individual reason. Price, in his *Review of the Principle Questions of Morals* (1758), is said to have anticipated Kant. However, in one crucial area he differed from him, namely he accepted that moral problems may be perplexing, and that it is simplistic to accept with Butler that all we need to do is to "honestly attend" to "the rule of right within." Although Price was an intuitionist, he did not go along with the current in the later Enlightenment to grant conscience sovereign authority. He accepted that even if we honestly attend to conscience we could not always be sure of what its dictates were. It was neither the blinding force of reason, nor an unassailable force of sentiment. Aware of the complexity of moral problems and deeply suspicious of enthusiasm, which he associated with compelling interior convictions that refused to submit themselves to the test of reason, he asserted that the central virtue was to act conscientiously by taking the trouble to examine ethical problems with utmost scrupulosity in all their aspects.[47] Thus, although obedience to conscience could accept certain pragmatic restraints, it also demanded the creation of an enlightened arena for free enquiry. His concern for conscience required the transformation of existing states; subjects needed to become citizens in order that they could develop fully their moral personalities. The guaranteeing of natural rights does not create a virtuous polity. It is religious liberty, the liberty to participate in political life, the separation of church and state, that establish the ideal conditions for virtuous civil society. At the heart of his stance is the demand for an open society enabling us to be free to govern ourselves, both at a personal level and at the level of civil society. Obedience to conscience was an enlightened version of the religious obligation constantly to seek out the God's truth and it was most satisfactorily fulfilled in an enlightened community of candid truth-seekers. As he wrote in an early letter to David Hume:

> Nothing is fundamental besides a faithful desire to find out and to practise truth and right.[48]

Some Concluding Observations

We have seen how religious toleration came to be viewed in a positive light in the Enlightenment, and how the claims of the religious conscience came to be accepted. In doing so we noted the trend to emphasize the enlightening of conscience as a means of combating enthusiasm. The Enlightenment was a moralizing force, and produced a rich vein of discussion of the moral conscience. Here there were two trends, one to emphasize the sovereignty of the natural moral conscience, and the other to be concerned about the enlightened pursuit of moral truth. Both, however, were concerned with creating conditions in which peoples, secure in their rights, would behave better toward each other.

Ideas of conscience undoubtedy were naturalized, universalized, made democratic and, to a degree, secularized. The Enlightenment was anticlerical, opposed to the theocratic state and favored the religious right of conscience. It was less clearly antireligious. It is true that its concerns were fundamentally ethical and increasingly focused on the natural rights of man, rights that could be translated into secular human rights. Such rights, however, were usually the expression of enlightened religion, which perhaps at its most characteristic was Deistic rational religion.[49] This strain of enlightened thinking was not without its problems. What is left of the notion of liberty of conscience if enlightened consciences all reason the same way and do not have to wrestle with moral complexity?[50] Perhaps a more serious worry, at least for the late twentieth century, is that the legacy of this sort of thinking is liberal complacency; the belief that all right-thinking people will have the same notion of the good and the true, irrespective of circumstance.

Others have worried not about the types of conformism caused by the enlightened conscience, rather they have seen secular anarchistic individualism as its consequence. Such fears have been exaggerated for the Enlightenment was a secularizing tendency rather than an exclusively secular movement. Moreover, it did not cut the umbilical chord between rights and duties.[51] Among the reasons for this are that Enlightenment thinkers retained a sense of the intimate relationship between the religious and moral dimensions of conscience and were well aware that the obligation to follow conscience ultimately arose from a religious duty; that the center of the late eighteenth-century demands for natural rights was a desire for renewal akin to spiritual renewal; that religious toleration still remained close to the top of the Enlightenment agenda; and finally because of the recognition, as Thomas Paine put it, that "spiritual freedom is the root of political liberty."[52]

Paine himself provides a fine instance of the tendency to assert the indefeasibility of conscientious rights, to demand natural rights rather than toleration, and to extend conscientious rights into the whole spectrum of secular affairs. Such thinkers provided the material for the many declarations of rights in the late eighteenth century. However, the late eighteenth-century rhetoric of rights has somewhat obscured the Enlightenment concern for creating the conditions in which the moral personality would flourish. This was most fully explored by those who were skeptical of the claims for conscientious infallibility. Indeed, it created some tension with natural rights claims for those who, like Richard Price, made the duty to inform as well as to obey conscience central, retained a measure of skepticism about the progress of truth, were more cautious in conceding equality to those who in their view were not sufficiently independent to meet the conditions for personal autonomy, insisted on the continuing importance of tolerance as well as toleration, and retained a lively sense of the correlation between rights and duties.

At its best, the Enlightenment integrated religious and moral concerns, created a set of minimal standards of human rights that are morally binding on states and individuals, and set out exacting standards for enlightened conduct and the creation of properly enlightened polities and communities. The lamentations of those who see the loss of diversity and particularity as a consequence of the universalizing and democratizing tendency of the Enlightenment miss one crucial point. Diversity and particularity were already under threat from a generalizing tendency far more dangerous than that of the Enlightenment, namely that of the burgeoning Leviathan state. This is the haunting specter of modern history. The Enlightenment, through its many-sided debate about conscience, at least set limits beyond which states transgressed universally accepted norms. If it is true that "freedom is ultimately a form of parole which they [states] grant their subjects to indicate a secure and untroubled polity," at least the Enlightenment helped to set and extend the terms of that parole.[53] The conscientious values delineated by the Enlightenment are weak but indispensable weapons in the struggle to preserve human dignity and freedom. Indeed it is indicative of the influence of Enlightenment that so many of the problems discussed in subsequent chapters occur within the parameters of Enlightenment norms. In particular, the enshrinement of Enlightenment ideas in public law has thrown into high relief the tension between those universal norms and their appropriate application for individuals and communities. The diverse ideas of conscience within the Enlightenment can still have a bearing on the way one chooses to resolve those problems.

Notes

1. J. M. Roberts, "Revolution and Improvement," *The Western World 1775–1847*, (London: Weidenfeld and Nicolson, 1976), pp. 65–66.

2. Isaiah Berlin, *Against the Current: Essays in the History of Ideas* (Oxford: Oxford University Press, 1981), p. 162.

3. Alan P. F. Sell, " 'Conscience' in Recent Discussion," *Theology: A Monthly Review*, lxvi, no. 522, Dec. 1963, pp. 498–504.

4. See Cardinal Newman's *Eighteen Theses on Liberalism* from his *Apologia Pro Vita Sua*, cit. J. C. D. Clark, *Revolution and Rebellion: State and Society in the Seventeenth and Eighteenth Centuries* (Cambridge: Cambridge University Press, 1986), pp. 172–73.

5. There is a large volume of literature on enlightened reform. The essential guide is H. M. Scott (ed.), *Enlightened Absolutism: Reform and Reformers in Later Eighteenth-Century Europe* (Houndsmill and London: Macmillan, 1990); on codification of civil law and its limitations, see Peter Stein, *The Character and Influence of the Roman Civil Law: Historical Essays* (London and Ronceverte: The Hambledon Press, 1988), pp. 142–47.

6. See "Luther's Answer before the Emperor and the Diet of Worms, 18 April 1521," in E. G. Rupp and B. Drewery, *Martin Luther* (London: Edward Arnold, 1970), p. 60.

7. John Plamenatz, *Man and Society*, Vol. 1, (London: Longman, 1963, 8th impress, 1974), p. 86; Preston King, *Toleration*, (London: George Allen and Unwin, 1976), p. 96, describes "conscience" as being for Bayle "the new religion."

8. Oscar Kenshur, *Dilemmas of Enlightenment: Studies in the Rhetoric and Logic of Ideology* (Berkeley, CA: University of California Press, 1993), pp. 85–86, 94, cites Bayle, *Commentaire Philosophique sur ces paroles de Jésus Christ "Contrains-les-d'entrer"* (1686). See P. Casini, "Newton's *Principia* and the Philosophers of the Enlightenment," *Notes and Records of the Royal Society*, 42, no. 1 (Jan. 1988), p. 36.

9. See T. C. W. Blanning, "Frederick the Great and Enlightened Absolutism," in H. M. Scott ed., *Enlightened Absolutism*, pp. 277–82.

10. "An Answer to the Question: 'What Is Enlightenment?' " (1784), in Hans Reiss (ed.), H. B. Nisbet (trans.), *Kant's Political Writing* (Cambridge: Cambridge University Press, 1970, reprinted, 1984), p. 58.

11. *Traité sur la Tolérance*, in Jacques Van den Heuvel (ed.), *Voltaire, L'Affaire Calas et Autres Affaires* (Paris: Gallimard, 1975), p. 173; R. R. Palmer, *The Improve-*

ment of Humanity: Education and the French Revolution (Princeton, NJ: Princeton University Press, 1985), pp. 52–59.

12. See P. Gay, *Voltaire's Politics: The Poet as a Realist* (2nd ed., New Haven, CN: Yale University Press, 1968), pp. 61–62.

13. See Voltaire, *Traité sur la Tolérance*, loc. cit., p. 174.

14. Mirabeau, *Les Économiques* (1769), cit. George Gusdorf, *Les Sciences Humaines et la Pensée Occidentale, IV, Les Principes de la Pensée au Siècle des Lumières* (Paris: Payot, 1971), p. 363.

15. Ibid., pp. 363–65.

16. I am indebted here to the entries on "conscience" and "laws of nature," in John W. Yolton, *A Locke Dictionary* (Oxford: Blackwell, 1993), pp. 49–51, 122–23.

17. There is a link, however, with religious notions of conscience for Locke describes reason as "natural revelation." Ibid., p. 238. The relevant sections of Locke's *Essay* are reprinted in Peter A French (ed.), *Conscientious Actions: The Revelation of the Pentagon Papers* (Cambridge, MA: Schenkman Publishing Co., 1974), pp. 140–47.

18. Yolton, *Locke Dictionary*, p. 122.

19. James Tully (ed.), Michael Silverthorne (trans.), *Samuel Pufendorf: On the Duty of Man and Citizen According to Natural Law* (Cambridge: Cambridge University Press, 1992), p. xviii.

20. Ibid., Bk. 2, ch. 18, cl. 9, p. 176.

21. Ibid., Bk. 1, ch. 1, cl. 4, pp. 17–18.

22. Ibid., Bk. 1, ch. 1, cls. 5–7, p. 18.

23. Here, Pufendorf was following in the footsteps of Hugo Grotius, whom he regarded as the founder of modern natural law theory. Grotius was more radical than Pufendorf in that he accepted that duty was not dependent on the existence of God. See Richard Tuck, "The 'Modern' Theory of Natural Law," in Anthony Pagden (ed.), *The Languages of Modern Political Theory* (Cambridge: Cambridge University Press, 1987), pp. 104–05.

24. Anthony Ashley Cooper, Third Earl of Shaftesbury, *An Inquiry Concerning Virtue, or Merit* (1699, corr. ed. 1711, 2nd ed. 1714) in D. D. Raphael (ed.), *British Moralists 1650–1800,* vol. 1, (Oxford: Clarendon Press, 1969), p. 177, sect. 207 and p. 186, sect. 220.

25. Stanley Green, *Shaftesbury's Philosophy of Religion and Ethics: A Study in Enthusiasm* (Columbus, OH: Ohio University Press, 1967), p. ix.

26. Shaftesbury, *Inquiry*, p. 188, sect. 223.

27. Locke could argue that he placed no restraints on religious liberty *as such*, yet his proposed restrictions on Catholics and indeed atheists would trespass on their

religious liberty. There is a similar contrariety in Bayle. See Kenshur, *Dilemmas of Enlightenment,* pp. 237–38, fns. 18 and 25.

28. Grean, *Shaftesbury's Philosophy,* p. 133.

29. See Roland Stromberg, *Religious Liberalism in Eighteenth-Century England* (Oxford: Oxford University Press, 1954), p. 156.

30. F. Hutcheson, *A System of Moral Philosophy* (London, 1754), bk. III, p. 316, fn.

31. Cit., Norman Hampson, *The Enlightenment* (Harmondworth: Pelican Books, 1968), p. 104.

32. Grean, *Shaftesbury's Philosophy,* p. 243.

33. D. O. Thomas, "Obedience to Conscience," *Aristotelian Society,* April, 1964, XIII, pp. 246–47.

34. Joseph Butler, ed. W. R. Matthews, *Fifteen Sermons Preached at the Rolls Chapel and A Dissertation upon the Nature of Virtue* (London: G. Bell & Sons Ltd., 1967), p. 53; cf. p. 63.

35. Ibid., p. 117.

36. Ibid., p. 242.

37. Cf. R. R. Palmer, *Catholics and Unbelievers in Eighteenth-Century France* (Princeton, NJ: Princeton University Press, 1939), pp. 39–41.

38. Norman Hampson, *The Enlightenment,* pp. 186–217.

39. Jean Starobinski, "Jean Jacques Rousseau," *Proceedings of the British Academy,* LXII (1976), London, 1977, p. 105.

40. Ibid., citing, *Émile,* book iv, Paris, Pléiade, vol. 6, p. 491; see also Roland Grimsley, *Rousseau and the Religious Quest* (Oxford: Clarendon Press, 1968), esp. pp. 61–63, and Robert Wokler, *Rousseau* (Oxford: Oxford University Press, 1995), pp. 85–88.

41. See Starobinski, p. 105; and D. O. Thomas, "Obedience to Conscience," loc. cit.

42. Immanuel Kant, *The Conflict of the Faculties*; *Der Streit der Fakultäten,* Mary J. Gregor (trans. and intro.), (New York: Abaris Books, 1979; repr. Lincoln and London: University of Nebraska Press, 1992), pp. 51–53.

43. Ibid., pp. 49, 57, 59.

44. Hans Reiss (ed.), *Kant's Political Writings,* pp. 55 and 59.

45. See ibid., *On the Common Saying: 'This May Be True in Theory, but It Does Not Apply in Practice'* (1792), p. 72, in which he argued that "everything in morals which is true in theory must also be valid in practice."

46. Jacques Godechot (ed.), *Les Constitutions de La France depuis 1789* (Paris: Garnier Flammarion, 1979), p. 34, Article 11 of the Declaration of the Rights of Man and of Citizens, August 26, 1789, incorporated into the constitution of 1791.

47. Richard Price, *A Review of the Principal Questions in Morals,* D. D. Raphael (ed.), (Oxford: Clarendon Press, 1974), esp. pp. 179–81, 225–26. The authoritative study of Price on conscience is D. O. Thomas, *The Honest Mind: The Thought and Work of Richard Price* (Oxford: Clarendon Press, 1977), esp. ch. 5.

48. D. O. Thomas, and Bernard Peach (eds.), *The Correspondence of Richard Price* (3 vols., Durham, NC and Cardiff: Duke University Press, University of Wales Press, 1983–1994), vol. 1: July 1748–1778, pp. 46–47, Price to David Hume, 24 March 1767.

49. See Allen W. Wood, "Kant's Deism," in Philip J. Rossi and Michael Wreen (eds.), *Kant's Philosophy of Religion Reconsidered* (Bloomington and Indianapolis: Indiana University Press, 1991), pp. 14–15.

50. See Alisdair MacIntyre, *A Short History of Ethics: A History of Moral Philosophy from the Homeric Age to the Twentieth Century* (London: Routledge and Kegan Paul, 1967, reprinted, 1991), p. 198; see also D. O. Thomas, "Obedience to Conscience," loc. cit.

51. See Owen Chadwick, *The Secularization of the European Mind in the Nineteenth Century* (Cambridge: Cambridge University Press, 1975), p. 27.

52. Moncure Daniel Conway (ed.), *The Writings of Thomas Paine* (4 vols., New York, 1902, reprinted, New York: Burt Franklin, 1969), vol. 1, xii, "Thoughts on Defensive War," (1775), p. 57.

53. J. H. Shennan, *Liberty and Order in Early Modern Europe: The Subject and the State 1650–1800* (London and New York: Longman, 1986), p. 126.

Chapter 5

Speech for the Soul:
Religion, Conscience, and Free Speech
in Antebellum America

Elizabeth B. Clark

Histories of free speech in the United States have often treated it as a secular matter, focusing on the political and constitutional struggles of the eighteenth century. This chapter will relocate the discussion of the arguments for a free speech model from the eighteenth to the nineteenth century, and from secular to religious sources. For while free speech was clearly of critical value in the founding constitutional scheme, its parameters were not fully developed in that period.[1] This chapter will focus on arguments for "rights of conscience"— largely free speech, but also the free press—as they were developed within a Boston circle that included transcendentalist Unitarians and Garrisonian abolitionists; and on the forms of both secular and religious free speech communities that those reformers envisioned as replacing older forms of hierarchically ordered communities. Liberal Protestant thinkers crafted a strong model of free speech with roots deep in the dissenting tradition of liberal Protestantism, particularly in the divine mandates of individual conscience; its strength came from antebellum religious liberals' fierce assertion of the right of private judgment against orthodox authority, in the course of the struggles that signaled an end to the reign of Calvinism. The recovery of conscience as a primary form of direct communication with God, and the corresponding freedom to express principles of conscience, were important parts of the assertion of individual moral agency in spiritual matters as against older, disabling forms of orthodox practice.

The right of private judgment, a cornerstone of the Protestant Reformation, had a distinguished trans-Atlantic career in the service of seventeenth-

and eighteenth-century Puritan dissenters.[2] By the time of the American Revolution, protection for conscientious religious belief had become a staple duty of the enlightened state as well.[3] The robust "Christian liberty" of dissenting groups like the Levellers, though, had been tamed by liberal political thought. The Founders' ideals of toleration and separation, while they created a private space for religious belief, also sought to limit the role of belief as an active force in the secular sphere. Lockeian liberalism, grounded as much in the individual's material interests and experiences as in the inner life of the spirit, defended the citizen's right to hold any set of beliefs, but downplayed the function of conscience as a way of knowing, a method of inquiry, or a dynamic component of communication between individuals engaged in a common moral quest. Sheldon Wolin has described Locke's distrust of conscience's role as an effort to limit it to "an internalized expression of external rules rather than the externalized expression of internal convictions."[4]

By 1830 the Lockeian demotion of private judgment did not sit well with liberal reformers in matters spiritual or political: the innate ideas that Locke had so convincingly dismissed reappeared in religious reform thought.[5] Transcendentalist Unitarians, among the most vocal proponents of private judgment, cast conscience as a universal moral faculty, an innate power— sometimes described as a voice—though which humans had a direct channel to God, unmediated by civil or ecclesiastical authorities.[6] Antebellum movements concerned with reasserting the moral authority of innate knowledge and the inner life reestablished conscience as a subjective and highly individualized function. Conscience both enabled the individual to determine what was right, and helped will her to act on it.[7] Transposing the traditional order of authorities, Unitarian reformers' priorities were clear: as Theodore Parker announced, "My own conscience is to declare that law to me, yours to you, and is before . . . the decision of majorities and a world of precedents."[8]

The antebellum resurgence of intuitionism and belief in private judgment gained strength from its location at the convergence of two different types of historical movements. First, liberal Protestantism flourished in the context of a broader intellectual shift characterized by the notion of subjective reason and experience as the touchstone of authenticity in movements as diverse as romanticism, transcendentalism, evangelicalism, and liberal Protestantism, a shift that G. Stanley Hall described as a "transition from the view that morality was a code of laws which God revealed in Scripture, to the view that his code was best studied in the innate intuitions and sentiments of man."[9]

Second, for many northerners the crisis of slavery tested and gave new scope to the role of conscience in public affairs, particularly after the fortification of the Fugitive Slave Law in 1850 brought the moral forces of private judgment into direct conflict with secular authorities.[10] As Sheldon Wolin has noted, conscience could easily be turned to political advantage, since it "was a response to power; it had to do with the individual as the object of compulsion in a governed order."[11] Although there was disagreement about its limitations, conscience, associated as it had traditionally been with piety and a heart open to God's will, commanded respect from a broad spectrum of antebellum Protestants from liberals to moderate evangelicals.[12] Despite its few formal victories, conscience claims occupied an important place in antebellum discourses about power precisely because they drew on two sources of energetic opposition: the struggles against the twin inhumane institutions of Calvinism and slavery.[13]

The emphasis on private judgment and the moral authority of the individual in liberal Protestant thought went hand-in-hand with a rethinking of the idea of central authority in both the church and the state. On spiritual turf, the struggle against Calvinist orthodoxy expressed itself in a revision or rejection of traditional sources of religious authority.[14] The liberal Christian was now to read the Bible with an interpretive eye; to listen to the minister with a critical ear; and to scrutinize the organized church's exercise of power through the filter of divine moral precepts, intuitively understood. As Parker suggested, Christianity was not a system of doctrines, but a method of truth seeking: "It lays down no positive creed to be believed in; commands no ceremonial action to be done; it would make the man perfectly obedient to God, leaving his thoughts and actions for Reason and Conscience to govern."[15]

In addition, as determinist theology gave way to systems that stressed the moral value of individual striving, personal religious speech and inquiry became more closely connected to the moral life and the possibility of salvation. Rights of conscience emanated from the duty to know God, whether through the public witness of a revival meeting, or the reasoned exchange over spiritual matters more favored by Unitarians. Judgment day was a lonely encounter, for which the individual must prepare: the "necessity of answering for himself at the bar of God, obliges every man to act an independent part."[16] Any form of censorship curtailing free inquiry—like that interrogating the moral status of slavery—denied to "the human mind the right to follow the guidance of the spirit of God; and to exult in deliverance from error, and in the glorious freedom of the truth."[17] God required each follower to search out and challenge instances of sin; for a "noble-hearted person wishes always, when convinced of error or evil, to manifest in some outward way, either by word or action, this consciousness."[18] Gerrit Smith, a Presbyterian come-outer who strongly critiqued orthodox religious practice, called free discussion "a home bred right. . . . Laws to gag men's mouths, to seal up their lips, to freeze up the warm flushings of the heart, are laws which the free spirit cannot brook; they are laws contrary alike to the nature of man and the commands of God; laws destructive of human happiness and the divine constitution, and before God and man they are NULL AND VOID."[19] For antislavery sympathizers, slavery provided the most glaring examples and most powerful metaphor for the stifling of the religious senses in situations where Christians were denied a forum for free expression and inquiry that might be crucial to their spiritual development.[20]

Religious speech also took on a new importance in the context of the more personal and less authoritarian spiritual relationships modeled in both liberal and evangelical denominations. Patterns of prayer changed, as more formal language of worship and adoration gave way to intercessory prayer of a more personal, substantive, and engaged sort, stressing the petitioner's wants and needs.[21] In a preface to a collection of Parker's prayers, Louisa May Alcott noted the chatty nature of his communication with God, "not cold and formal . . . It was a quiet talk with God, as if long intercourse and much love had made it natural and easy for the son to seek the Father."[22] While intimate communion with God was always an important part of a Protestant's spiritual formation, antebellum religionists decidedly rejected set prayers in favor of spontaneous expressions of religious feeling, bursting forth from the inner self: "Prayer is the unfeigned language of the heart."[23] In a way that was reminiscent of both romantic and sentimental literary forms, religious manuals constructed prayer as the urgent expression of the authentic self, with the moment of consummation being not the fulfillment of the prayer but the utterance itself.

> Every emotion, just as naturally as it rises within us, seeks expression. Its nature is to manifest itself outwardly in various ways, by the eyes, the countenance, the lips and the life. And moreover it acquires in this way a force which it would otherwise lack. . . . It is the office of language, words, not only to communicate to others our thoughts and emotions, but to give them a habitation and a name in our own consciousness, increased power in our own hearts. . . . We give utterance . . . because nature prompts such an utterance, and the act tends to render the natural feeling which it expresses more pure and true.[24]

The right of members of a congregation to express themselves on all theological and moral matters became a cornerstone of the liberal reform agenda. In the conflict over church polity, liberal reformers brought to bear a theory of power that was clearly influenced by the political values of democracy and Christian humanism.[25] Indeed, reformers commonly criticized religious institutions as "undemocratic," and used the ideals of democracy as the yardstick against which religious groups were measured. Theodore Parker characterized early Puritan theocracy in political terms, calling it a state of "tyranny," and suggested that it was "the democratic idea" that had eroded its dictatorial practices.[26] For William Goodell, a religious establishment exercised an abusive control analogous to civil government, including "the lawmaking or legislative power... the promulgation of decretals, canons, rules, digests, or disciplines; all these backed up with corresponding judicial action, trials, decisions, sentences, excommunications..."[27] This kind of power, predicated on rigid external controls and a monopoly over a critical, esoteric body of knowledge, offended a number of powerful liberal tenets, including beliefs in free expression, spontaneous self-government, and democratic participation.[28]

Writers sympathetic to the liberal cause characterized the church in its ideal form as a "simple democracy." William Goodell portrayed the connection between democracy and Christianity as so strong that "men would refuse to recognize the one, where the claims of the other were spurned aside. Christianity and Democracy would be seen walking hand in hand..."[29] Himself a person of unquestioned personal faith, Goodell nonetheless unselfconsciously revealed the plasticity of religious thought in this period by outlining the evolution of God's character from the autocratic progenitor of divine-right kings, to the "Christian" ideal of God, who governed much more democratically.[30]

Within congregations the language of Christian brotherhood was common across the denominational spectrum, and always carried with it leveling connotations.[31] But liberal rhetoric stressed fraternity's egalitarian message as a critique of authoritarian religious power. Conscience or individual moral authority was again the key to the theory of democratic church polity. In Channing's words,

> It is because I have learned the essential equality of men before the common Father, that I cannot endure to see one man establish his arbitrary will over another by fraud, or force, or wealth, or rank, or superstitious claims. It is because the human being has moral power, because he carries a law in his own breast and was made to govern himself, that I cannot endure to see him taken out of this own hands and fashioned into a tool by another's avarice or pride.[32]

The fact that each individual possessed a conscience and an innate moral sense that provided a direct conduit to God's will meant not just that spiritual knowledge was accessible to all, but that it was impossible for the few to monopolize. In Channing's words, "Religion must be viewed, not as a monopoly of priests, ministers, or sects... not as an instrument by which the few may awe the many... but as the property of every human being, and as the great subject for every human mind."[33] Parker, too, denied that an "inspired man" was needed "to stand between mankind and the inspired Word," noting that the Reformation tradition had been right to challenge the established church, but had limited the "power of private inspiration" and so blocked access to a main source of religious truth.[34]

The vision of religious society that liberals imagined, by contrast to the stratified orthodox community, was modeled along a horizontal axis. Both religious groups commonly labeled "liberal" and "evangelical" challenged the orthodox exercise of authority in the first decades of the century, and both produced relatively decentralized new models for relations within Christian communities. But these models were different in fundamental respects. The evangelical style, epitomized in revivalism, relied heavily on the creation of affective bonds between congregants founded in the shared experience of opening the heart to God.[35]

Liberal Protestants were not immune to the attractions of religious sentiment;[36] but for them the primary bonds of the new religious community were formed through more formally rational pursuits of debate and discourse. Indeed, in the 1830s, Boston's liberal reform circle institutionalized the "conversational" method of truth-seeking in both religious and social settings. Two transcendentalists with strong followings among reformers, Bronson Alcott and Margaret Fuller, popularized an organized conversational format in which "spontaneous" dialogue among the participants was thought to "mimic the deeper spiritual truths that written or 'frozen' language could never capture, and because . . . they promote originality and self-reliance."[37] This fluid form of speech offered two benefits: it provided the intuitive spiritual and moral truths accessible to the authentic self; and the revelation of this subjective truth, in exchange with spontaneous others, provided a forum in which the insight of an individual conscience could begin to accommodate itself to the intuitions of others, in progress toward a common understanding of moral and social problems.[38] Charles Follen, a Unitarian abolitionist with transcendentalist sympathies, suggested that the individual's religious interests were best secured by "relying wholly and solely on the principles of individual freedom, and intimate spiritual intercourse among men . . ."[39] The individual conscience, the legislator within, was still paramount, and "whilst consulting others, inquires still more of the oracle within itself." But in Channing's and other liberal Protestants' views, it was in the community of Christians simultaneously struggling to interpret God's laws that the mind "receives new truths as an angel from heaven . . . and uses instructions from abroad, not to supercede but to quicken and exalt its own energies."[40] A number of progressive Unitarian ministers including Clarke, Parker, and William Henry Channing instituted open discussion groups as supplements to the Sunday service, to serve the obligation of individuals in a religious community to speak and listen, and to engage with others around spiritual questions as a form of truth-testing in the pursuit of spiritual knowledge. All of these discussion groups downplayed the spiritual authority of the minister, stressing rather the primacy of individual intuition and expression.[41]

Liberal Protestant reformers' extreme solicitude for free speech was undoubtedly fueled by their own position as dissenters in both the religious and political spheres; they often accused the orthodox of conspiring to silence them within the church, both on questions of religious doctrine, and on the abolitionist views which many held fervently.[42] Citing Luther as their hero, liberals proclaimed that the freedom to challenge received wisdom was "essential to liberty in Church and State. . . . The blood in our veins is not more important to the health of the body, than free speech in our mouths is to the health of the Church."[43]

All in all, liberal religious advocates laid out a role for free speech that was more compelling in the context of nineteenth-century culture than the model bequeathed by eighteenth-century political thinkers. An earlier generation of dissenters, including Thomas Paine and Joseph Priestly, had defined rights of expression as natural, and therefore inalienable, rights, thus distinguishing them from the political liberties such as the vote that were acknowledged as within the control of the state.[44] But Channing, Emerson, and others went further, to link free speech more fully with ascendent romantic notions of the authentic self, and with an experimental form of spontaneous inquiry that many liberals believed to be the only way to gain true knowledge, in light of the demotion of revelation and other authoritarian forms of ordering. The "natural" quality of speech here, whether prayer or discussion, was intimately tied to the inner moral life and ultimately to the possibility of salvation.

In the end, liberal reformers' vision of free speech and inquiry transformed their model of social relations, as it had their model of church relations. "Society" in reform argot stood for every good thing that government did not: it represented a public sphere where citizens could meet in voluntary association and mutual exchange, unregulated by positive law or social hierarchy; a sphere where humans made manifest the "invisible, refined spiritual ties, bonds of the mind and heart. Our best powers and affections crave instinctively for society . . ."[45] Given their championship of liberal, deregulatory schemes, it should not be surprising that liberal Protestant reformers laid out a model of a free speech community that in some respects foreshadowed later conceptions of the "marketplace of ideas," extolling the mutual exchange of ideas in a decentralized setting. In his 1838 Harvard Divinity School Address, a controversial paean to intuitionism, Emerson proclaimed that "truly speaking, it is not instruction, but provocation, that I can receive from another soul."[46] The friction of two ideas rubbed together created the "electricity of thought, of truth, of freedom for the Word of God . . ."[47] Of course, the notion of a group of autonomic individuals simultaneously baring their souls raises the specter of both cacaphony and conflict. But reformers had such faith in the moral harmony of the overarching scheme that they believed that mutual dialogue would result in the development of a "public conscience," the only force that could save America from the "iniquities of judges and politics."[48]

The formation of public opinion, of course, required some effort, "to bring public opinion and public affairs to the standard of truth and rectitude."[49] In this enterprize, discussion was action. Channing defined spiritual freedom as "moral energy or force of holy purpose put forth against the senses, against the passions, against the world, and thus liberating the intellect, conscience, and will, so that they may act with strength and unfold themselves for ever."[50] Reformers believed strongly in the transformative power of decentralized, participatory, grass roots discussion. The anarchist Nathaniel Rogers described a model Fourth of July celebration, where instead of the customary "prostituted, rum-soaked, powder-soaked anniversary," citizens gathered for

> such a discussion as the republican old dragon cannot long stand. They had no lecture—and they needed none. They discussed the subject like independent, intelligent, patriotic, christian men—at home—in their own meeting house . . . —a neighborhood discussion— . . . The people must meet—discuss—decide—and sentence. That slavery has lasted thus long is owing to the fact that the *people have not discussed it* in primary, home assemblies.[51]

Similarly, Henry C. Wright described going over the heads of the clergy to the people: "When meeting houses were closed, we went into school houses, private houses, log houses and into the streets and market places."[52]

Liberals' strong conviction that each individual had direct access to spiritual truth and that no one could lay claim to innately superior knowledge had radically democratic implications. In the antebellum period, as the force of universalist enlightenment thought waned, Christian egalitarianism became for a time the vehicle for notions of equality, strongly premised on the assertion that each individual had direct access to the "authority of conscience."[53] The essence of nonpolitical reform was pressure on the body politic.[54] Liberal reformers prized free speech, as their revolutionary forebears had, for its capacity to challenge oppressive authority by speaking truth to power, whether civil or religious.[55] In their view, an egalitarian free speech community was one in which, unrepressed by the establishment "dough faces" who sought to silence them, "men may put forth their powers, and act from themselves."[56]

While their confidence in the working out of God's will was strong, liberal reformers also had a pragmatic earthly understanding of the public relations struggle necessary to form the public conscience, particularly in opposition to the wily proslavery "priesthood," a "religious aristocracy" whose familiarity with parishoners allowed them to "mold public opinion" at weddings, funerals, sick beds, and occasions "when the mind is peculiarly tender, and susceptible of deep and lasting impressions."[57] Aware of the expanding power and scope of the popular press, Channing called for an oppositional press to fight the established press, making it

> their steady aim to form a just and lofty public sentiment . . . In the present stage of society when newspapers form the reading of all classes, and the chief reading of the multitudes, the importance of the daily press cannot be overrated. . . . It may and should take rank among the most effectual means of social order and improvement. It is a power, which should be wielded by the best minds in the community.[58]

Although their commitment to change through the cultivation of "public opinion" or "public sentiment" was severely tested by the course of events, the transcendentalist reformers maintained a strong belief that public sentiment, rather than the formal mechanism of government, was the root of social ordering and the key to social change.[59] Theodore Parker spoke for reformers of all stripes when he described government as carried by two agencies, public opinion and public law, with the former always preceding and shaping the latter.[60] From our vantage point, it is difficult to assess this claim realistically. Critics accuse Christian reformers of naïveté for their belief in nonpolitical reform, and picture moral suasion as inevitably displaced by more mature forms of political abolitionism manifested in the legislative campaigns of the 1840s and 1850s.[61] At the same time, a coalescing public sentiment in the north critical of slavery certainly seems to be one prominent feature of the antebellum political landscape, particularly after the publication of *Uncle Tom's Cabin* in 1852.

A lively exchange over the role of public dialogue in liberal society and the efficacy of social norms generated through public debate has recently engaged political theorists. Jurgen Habermas in particular sees the "rational-critical debate" carried on in a public sphere lodged between the domestic world and the state as capable of producing a weighty mass of opinion that can effectively oppose or shape policy at the level of institutional government.[62] Rather than positing a transcendent model, though, Habermas grounds this public sphere historically, seeing it operating most fully in the bourgeois world of developing democratic nations from the seventeenth to the mid-nineteenth century. The immediate conditions for the operation of Habermas's public debate look very much like the world that Channing envisioned: an unregulated, nonhierarchical space in which reasoned argument and not status held sway; a debate that enabled the "consensual generation of general norms of action through practical discourses";[63] and the use of new, social forms of both oral and print culture (magazines, newspapers, the wide-ranging Lyceum lecture series) to bring questions of social importance to the fore, and to aid in molding disparate voices into a mass with enough coherence to label it "public opinion." Throughout Habermas's work there is a tension between the descriptive and the normative; and he has been criticized for exaggerating a "golden age" of democratic practice, and the radical potential of the bourgeois commitment to "free speech."[64] But Channing and his cohort certainly envisioned "public opinion" or "public sentiment" as a new force to be both cultivated and reckoned with, and understood it as having a formative role in shaping policies and governing practices. Their model was profoundly democratic, in that it privileged no voice above any other; but it worked more on a consensual than a majoritarian model of conflict resolution. For Christian reformers, free speech started and was rooted in the spiritual autonomy of the individual; but it played an important role in the shaping of public opinion, and ultimately in the crafting of public policy as well.

Notes

1. Leonard W. Levy, *Legacy of Suppression: Freedom of Speech and Press in Early American History* (Cambridge, MA: Harvard University Press, 1960).

2. John Van Til, *Liberty of Conscience: The History of a Puritan Idea* (Phillipsburg, NJ: P&R Publishing Co., 1972; reprint, 1992); Kevin T. Kelly, *Conscience: Dictator or Guide? A Study in Seventeenth-Century English Protestant Moral Theology* (London: Geoffrey Chapman, 1967); Geoffrey F. Nuttall, *The Holy Spirit in Puritan Faith and Experience* (Chicago: University of Chicago Press, 1946; reissued, 1992, with an introduction by Peter Lake); Norman Fiering, *Jonathan Edwards's Moral Thought and Its British Context* (Chapel Hill: University of North Carolina Press, 1981), esp. pp. 62–80.

3. Leonard Levy, *The Establishment Clause: Religion and the First Amendment* (New York: MacMillan, 1986); John Noonan, *The Believers and the Powers That Are: Cases, History, and Other Data Bearing on the Relation of Religion and Government* (New York: Macmillan Publishing Co., 1987), pp. 93–126; J. R. Pole, *The Pursuit of Equality in American History* (Berkeley: University of California Press, 1978), pp. 59–86.

4. Sheldon Wolin, *Politics and Vision: Continuity and Innovation in Western Political Thought* (Boston: Little, Brown and Co., 1960), pp. 274, 338.

5. Staughton Lynd, *Intellectual Origins of American Radicalism* (New York: Vintage Books, 1968), p. 23.

6. Theodore Parker, "The Previous Question Between Mr. Andrews Norton and His Alumni," by "Levi Blodgett" (Boston, 1840); "Rights of Conscience," *Liberator*, Nov. 23, 1838, 188; Daniel Walker Howe, *The Unitarian Conscience: Harvard Moral Philosophy, 1805–1861* (1970; reissued, Middletown, CN: Wesleyan University Press, 1988), pp. 53–56; Theodore Parker, *The Function and Place of Conscience in Relation to the Laws of Men* (Boston, 1850).

7. Howe, *Unitarian Conscience*, pp. 53–64.

8. Parker, *Function and Place of Conscience*; see also Lydia Maria Child, *The Duty of Disobedience to the Fugitive Slave Act: An Appeal to the Legislators of Massachusetts* (Boston, 1860).

9. Quoted in Donald Meyer, *The Instructed Conscience: The Shaping of the American National Ethic* (Philadelphia: University of Pennsylvania Press, 1972). See also William R. Hutchison, *The Transcendentalist Ministers: Church Reform in the New England Renaissance* (Boston: Beacon Press, 1959).

10. Lynd, *Intellectual Origins*, pp. 23–34, 45–46, 54, 100–29.

11. Wolin, *Politics and Vision*, p. 187.

12. Meyer, *Instructed Conscience*, chap. 4; Edward Madden, *Civil Disobedience and Moral Law in Nineteenth-Century American Philosophy* (Seattle: University of Washington Press, 1968), chaps. 3, 4. From the evangelical side, see Lewis Tappan, *The Fugitive Slave Bill: Its History and Unconstitutionality* (New York, 1850). On Quakers and conscience, see Peter Brock, *Radical Pacifists in Antebellum America* (Princeton: Princeton University Press, 1968), Appendix. On Unitarians, see Howe, *Unitarian Conscience*, chap. 2; and James Duban, "Conscience and Consciousness: The Liberal Christian Context of Thoreau's Political Ethics," *New England Quarterly*, vol. 60 (1987).

13. Lydia Maria Child, *Lydia Maria Child, Selected Letters, 1817–1880*, Milton Meltzer and Patricia G. Holland (eds.), (Amherst: University of Massachusetts Press, 1982), p. 335.

14. See Daniel Walker Howe, "The Decline of Calvinism: An Approach to Its Study," *Comparative Studies in Society and History*, vol. 14, 1972; Joseph Haroutunian, *Piety Versus Moralism: The Passing of New England Theology* (New York: H. Holt, 1932); Nathan Hatch, *Democratization of American Christianity* (New Haven: Yale University Press, 1989), pp. 170–83.

15. Theodore Parker, *Discourse of Matters Pertaining to Religion*, Frances Power Cobbe (ed.), (London, 1863), pp. 188–89.

16. William Hosmer, *Slavery and the Church* (1853; reprinted, New York: Negro Universities Press, 1970), p. 184; William Hosmer, *The Higher Law in Its Relations to Civil Government, with Particular Reference to Slavery, and the Fugitive Slave Law* (1852; reprinted, Miami: Mnemosyne Publishing Co., 1969), chaps. 4, 5; Daniel Rodgers, "Rights Consciousness in American History," in James W. Ely and David J.

Boderhamer (eds.), *Bill of Rights in Modern America: After 200 Years* (Bloomington, IN: Indiana University Press, 1993).

17. Proceedings of the Illinois Anti-Slavery Convention Held at Upper Alton . . . 1837 (Alton, 1838), p. 26; Charles Follen, *Religion and the Church* (Boston, 1836); Gerrit Smith, *A Discourse on Creeds and Ecclesiastical Machinery* (Boston, 1858); William Ellery Channing, *The Works of William E. Channing, D.D., 8th Complete Edition*, (6 vols., Boston, 1848), vol. 1, "Introductory Remarks," p. xx. Note also support among evangelical abolitionists: Lawrence Lesick, *The Lane Rebels: Evangelicalism and Antislavery in Antebellum America* (Metuchen, NJ: Scarecrow Press, 1980), p. 135.

18. James Freeman Clarke, *The Doctrine of Christian Prayer. An Essay* (Boston, 1856), p. 283.

19. Gerrit Smith, *Liberator*, Nov. 14, 1835, p. 181.

20. Lydia Maria Child, *An Appeal in Favor of That Class of Americans Called Africans* (Boston, 1833), p. 4.

21. Sandra Sizer, *Gospel Hymns and Social Religion: The Rhetoric of Nineteenth-Century Revivalism* (Philadelphia: Temple University Press, 1978), pp. 50–51; W. H. Furness, *Domestic Worship* (Boston, 1842).

22. Theodore Parker, *Prayers by Theodore Parker, a New Edition with a Preface by Lousia M. Alcott, and Memoir by F. B. Sanborn* (Boston, 1882), p. iii.

23. Otis A. Skinner, *Family Worship: Containing Reflections and Prayers for Domestic Devotion* (Boston, 1860); see also Clarke, *Doctrine of Christian Prayer*, pp. iii, 118, 141–45, 158–59; Furness, *Domestic Worship*, p. xiii; Lewis Perry, " 'We Have Had Conversation in the World:' The Abolitionists and Spontaneity," *The Canadian Review of American Studies*, vol. 6, no. 1 (Spring, 1975).

24. Furness, *Domestic Worship*, pp. viii, x. Emerson asserted the overriding autonomy of expression in his reply to a critic of his Divinity School Address: "I do not know what arguments mean in reference to any expression of a thought." Quoted in Hutchison, *Transcendentalist Ministers*, p. 79.

25. On the influence of the Enlightenment on Boston Unitarians, see Henry F. May, *The Enlightenment in America* (New York: Oxford University Press, 1976), pp. 350–57. Howe places Harvard Unitarianism in the tradition of the "Christian Enlightenment." See *Unitarian Conscience*, especially pp. 5–6.

26. Theodore Parker, "The Progress of America" (Boston, 1854).

27. William Goodell, *The Democracy of Christianity, or an Analysis of the Bible and Its Doctrines in Their Relation to the Principle of Democracy* (New York, vol. 1, 1849; vol. 2, 1852), vol. 1, p. 206.

28. On liberalism, see Richard O. Curry and Lawrence B. Goodheart, "Individualism in Trans-National Context," in Richard O. Curry and Lawrence B. Goodheart (eds.), *American Chameleon: Individualism in Trans-National Context* (Kent, OH: Kent State University Press, 1991).

29. Smith, *Discourse on Creeds*; Goodell, *Democracy of Christianity*, p. iii.

30. Goodell, *Democracy of Christianity*, vol. 2, chap. 1.

31. Hosmer, *Slavery and the Church*, pp. 119, 121; Goodell, *Democracy of Christianity*, vol. 1, chap. 1.

32. Quoted in Vernon Parrington, *The Romantic Revolution in America, 1800–1860* (New York: Harcourt, Brace and Co., 1927), p. 326.

33. William Ellery Channing, "Spiritual Freedom," *Works*, vol. 4, pp. 85–86.

34. Parker, *Discourse of Matters Pertaining to Religion*, p. 289.

35. See Lesick, *Lane Rebels*. On the way in which public prayer created a horizontal network in an evangelical community, see Sizer, *Gospel Hymns*, p. 64; one minister wrote that "moral influence is at its highest when it moves from one heart to another . . . The gospel gets an impulse in passing through a human heart which it could not have if it were shot through the lip of an archangel" (ibid., p. 115).

36. Parker, "The Previous Question"; Howe, *Unitarian Conscience*, chap. 6.

37. Charles Capper and Margaret Fuller, *An American Romantic Life: The Private Years* (New York: Oxford University Press, 1992), pp. 291–96; Hutchison, *Transcendentalist Ministers*, p. 33. See also Thomas Bender, *New York Intellectual* (New York: Oxford University Press, 1987), p. 39.

38. Capper, ibid.; Perry, " 'We Have Had Conversation in the World.' "

39. Follen, *Religion and the Church*.

40. Channing, "Spiritual Freedom," pp. 72, 73; Edward Barber, *Mr. Barber's Oration, Delivered Before the Addison County Anti-Slavery Society . . . 1836* (Middlebury, 1836); see also Madden, *Civil Disobedience*, pp. 88–89, quoting Emerson, "We must leave our pets at home when we go into the street, and meet men on broad grounds of good meaning and good sense."

41. Hutchison, *Transcendentalist Ministers*, pp. 147–48, 151, 174, 185–88. On the ways in which revivalism centered religious practice on the individual rather than formal church government, see Charles C. Cole, Jr., *The Social Ideas of the Northern Evangelists, 1826–1860* (1954; reprinted, New York: Octagon Books, 1977), pp. 6–7.

42. Channing, "Spiritual Freedom," pp. 72, 88; *Proceedings of the New England Anti-Slavery Convention . . . 1837* (Boston, 1837), p. 108; *Liberator*, Aug. 18, 1837, p. 134. For cites to the pulpit exchange controversy, see Hutchison, *Transcendentalist Ministers*.

43. Hosmer, *Slavery and the Church*, p. 148; see also *Proceedings of the New England Anti-Slavery Convention . . . 1837*, p. 64. On the reformers' construction of Luther in America, see Hartmut Lehmann, *Martin Luther in the American Imagination* (Munich, 1988).

44. See Steven H. Shiffrin, *The First Amendment: Democracy and Romance* (Princeton: Princeton University Press, 1990); Lynd, *Intellectual Origins*, p. 54.

45. Channing, "Spiritual Freedom," p. 91; Corrine Jacker, *Black Flag of Anarchy: Antistatism in the United States* (New York: Charles Scribner's Sons, 1968), pp. 27–35. On the formation of evangelical communities around more affective models, see Jane Tompkins, *Sensational Designs: The Cultural Work of American Fiction, 1790–1860* (New York: Oxford University Press, 1985), pp. 132–33; and Sandra Sizer, *Gospel Hymns*, pp. 52, 59, 68, 70–72.

46. Ralph Waldo Emerson, "The Divinity School Address," in Conrad Wright (ed.), *Three Prophets of Religious Liberalism: Channing, Emerson, Parker* (Boston: Beacon Press, 1961), p. 95.

47. George B. Cheever, *The Commission from God of the Missionary Enterprise Against the Sin of Slavery: . . . An Address, Delivered in Tremont Temple, Boston, Thursday, May 27, 1858* (Boston, 1858), p. 32.

48. Cheever, *Address Delivered at Tremont Temple.*

49. William Ellery Channing, "Duty of the Free States," part II, *Works*, vol. 5, p. 283; see also Goodell, *Democracy of Christianity*, p. 346.

50. Channing, "Spiritual Freedom," p. 71.

51. *Liberator*, July 14, 1837, 114.

52. *Liberator*, August 4, 1837, 126.

53. Channing, "Duty of the Free States," part II, p. 286. On Christian egalitarianism see Elizabeth B. Clark, "The Sacred Rights of the Weak: Pain, Sympathy, and the Culture of Individual Rights in Antebellum America," *Journal of American History*, vol. 82 (1995): pp. 463–93, esp. pp. 474–75.

54. Bertram Wyatt-Brown, *Lewis Tappan and the Evangelical War Against Slavery* (Cleveland: Case Western University Press, 1969), pp. 269–70; Theodore Parker, "The Present Aspect of the Anti-Slavery Enterprise" (1856), in *The Rights of Man in America*, F. B. Sanborn (ed.), (1911; reprinted, New York: Negro Universities Press, 1969), pp. 407–09.

55. Channing, "Spiritual Freedom," pp. 72–73.

56. Cheever, *Address Delivered in Tremont Temple*; Channing, "Spiritual Freedom."

57. Stephen S. Foster, *The Brotherhood of Thieves: Or, a True Picture of the American Church and Clergy* (Concord, NH, 1886), pp. 29–30. On the power of the church to influence opinion, see also Channing, "Spiritual Freedom," p. 88; William Furness, *Two Discourses Occasioned by the Anniversary of the Declaration of Independence* (Philadelphia, 1843), p. 20; Hosmer, *Slavery and the Church*, p. 173.

58. *Liberator*, January 21, 1837, 13.

59. William Ellery Channing, "Letter on Catholicism," in *Works*, vol. 2, p. 266; Channing, "Spiritual Freedom," p. 98; Abby Kelly, "What Is Real Anti-Slavery Work?" in *Liberty Bell* (Boston, 1845), p. 203.

60. Theodore Parker, "The State of the Nation" (1851), in *Discourses of Politics*, by Theodore Parker (ed.), Frances Power Cobbe (London, 1863), p. 13; Parker, "The Present Aspect of the Anti-Slavery Enterprise," 407; Jane H. Pease and William H. Pease, *The Fugitive Slave Law and Anthony Burns: A Problem in Law Enforcement* (Philadelphia: J. B. Lippincott Co., 1975), pp. 7–8. For similar sentiments from evangelicals, see Theodore Dwight Weld, *American Slavery as It Is: Testimony of a Thousand Witnesses* (1837; reprint, New York: Arno Press, 1969), p. 143; Lewis A. Drummond, *Charles Grandison Finney and the Birth of Modern Evangelism* (London: Hodder and Stougton, 1983), p. 205.

61. See, for example, Lori Ginzberg, " 'Moral Suasion is Moral Balderdash': Women, Politics, and Social Activism in the 1850s," *Journal of American History*, vol. 73 (1986): pp. 601–622. Critics of Garrisonian abolitionism have similar criticisms, including Garrison's biographer John L. Thomas in *The Liberator: William Lloyd Garrison, A Biography* (Boston: Little, Brown and Co., 1963). For a corrective view, see Aileen Kraditor, *Means and Ends in American Abolitionism* (New York: Pantheon Books, 1969).

62. Jurgen Habermas, *The Structural Transformation of the Public Sphere: An Inquiry into a Category of Bourgeois Society*, trans. Thomas Burger (Cambridge: MIT Press, 1991); see also Craig Calhoun (ed.), *Habermas and the Public Sphere* (Cambridge: MIT Press, 1993), especially Calhoun, "Introduction"; and Seyla Benhabib, "Model of Public Space: Hannah Arendt, the Liberal Tradition, and Jurgen Habermas." Other writers on liberal dialogic communities include Bruce Ackerman, *Social Justice in the Liberal State* (New Haven: Yale University Press, 1980).

63. Benhabib, "Models of Public Space," p. 85.

64. On the "golden age" question, see Michael Schudson, "Was There Ever a Public Sphere? If So, When? Reflections on the American Case," in Calhoun (ed.), *Habermas and the Public Sphere*; and Moishe Postone, "Political Theory and Historical Analysis," ibid.

Chapter 6

Jewish Nongovernmental Organizations, Religious Human Rights, and Public Advocacy in the Twentieth Century

Irwin Cotler

This chapter is being written at a critical juncture in the struggle for human rights in general and religious human rights in particular; and at a defining moment in the role of human rights nongovernmental organizations (NGOs) generally, and Jewish NGOs in particular.

On the one hand, there has been a literal explosion of human rights, where human rights is the organizing idiom of our political culture, where human rights has emerged, as it were, as the "new secular religion of our times." At the same time, however, in the dialectics of revolution and counter-revolution in human rights, the violations of human rights continue unabated. The homeless of America, the hungry of Africa, the imprisoned of Asia and the Middle East can be forgiven if they think the human rights revolution has somehow passed them by; while the silent tragedy of the Kurds, the ethnic cleansing in the Balkans, the horror of Sarajevo, the agony of Angola and Rwanda are metaphor and message of the assault on, and abandonment of, human rights in our time.

And what is true of the human rights revolution and counterrevolution is also true of the state of religious human rights.

On the other hand, freedom of religion is one of the most fundamental of human rights—the "firstness" of the rights constitutionalized in both the American Bill of Rights and the Canadian Charter of Rights and Freedoms—and anchored in the corpus of contemporary international law. It is entrenched in each of the major international human rights treaties.[1]

However, notwithstanding this "critical mass" of protection for freedom of religion in both constitutional and international law, freedom of religion remains "the most persistently violated human right in the annals of the species."[2] Indeed, "religious intolerance has generated more wars, misery and suffering than any other type of discrimination or bias,"[3] and is not unrelated to much of the ethnic, tribal, or "civilizational" conflict of our day.

Interestingly enough, this dialectical character of religious human rights—with its consecration in law, on the one hand, and in its massive violations of religion, on the other—finds expression in the historiography of the Jewish religion and the experience of the Jewish people.

On one level, the Jewish religion or Jewish religious rights—like religions generally—are at the core, the foundation for universal human rights as a whole; in a word, if human rights has emerged as the new "secular religion" of our time, then the Jewish religion (or Christian, Moslem, Hindu) is at the core of this new "secular religion" of human rights—the whole symbolized by the normative exhortation in the Jewish religion of "Tikun Olam"—the responsibility to "repair the world."[4]

This responsibility, as well as the notion of "B'Tselem"—that we are all created in the image of G-D—is the essence of religions organized around the inherent dignity of the human person, and the equal dignity of all persons. Jewish lore has often elaborated on this theme, as reflected in the following story from the Talmud: "What is the most important verse in the whole Bible?" asked a Talmudic sage, Ben Azai. And his answer was, "The verse from the Book of Genesis that says: 'Man was created in the Divine image.' " That verse establishes for Jews—and for Jewish NGOs—the fundamental relationship between one person and another. All were created in the image of G-D. Therefore, all are entitled to equal respect for their dignity and worth.

Similarly, the Talmud provides that when a witness in a capital case comes to the witness stand, he must be admonished in the following words:

A single man was created in order to teach you that if one destroys a single person, it is as though he had destroyed the population of the world. And if he saves the life of a single person, it is as though he had saved the whole world.[5]

And yet, notwithstanding this profound commitment to human rights anchored in the Jewish religion, in the very history of the Jewish people and in the prophetic tradition, or perhaps because of it, as Norman Cohn put it,[6] violations of Jewish religious rights—be they through forced conversions, expulsions, inquisitions, pogroms, and yes, genocide—have been one of the most persistent and enduring hatreds in all of human history.

It is not surprising, therefore, that Jewish NGOs, regarding themselves as legatees of the Jewish past and trustees of the Jewish future, should have committed themselves to the promotion and protection of human rights in general, and religious rights in particular; and to combating human rights violations in general, and the violations of freedom of religion in particular.

A word about definition. In referring to "Jewish" NGOs I have adopted a definition of the term *Jewish* that is anchored both in a more inclusive notion of what being Jewish means, as well as in an appreciation of what Jewish NGOs in fact do. More particularly, I have not restricted or limited the term *Jewish* to its religious or sectarian definition of a Jew as a person born of a Jewish mother or who has converted to Judaism;[7] rather, the term *Jewish* will refer to the intersecting religious, cultural, ethnic, and national identities whose composite defines what it means to be Jewish,[8] and which in fact is the mosaic that defines Jewish NGOs, or the mosaic by which these NGOs define themselves.

This chapter examines the human rights advocacy of Jewish NGOs in comparative perspective, with particular reference to the protection of religious human rights.[9] In particular, I consider the contribution of Jewish NGOs to the development of human rights law and the different strategies employed in the United States and Canada by Jewish NGOs in attempting to secure respect for religious human rights.

Jewish NGOs and Securing Religious Rights in International Law

During the nineteenth century, and up to World War II, Jewish NGOs were instrumental in the development of five fundamental principles that constitute the foundation of contemporary international human rights law; after World War II these groups made notable contributions to the creation of important instruments of international human rights law.

Although contemporary international human rights law is popularly regarded as a post–World War II phenomenon, the "historic antecedents" of international human rights, as Thomas Buergenthal put it,[10] are rooted in developments that found expression first during the decades from the Congress of Vienna in 1815 to the Treaty of Berlin in 1878 and beyond. These included interventions on behalf of Jewish populations, such as the American intervention on behalf of Romanian Jewry in 1902 and the U.S. intercession in the Kishinev Pogrom of 1905. They ended with the Treaty of Paris 1919–1920 and the Minorities Treaties of 1921.

In terms of Jewish experience during the period from 1815 to 1921, it was yet another century long example or expression of Jewish persecution, what Robert Wistrich has called the "enduring hatred"[11] of the Jews. On another level, however, the nineteenth century constituted a historic watershed in the development of international human rights law in general, and religious human rights in particular. The period from 1815 to 1921 witnessed for the first time the development of international human rights law in response to the violations of that period that offended one or more of the powers that sought to secure international order.

Professor Feinberg has expressed the historical role of Jewish organizations in the promotion and protection of human rights in general, and Jewish human rights in particular.[12] His comments on the hundred years between 1815 and 1914 are of particular relevance to the understanding of Jewish NGOs and their role today, and the "human rights" motif that drives their public advocacy. He writes:

> The oppression, persecutions and sufferings which were the lot of Jewry in many lands stirred the conscience of the world in the period between the Congress of Vienna and the Paris Peace Conference and prompted the Great Powers to intervene from time to time on their behalf. Throughout that period, and at the Conference itself, the Jews applied all their energy and initiative in the international arena to the struggle against oppression and for the assurance of Jewish rights and of respect for Jewish dignity. In doing so, they made a noble contribution to the furtherance of fundamental human rights and Man's basic freedoms, and to the development of public international law.[13]

The experience of Jewish communities, the advocacy of Jewish NGOs and the response of the international community contributed to the conceptualization of five international legal doctrines that were to form the foundation of contemporary international human rights law, particularly in the area of religious human rights. These doctrines, or principles, included first, the Doctrine of Humanitarian Intervention: namely, the principle that a state may intervene in the affairs of another state if that other state engages in inhumane or uncivilized conduct that shocks the conscience of mankind; second, the principle that the *recognition of the independence of a state is contingent on that state's guarantee of freedom of religion and eschewal of discrimination on the grounds of religion*; third, *the protection of minorities*—which found expression at the Paris Peace Conference in 1919–1920 where the Minorities Treaties were drafted[14]; fourth, the principle of *universalization of rights*—including religious human rights—and the *very idea of a United Nations*, which principle and idea grew out of the Minorities Treaties themselves; and finally, out of the doctrine of humanitarian intervention—or the protection of vulnerable peoples from actions that "shock the conscience" of mankind—a fifth international legal doctrine, namely, the principle of Accountability for Crimes Against Humanity, which became the cornerstone of the Nuremberg Principles following World War II.

Given this moral and jurisprudential legacy, it is not surprising that Jewish NGOs should have made a notable contribution, *inter alia*, to the creation of important post–World War II international human rights instruments.

Jewish NGOs were not only "present at the creation," but played a formative role in the events leading up to the San Francisco Conference in 1945 and in the formulation of the UN Charter itself. In the ashes of the Holocaust, and in the wake of the collapse of the special guarantees in the Minorities Treaties, Jewish NGOs were prominent among those organizations who, even before the United Nations Founding Conference in San Francisco joined in publishing in December 1944, a "Declaration of Human Rights" asserting that "an International Bill of Human Rights must be promulgated."[15] In language reminiscent of contemporary international human rights law doctrine, they affirmed that "no plea of sovereignty shall ever again be allowed to permit any nation to deprive those within its borders of those fundamental rights."[16] They affirmed their belief in "the equal and inalienable rights of all members of the human family." In the words of Sidney Liskofsky, they acted on the credo "that the human rights of Jews would be respected and secured in the degree that the rights of all men were honoured and safeguarded."[17]

As Lerner put it, "The WJC, the American Jewish Conference and the Board of Deputies of British Jews made joint representations to the San Francisco Conference, while their representatives approached delegations, expressing their concern that an effective system of human rights should be adopted."[18] Indeed, "the fate of the Jews at Hitler's hands was a major impetus for the decision to make the protection of human rights a principal purpose of the United Nations."[19]

Jewish NGOs in the United States and Canada, Constitutional Law and Religious Human Rights

The record of Jewish NGO involvement in the United States and Canada in matters of religious human rights reflects the hard work and passionate commitment of earlier initiatives in Europe and on the international plane by Jewish organizations and advocates. Although the efforts of the NGOs in both countries are dedicated to the common goal of furthering human rights, including religious rights, strategies and philosophies have been affected by the difference in political and legal cultures between the two nations. Accordingly, different interpretations of what "rights" comprehend, and how best to protect and better them have emerged.

United States

The activities of Jewish NGOs in the United States in the formulation of constitutional and statute law regarding religious human rights have been organized around three basic themes:

1. Ensuring guarantees of the freedom to manifest and maintain one's own belief (without coercion)
2. Ensuring maintenance of the boundaries between religion and politics—that is, the separation of church and state—in accordance with the United States Constitution
3. Ensuring the right to equality, equal citizenship, and non-discrimination in matters of religious human rights

The activities of three major U.S. "Jewish defense organizations"[20] in the promotion and protection of religious human rights—largely through the courts, and largely in relation to issues of separation of church and state—are a case study of the role of Jewish NGOs in the promotion and protection of religious human rights in general. In addition, they demonstrate the organizing principle underlying their advocacy—of "promotion and protection"—"that the rights of Jews would only be secure when the rights of people of all faiths were equally secure."[21] Indeed, the three Jewish NGOs have filed more amicus briefs on behalf of the rights of non-Jews than of Jews.[22]

The first major case in which the American Jewish Committee (AJC), the Anti-Defamation League (ADL), and the American Jewish Congress filed a legal brief—*Pierce v. Society of Sisters of the Holy Names of Jesus and Mary*[23]—had nothing to do directly with the religious human rights of Jews—as the name of the case itself implied. The AJC filed a brief in the *Pierce* case to challenge an Oregon law, inspired by the Ku Klux Klan, that required all children to attend public schools.

The real intent—and ultimate prospective effect—of the law was to put Catholic parochial schools out of business. There were, however, no Jewish parochial schools in Oregon, and one might wonder what the "nexus" of this case was to a Jewish NGO. But this case was to emerge as a "defining moment" in the litigation strategy of the AJC and its sister organizations. For it was through this case that these Jewish NGOs were to declare and establish the underlying theme of their litigation strategy—that the security of the religious rights of Jews is dependent on the security of the religious rights of people of other faiths. Hence, even though there were no Jewish parochial schools in Oregon at that time, the AJC filed its brief on the side of the Catholic schools. The Supreme Court unanimously struck down the law holding that it interfered with the liberty of parents to educate their children as they wished. This decision, as Samuel Rabinove, legal counsel to the Committee put it, "has been termed the Magna Carta of Parochial Schools."[24]

The *Pierce* case was the first of a series of cases in which the AJC was to uphold religious rights, freedoms, and practices for people of all faiths. For example, in the 1943 case of *West Virginia v. Barnette*,[25] the compulsory "flag salute" case, the AJC supported the right of Jehovah's Witness children, in accordance with their parents' religious convictions, to refuse to salute the flag in public school. Again the Court upheld the right of a religious minority to act according to the dictates of its faith and beliefs.

In the 1963 landmark case of *Sherbert v. Verner*,[26] the AJC filed a brief in support of the right of a Seventh-Day Adventist to receive unemployment compensation benefits where she had refused to accept employment requiring her to work on Saturday. The Supreme Court held that for the state to disqualify Mrs. Sherbert for such benefits solely because she refused to work on Saturday, a decision based squarely on her religious beliefs, imposed an unconstitutional burden on her free exercise of religion.

More recently, however, in a series of cases where secular and liberal Jewish NGOs joined conservative and sectarian ones in filing amicus briefs in support of the free exercise of religion, the decisions of the Supreme Court have raised some serious—and as yet unanswered questions—about the nature, scope, and efficiency of the Free Exercise Clause. For example, in the case of *Goldman v. Weinberger*,[27] also in 1986, AJC joined with the Christian Legal Society in upholding the right of an Orthodox Jew in the Air Force to wear his yarmulke indoors while on duty. The Court held that the denial of this right was not a breach of the "free exercise clause."[28]

But while the AJC and its sister Jewish NGOs have been "vigorous proponents of the free exercise of religion,"[29] they have opposed, no less vigorously, any state "entanglement" with religion "or breach in the wall of separation between Church and State,"[30] be it by way of religion in the public schools, or government aid to religious schools, or religious symbols on public property.

For example, the AJC filed Amicus briefs in a series of cases involving state-sponsored organized prayer and Bible reading in public schools.[31] These cases are compelling examples not only of the church-state "separation" controversy in the United States, but of the adherence of the major liberal and secular Jewish NGOs to the "separationist" ideology. The issue came to a head in the landmark cases of *Engel v. Vitale*[32] and *Abington School District v. Schempp*,[33] where the Supreme Court held that such state-sanctioned conduct violated the Establishment Clause. While in *Engel* the Court struck

down a state-composed prayer for public school use, *Schempp* went beyond
that to rule that state-sponsored recitation of *any* prayer, or devotional reading
from the Bible, breached the Establishment Clause. The decisions, which
caused a furore at the time, and were widely denounced as being antireligious, anti-Christian and un-American—engendered a certain backlash against
the Jewish NGOs, who were accused, along with the Supreme Court, "of
trying to remove G-D from the classroom." While subsequent attempts during
the Reagan, Bush and Clinton administrations to amend the First Amendment
to permit organized school prayer have not been successful, the more recent
Republican "Contract with America," supported by a Republican-controlled
Congress and with conservative democrats in support, might make it a reality;
and Jewish NGOs are once again at the forefront of the opposition.

As for government aid to religious schools, just as there are those who
believe that the Establishment Clause does not prevent state organized prayer
in the public schools, there are also those who believe that it does not bar a
state from subsidizing parochial schools, even if their reason for being is to
propagate a religious faith; and indeed, the U.S. Supreme Court has upheld
certain kinds of state aid to religious schools in the form of bus transportation
(the *Everson*[34] case), secular textbooks loans (the *Allen*[35] case), and services
for the health and welfare of the student (the *Wolman*[36] case), provided the
performance of these services is essentially secular.

Equally, however, the U.S. Supreme Court has said, and the three Jewish NGOs have so argued, that it is not a proper function of government to
advance the religious mission of parochial schools, and so it has struck down
state attempts to fund specific educational activities within parochial schools.[37]
As the AJC has put it, "The predominant view of the Jewish Community is
that all religions will flourish best if government keeps its hands off, neither
to hinder nor to help them."[38]

Canada

The Canadian experience, and the role of Canadian Jewish NGOs in
the matter of religious human rights, contrasts sharply with the situation in
the United States. This contrast reflects not only the different "rights cultures" of the two countries—and the different constitutional history—but
the different "rights perspectives"—or "Jewish perspectives"—of Jewish
NGOs in the United States and Canada. These differences find expression
in the manner in which, both through litigation strategy and otherwise,
Jewish NGOs in the two countries have adopted dramatically different—if
not opposite—principles and policies. Indeed, the "constitutionalist" and
normative perspectives of Canadian Jewish NGOs invite one to ask some

serious questions about the seemingly "self-evident truths" as held out by the American Jewish organizations.

Canadian Constitutional Law Prior to the Charter of Rights

For the first 115 years of the Canadian Constitutional experience, Canada, unlike the United States, did not have any entrenched Bill of Rights.

Traditional constitutional analysis and reform revolved around the division of powers between the federal government and the provinces—otherwise known as "legal federalism"—as distinct from the American preoccupation with limitations on the exercise of power, whether federal or state, otherwise known as "civil liberties." The outcome in Canada was a political or legal theory in which the constitutional discourse was about federalism or "power," and not about "rights" or people.

In a word, constitutional law developed in Canada as a "powers process," a battle of "sovereign jurisdictional rivalry" between the federal government and the provinces, with the courts as the arbiters of that process, rather than as a "rights process" with the courts as the guardians of those rights. It is not surprising, therefore, that while in the United States the popular metaphor of the American Constitution—"life, liberty and the pursuit of happiness"—is a rights-oriented, people-oriented metaphor, historically the popular metaphor in the Canadian constitution, until the Charter, was "peace, order, and good government"—a power-based, government-oriented metaphor, with a clear federalist—if not centralist—orientation.

Professor Bora Laskin, later Chief Justice of the Supreme Court of Canada, summed up this constitutional experience in one pithy sentence: "The basic constitutional question was which jurisdiction should have the power to work the injustice, not whether the injustice itself should be prohibited,"[39] or as he otherwise put it, "The constitutional issue is simply whether the particular suppression is competent to the Dominion or the Province, as the case may be"[40]—a constitutional issue—or power process—in which Canadian Jewish NGOs, like other NGOs, had no particular "standing," or constitutional basis for "rights-based" advocacy.

And so it was then, that legislation offending religious human rights was either upheld or invalidated on jurisdictional grounds only. Accordingly, in the *Saumur*[41] case, for example, a Quebec City by-law which effectively prohibited Jehovah Witnesses from distributing their religious tracts was struck down on the grounds that it trespassed on federal jurisdiction in relation to criminal law. It is not surprising, then, that Canadian constitutional law does not record any Jewish NGO involvement in these "religious rights" controversies; for the "rights" issues were merely adjuncts to the "jurisdictional" issues, and with NGOs just bystanders to an inter-governmental power process.

Freedom of Religion Under the Charter

With the adopting of the Charter of Rights in 1982, and the constitutionalization of rights in Canada, a historical transformation occurred. There was, in Kuhn's language, a "paradigm shift" from a "powers process" to a "rights process," with the courts as "guardians of rights," citizens as "rights bearers," and NGOs as prospective "intervenants" on behalf of human rights. Now any law that affected freedom of religion, as in the *Saumur* case above, was vulnerable to challenge under S.2(a) of the Charter, which guaranteed to everyone the "fundamental freedom" of "freedom of conscience and religion."

Accordingly, in 1985—three years after the adoption of the Charter—the Supreme Court of Canada, in *R. v. Big M Drug Mart*,[42] struck down the Lord's Day Act, the federal Sunday Observance legislation that mandated store closings on Sundays and other days on religious grounds, that is, Christian holidays—and an Act that for seventy-five years had withstood constitutional challenge. Chief Justice Dickson offered the following definition of freedom of religion:

> The essence of the concept of freedom of religion is the right to enter-
> tain such religious beliefs as a person chooses, the right to declare
> religious beliefs openly and without fear of hindrance or reprisal, and
> the right to manifest religious belief by worship and practice or by
> teaching and dissemination.[43]

In 1988, in the *Zylberberg*[44] case, the Ontario Court of Appeal struck down an Ontario regulation mandating religious exercises, including prayer in the public schools, on the grounds that it "imposed Christian observances upon non-Christian pupils, and religious observances on non-believers";[45] while in 1990, in *Canadian Civil Liberties Association* v. *Ontario*, the same court struck down another regulation requiring a public school to devote two periods per week to religious education on grounds that this was "Christian" education.[46] The government of Ontario did not appeal these decisions, while the Canadian Jewish Congress intervened in both cases to challenge the Ontario legislation as contrary to Section 2(b) of the Charter, something that would not have even been possible in the pre-Charter law.

The Charter has wrought a constitutional revolution in Canada to the point that, as Madame Justice Claire L'Heureux-Dubé of the Supreme Court put it in 1987, "The Court has stretched the cords of liberty more in five years than the U.S. Supreme Court has in 200."[47]

Although these decisions have obvious parallels in American jurisprudence, in other respects the role and positions of Canadian Jewish NGOs in seeking protection of religious human rights had been markedly different from that of their counterparts in the United States.

In contrast to American Jewish NGOs challenge to government aid to Jewish education, Jewish NGOs have supported such government assistance in Canada; indeed, Jewish NGOs like the Canadian Jewish Congress have even gone to court to secure government support for Jewish education precisely on the grounds that the absence of such support constitutes a denial of *both* the "freedom of religion" and the "equality" provisions of the Canadian Charter of Rights and Freedoms. In this sense, then, Jewish NGOs in Canada have interpreted the promotion and protection of religious human rights in the matter of government aid to education in a manner exactly opposite to their counterparts in the United States.

Jewish NGOs in the United States have been steadfast in limiting government aid to public schools only—and have eschewed any government recognition of a state-supported private school system on both constitutional and policy grounds. By contrast, Jewish NGOs in Canada have sought equal standing for Jewish schools within, for example, the Quebec school system— on the grounds that the public school system in Quebec and Ontario under the Canadian Constitution is effectively confessional.[48] It authorizes government aid to Catholic and Protestant denominational schools. Rather than challenge the constitutionality of the "confessionality" principle in the Quebec public school system, they have sought to be recognized as another component of it. More recently in Ontario, Jewish parents supported by the Canadian Jewish Congress, have gone to court to secure standing and assistance for Jewish parochial schools not unlike that which has been part of the "constitutional practice" in Quebec.[49]

American Jewish NGOs have filed amicus briefs challenging a variety of breaches of the "wall of separation." For their part Canadian Jewish NGOs have not espoused any constitutional principle of "separation." Indeed, Section 29 of the Canadian Charter of Rights—which expressly incorporates the "confessionality" principle from Section 93 of the British North America Act—effectively constitutionalizes the role of the state in religion; Canadian Jewish NGOs are now seizing on this principle—and the equality rights principle in Section 15 of the Charter—to seek support for government assistance to Jewish schools.[50]

Why, then, the difference in the approach of Jewish NGOs to the protection of religious human rights in the United States and Canada? The answer may well lie in the different political and legal cultures of these two countries.

American constitutionalism is organized around an "individual rights" theory and culture; Canadian constitutionalism is organized as much around group rights and communitarian sensibilities as individual rights—a legal "culture" reflected both in the provisions protecting group rights and individual rights in the Canadian Charter of Rights and Freedoms, as well as in the case law interpreting and applying the Charter.[51] Indeed, the Canadian Supreme Court's definition of the values underlying a "free and democratic society" like Canada have included express reference to "cultural pluralism and group identity."

The United States eschews any relationship between Church and State. For the mainstream American Jewish NGOs, this notion of "separationism" emerges as much an article of "faith" as a principle of constitutionalism. In Canada, however, the Charter of Rights acknowledges the relationship or comingling of the two—certainly as far as denominational rights in education are concerned—and the Supreme Court of Canada has upheld this "relational" principle,[52] with Canadian Jewish NGO support.

The sociocultural imaging of the United States has been that of a "melting pot," or at least, a legal culture uncomfortable with the recognition of "multiculturalism" as a cultural, let alone juridical norm; in Canada the sociocultural imaging has been that of a "mosaic," while "multiculturalism"—a highly divisive code word in the U.S. lexicon—is entrenched as a constitutional norm in Section 27 of the Canadian Charter of Rights and Freedoms.[53]

There is also a difference between the two countries in the extent to which the religious heritage of each is given consideration and recognition. The United States Constitution makes no reference to G-D, while the Canadian Charter of Rights—in its opening Preamble—speaks of a Canada founded on principles that recognize the "supremacy of G-D and the rule of law."[54]

Americans, born of revolution—and having endured the ravages of a Civil War—tend to regard their government as more adversary than ally; Canadians, used to the doctrine and reality of Parliamentary soverignty and spared the fallout of revolution, have tended to regard their government as more ally than adversary, though the rights culture is admittedly modifying that notion.

But even apart from different constitutions and cultures in Canada and United States, there is also a different Jewish sensibility regarding the particular promotion and protection of religious human rights, and a different public advocacy deployed to achieve it.

First of all, in the United States the notion of separation of church and state not only protects Jews from "established" religion generally, but protects them from their own inner religious establishment as well. In Canada, Jews have been more generally responsive to a traditional sensibility, which has caused them to view religious human rights as essential to group as well as individual experience.

Second, in the United States, Jewish NGOs have been largely secular activist organizations—with even religiously Jewish NGOs more prominently associated with Reform Judaism and espousing a "separationist" ideology. In Canada, Jewish NGOs, while also secular activist organizations, tend to have a more "traditionalist" view, while religious Jewish NGOs tend to be more orthodox, and traditional, eschewing a "separationist" ideology.

The mainstream American Jewish NGOs, like other human rights NGOs, are highly "Americanized" and "secularized" in their identity, generally eschewing more "tribal" configurations, let alone government aid for Jewish "parochial" education. Canadian Jewish NGOs, like other Canadian ethnocultural NGOs, assert the "ethnocultural"—or Jewish—configuration of their identity; and they seek government support for their "Jewish" schools—as much as an expression of the multicultural mosaic to which they belong, as an assertion of the "tribal" requisites for their development as a "community," if not as a "People." The factums of the Jewish Appellants in the *Adler* case—and of the Intervenant Canadian Jewish Congress—resonate with a communitarian and traditionalist Jewish discourse and sensibility that would simply be inconceivable in the *amicus* briefs of the secular and liberal American Jewish NGOs.

Third, American Jewish lawyers and academics—the legal support system for American Jewish NGOs in their litigation strategy—have largely shared an "American Civil Liberties Union" (ACLU) sensibility—they can be found therefore, for the most part, on the same side as the ACLU in church-state litigation; in Canada, the core NGO support group of Canadian Jewish lawyers and academics have regarded their Jewish and human rights sensibilities as complementary and convergent—and anchored in the values of equality, human dignity, group identity, multiculturalism, and the like—a community sensibility. These are also the very values that the Canadian courts—and the Canadian constitution—have held out as the normative referents of a "free and democratic society."

It is not surprising, then, that in the most important church-state case ever to have reached the Supreme Court of Canada—the *Adler* case—Canadian Jewish NGOs and the Canadian Civil Liberties Association (CCLA) are on opposite sides of the issue.[55] Indeed, the CCLA factums could well have been written by the mainstream American secular and liberal Jewish NGOs; but it could never have been written or supported by the mainstream Canadian

Jewish NGOs, or the legal academics or lawyers who served as their legal support system.

Fourth, the litigation strategy itself is more of an American phenomenon, though, admittedly, the Charter is operating its own "rights-based" litigation and "intervention" strategy in Canada. But Canadian Jewish NGOs—even with the advent of the Charter and their prospective role as "intervenants"—continue to prefer the "parliamentary" or "representational" advocacy, which has not yet been "impoverished" by the Charter culture.

Finally, the American Jewish NGOs have not only focused more on a litigation strategy than their Canadian counterparts, but the very notion of a "litigation" strategy is absent from the Canadian Jewish NGO approach. The American Jewish organizations have developed a "strategic public advocacy" that is far more developed, organized, and well funded than their Canadian cohorts.

With some notable exceptions, Canadian Jewish NGOs have been prepared, or obliged for budgetary considerations, to consign "human rights" advocacy to other human rights NGOs, reserving for themselves a more narrow, and limited, conception of their role in Charter litigation to one where there has been a direct "Jewish nexus." Effectively, then, they have not embraced the principle that guided American Jewish NGO involvement in the religious liberty cases, namely, that the human rights of Jews would be respected and secured in the degree that the rights of all people were safeguarded and respected.

Also, by absenting themselves from human rights litigation where they did not discern a Jewish nexus, Canadian Jewish NGOs missed the opportunity of mapping and identifying Jewish concerns about religious human rights. This absence of the Jewish voice has been most noticeable in Equality Rights litigation.

Most important, the absence of a clear strategy on these issues has meant that the Canadian Jewish Congress (CJC) has not intervened in some cases where a Jewish nexus was discernible. This was true, for instance, in the historic "Sunday Observance" cases, whose outcome was of direct interest and consequence for Canadian Jewry.[56]

To be fair, the CJC, like any NGO, had to adjust commitments to capacities; and, in the absence of any legal department within the organization, such as exists with the American Jewish NGOs, its court involvement has necessarily been much more restrained. Nevertheless, the CJC and the League for Human Rights of Bnai B'rith have made an important contribution in the cases and areas where they did intervene.

If there is one area—and issue—that has galvanized the involvement of every single Canadian Jewish NGO, it has been the right of minorities to protection against group vilifying speech.

Indeed, all of the major Canadian Jewish NGOs supported the enactment of the antihate laws—as they had supported earlier federal and provincial antidiscrimination legislation—and have regarded such antihate legislation as part of the "genre" of legislation protecting, *inter alia*, against discriminatory practices. Moreover, they have also intervened in support of the constitutionality of the legislation in *every hate speech case* that has come before the Supreme Court of Canada, including supporting the constitutionality of the criminal law remedy—or "group libel" legislation—prohibiting the public and willful promotion of hatred against an identifiable group.[57] By contrast, all the major American Jewish NGOs regard hate speech as protected speech under the First Amendment, and have filed *amicus* briefs in support of the constitutionality of hate speech, or have challenged legislation seeking to combat it.

Canadian Jewish NGOs have regarded hate speech not as "protected" speech, but as "assaultive" speech; not as protective of the core values underlying free speech, but as assaultive of these values; not as contributing to a free and democratic society, but as destructive of such a society, particularly a multicultural domestic polity; not as expressive of the autonomy of the individual, but as subversive of the inherent dignity of the human person, let alone the equal dignity of all persons; not as "political speech" with the government as censor, but as "abhorrent speech" with minorities as targets— and parliament as protector; not as a "libertarian" issue, with hate speech as protected speech, but as an equality issue, and hate speech as a discriminatory practice; not as abstracted from international obligations—or the comparative experience of other free and democratic societies—but as anchored in international human rights law, prohibiting such racist hate speech; or in the jurisprudence of other liberal democracies that have upheld such antihate legislation in order that such societies remain free and democratic.

Clearly, the hate speech issue provides a looking glass into the dramatically different perspectives—and sensibilities—underlying the public advocacy of American and Canadian Jewish NGOs. To a Canadian observer—the sensibility of the American Jewish NGO appears as secular, individualistic, libertarian, and ahistorical—an "American" sensiblity, while the sensibility of the Canadian Jewish NGO appears as multicultural, communitarian, egalitarian, historical; a Jewish "ethno-cultural-religious" sensibility.

The Importance of Religious Human Rights to the Agenda of Jewish NGOs

This inquiry shows that the articulated major premise for Jewish NGO advocacy in the matter of religious human rights reposes in the teachings of the Jewish religion itself. Indeed, the teachings of the Jewish religion find expression in the very mission statements of the Jewish NGOs, which speak of the responsibility that Jews have for the "repair" of the world, as they do for each other; or that the saving of a single life is tantamount to saving the entire world, because we are all created in the image of G-D.

The study also demonstrates that Jewish NGOs relying on this religious foundation for human rights have through their advocacy on both the international stage and within the borders of individual states contributed greatly to the development of both international and national human rights regimes and sensitivities, particularly during the twentieth century. As we have seen, the context and objectives of the promotion of religious human rights by the Jewish organizations may vary at a national level because of differences in political and legal cultures, and in particular as societies tend toward individualist or also embrace group rights notions. Despite these differences, however, they reflect a common religious inspiration and a common commitment to benefit Jews as well as others in terms of protection and respect. The advocacy and litigation strategy of the major American Jewish human rights NGOs in the matter of religious human rights proceeds from the assumption that the "human rights of Jews would be respected and secured to the degree that the rights of all people were safeguarded and respected." The working out of this principle has emphasized an American concern to shield the individual, and to seek to demarcate church and state as separate spheres. Canadian Jewish NGOs have sought to use the Jewish experience to enhance the importance of group religious rights to invoke the initiative of the state in combating discrimination on religious as well as secular grounds. Both approaches have had a significant impact in imbedding rights discourse and practice in the United States and Canada and in providing models for other societies grappling with these issues. Moreover, despite the difference in approach, the advocates from North American Jewish NGOs have been at one in pressing for respect for religious human rights elsewhere, while recognizing in common with other religious traditions the need for greater equality within Jewish communities.

Notes

1. These include, *inter alia*, Articles 1(2) and 55(c) of the UN Charter, Article 18 of the 1948 Universal Declaration of Human Rights, Article II of the Convention on the Prevention and Punishment of the Crime of Genocide, Article 4 of the 1965 International Convention on the Elimination of all Forms of Racial Discrimination, Article 18 of the 1966 International Covenant on Civil and Political Rights, Principle VII of the 1975 Final Act of the Helsinki Conference on Security and Cooperation in

Europe, Article 7 of the International Convention on the Elimination of All Forms of Discrimination Against Women, and Article 14 of the 1989 Convention on the Rights of the Child.

2. Y. Dinstein, *Freedom of Religion and the Protection of Religious Minorities* (1981), American Jewish Committee, p. 2.

3. Ibid.

4. This moral injunction is found in the Jewish prayer "Aleinu," which is said three times daily.

5. M. Sanhedrin 4:5.

6. Norman R. C. Cohn, *Warrant for Genocide: The Myth of the Jewish World Conpiracy* (Chico, CA: Scholars Press, 1981).

7. Yitzchak Englard, "Religion and State in Israel," *American Journal of Comparative Law*, 35 (1987): 185.

8. See, for example, the "multi-issue" public affairs agenda of the National Jewish Community Relations Advisory Council (NJCRAC), the umbrella planning and coordinating body for the organized Jewish community in the United States. Its advocacy agenda reflects and represents the Jewish mosaic.

9. The universe of Jewish NGOs in the U.S. and Canada is broad, embracing international, regional, and national organizations; religious and secular organizations; human rights and aid organizations; and service and advocacy organizations. The mission statements of all the major international—and national—Jewish NGOs include reference, in some form, to the "survival, security, and well-being of the State of Israel." Indeed, an appreciation not only of the mission statements but the advocacy of Jewish NGOs demonstrates the extent to which Israel has emerged as the "civil religion" for organized Jewry.

10. T. Buergenthal, *International Human Rights* (St. Paul: West Publishing, 1988), p. 1.

11. R. Wistrich, *Antisemitism: The Longest Hatred* (London: Thames Methuen, 1991).

12. N. Fineberg, "The International Protection of Human Rights and the Jewish Question," *Israel Law Review* 3 (1968): 487.

13. Ibid., at p. 500.

14. Fineberg described these initiatives as an historic step "towards the recognition of human rights as an integral part of international law." Ibid.

15. Ibid.

16. Ibid.

17. Ibid, at 278.

18. Natan Lerner, "The World Jewish Congress and Human Rights," *World Jewish Congress*, 1978, p. 7.

19. S. Liskofsky, "The International Protection of Human Rights," in L. Henkin (ed.), *World Politics and the Jewish Condition: Essays to a Task Force in the World of the 1970s and the American Jewish Committee* (New York: Quadrangle Books, 1972), at p. 277.

20. The American Jewish Committee, the Anti-Defamation League, and the American Jewish Congress.

21. Jacob Blaustein, Mission Statement, JDC, 1994, published on the occasion of eightieth anniversary of its founding in 1914, cited in S. Liskofsky, p. 277 and J. Shestack, "Judaism and Human Rights," *American Jewish Committee*, 1983, p. 11.

22. More recently, and in the last ten years in particular—the shared, albeit distinctive perspectives and litigation strategy of these three Jewish NGOs have increasingly been challenged by religiously orthodox Jewish NGOs. In particular, the Commission on Law and Public Affairs, the litigation arm of Agudath Israel, has filed opposing *amicus* briefs in matters pertaining to the litigation of religious human rights in general, and matters of separation of church and state in particular.

23. 268 U.S. 510 (1925).

24. S. Rabinove, "How—And Why—American Jews Have Contended for Religious Freedom: The Requirements and Limits of Civility," *The Journal of Law and Religion*, vol. 8, no.'s 1 and 2 at 141.

25. 319 U.S. 624 (1943).

26. 374 U.S. 398 (1963).

27. 475 U.S. 503 (1986).

28. See also *Lyng v. Northwest Indian Cemetry*, 108 S.Ct. 1319 (1988), and *Oregon Department of Human Resources v. Smith*, 110 S.Ct. 2604 (1990) in which an Indian burial site and peyote use for religious purposes were found not worthy of protection under the "free exercise" clause. The effect of *Goldman, Lyng*, and *Smith* was somewhat mitigated by *Lukumi*, 936 F.2d 586, (1991), *rev'd*, U.S.L.W. 4587. In this decision the Supreme Court struck down city ordinances prohibiting religious animal sacrifice.

29. S. Rabinove, "Separationism for Religion's Sake," *First Things*, 1990.

30. "Wall of Separation" principle (*Everson v. Board of Education*) cited by S. Rabinove, "The Supreme Court and the Establishment Clause," American Jewish Committee, 1994, p. 1.

31. See, for example, AJC briefs in *Zorach, Engel, Schempp,* and *Weisman* cases.

32. 370 U.S. 421 (1962).

33. 374 U.S. 203 (1963).

34. *Everson v. Board of Education of the Township of Ewing*, 330 U.S. 1 (1947).

35. *Board of Education of Central School District No. 1 v. Allen*, 392 U.S. 236 (1968).

36. *Wolman v. Walter*, 433 U.S. 229 (1977).

37. S. Rabinove, *Supra*, Note 30.

38. For a decision eroding this position, see *Zobrest v. Catalina Foothill School District*, 125 L.Ed. 2d 1; 113 S.Ct. 2462 (1993). On the issue of religious symbols on public property, see *Lynch v. Donnolley*, 465 U.S. 668 (1984), and *County of Allegheny v. ACLU*, 109 S.Ct. 3086 (1989).

39. P. Hogg, *Canadian Constitutional Law*, 3rd ed. (Toronto, Carswell, 1992).

40. B. Laskin, *Canadian Constitutional Law*, 2d ed. (Toronto, Carswell, 1960) at 939.

41. *Saumur v. Quebec* [1953], 2 S.C.R. 299.

42. (1985), 18 D.L.R. (4th) 321 (S.C.C.).

43. Ibid., at 336.

44. *Zylerberg v. Sudbury Board of Education* (1988), 52 D.L.R. (4th) 577 (Ont. C.A.).

45. Ibid., at 654.

46. (1990) 71 O.R. (2d) 341 (C.A.).

47. Statement made by Madam Justice Claire L'Heureux-Dubé at McGill University in 1987.

48. *Hirsch v. Protestant Board of School Commissioners of Montreal* [1928] 1 D.L.R. 1041 (Can. P.C.).

49. *Adler v. The Queen* (1994), 19 O.R. (3d) (Ont. C.A.), aff'd. (1996), 140 D.L.R. (4th) 385 (S.C.C.)

50. M. Prutschi, "Church-State Separation in Canada," *Reconstructionist*, Jan.–Feb. 1986, p. 17.

51. See, for example, Sections 16–23 of the Charter of Rights, protections of minority language rights in education; Section 25 respecting aboriginal rights; Section 27 respecting multiculturalism; Section 28 respecting womens' rights; and Section 29 respecting denominational rights in education.

52. *Reference re Bill 30, An Act to amend the Education Act to provide full funding for Roman Catholic Separate High Schools* [1987] 1 S.C.R. 1148.

53. Section 27 reads: "The Charter shall be interpreted in a manner consistent with the preservation and enhancement of the multicultural heritage of Canadians."

54. The Preamble reads, in full: "Whereas Canada is founded upon principles that recognize the supremacy of God and the rule of law."

55. See note 49, supra.

56. *R. v. Big M Drug Mart Ltd.* [1985] 1 S.C.R. 295; *Edwards Book & Art Ltd. v. The Queen* [1986] 2 S.C.R. 713; *Hy and Zel's Inc. v. Ontario (Attorney General)* [1993] 3 S.C.R. 675.

57. *R. v. Zundel* [1992] 2 S.C.R. 731; *R. v. Keegstra* [1990] 3 S.C.R. 713; *Canada (Canadian Human Rights Commission) v. Taylor* [1990] 3 S.C.R. 892.

Chapter 7

Communal Property and Freedom of Religion: *Lakeside Colony of Hutterian Brethren v. Hofer*

Alvin Esau

Introduction

In *Lakeside Colony v. Hofer*,[1] a majority within a Hutterite colony in Manitoba went to court to seek the assistance of the state in the form of the police power to force a minority group at the colony to leave.[2] The majority group had allegedly excommunicated the minority group from membership in the colony. After the Supreme Court of Canada declared the excommunications to be invalid, a second round of excommunications and litigation commenced.[3] In the end the majority was successful at law, but at a cost to Hutterian autonomy. The courts insisted that a person could only be removed from the communal property if the colony had followed the procedural norms of "natural justice."

While the *Lakeside* case raises issues of the jurisdiction of the civil courts to review and enforce ecclesiastical judgments, and the standard of review employed by the courts,[4] I want to focus in this chapter on the communal property issues in the case. The minority group was not only forced off the colony, they also had to leave without any share in the colony assets to start a new life elsewhere. While upholding this aspect of the communal property regime, judicial regrets were expressed,[5] indicating some uncertainty as to the continued judicial accommodation of this aspect of the Hutterian regime in the name of freedom of religion.

Hutterites

The Hutterites are an Anabaptist group founded in 1528 in Moravia.[6] They eventually acquired their name from one of the early leaders of the group, Jacob Hutter, who was burned at the stake in 1536. Peter Rideman, one of the subsequent leaders, wrote a confession of faith while in jail in 1540, and this work has nearly the authority of scripture for Hutterites to this day.[7] Hutterites share with the Mennonites and Amish certain Anabaptist fundamentals such as adult voluntary baptism; the separation of the church from the fallen host society, including the state; and the church as a community that radically follows Jesus in all areas of life, including nonresistance, the refusal to bear arms for the state or for yourself.[8]

What makes the Hutterites distinctive from other Anabaptist groups is that the communitarian view of the separated church includes the notion of community of property. While some forms of property such as radios, television sets, and cars are prohibited on colonies, and many matters of personal dress and personal consumption are regulated, generally the Hutterites embrace modern technology in their economic enterprises. This is in contrast to the Amish, for example, who often reject various technological innovations.[9]

The Hutterites came from Russia to what is now South Dakota in 1874.[10] Two groups came in that year and established two separate colonies, with a third group arriving in 1877. Altogether the three groups only numbered about 350 adults and children. Yet out of these three original colonies in 1874 we now have about 350 Hutterite colonies and about 35,000 persons living on them in the great plains region of Western Canada and the United States.[11] This growth is based on a very high Hutterian birth rate (most families have ten children or more), as well as the phenomenal economic success of the colonies.[12] After a colony is established, assets are built up so that the colony can eventually split and establish a new colony. Then both the mother colony and the new daughter colony build up assets for the time when both of them will establish new colonies again. This constant creation of new colonies, given the high birth rates, controls the size of a colony to allow for meaningful relationships and work opportunities. Generally colonies are composed of around one hundred people.

The colonies today are associated into three separate conferences all going back to the three original colonies in South Dakota. The first colony to be established in 1874 was headed by a blacksmith by trade and all those colonies tracing their roots back to that colony are part of the Schmied-Leut conference. The second colony was headed by an individual whose first name was Darius, so now there is a group of Hutterites called the Darius-Leut. The third group was headed by a teacher by trade and the colonies derived from this group are part of the Lehrer-Leut conference. There are around ninety

Hutterite colonies in Manitoba, all historically part of the Schmied-Leut.[13] The colonies in Saskatchewan and Alberta are either Darius or Lehrer. Almost all the Hutterites fled the United States and came to Canada in 1918 due to severe persecution by the host society. However, eventually a more hospitable environment developed again, and in the face of restrictive opportunities to expand in Canada, daughter colonies were again established in the United States.

There is a fourth group calling themselves the "Eastern Hutterites," more properly called the Bruderhof or Society of Brothers, sometimes also referred to as the Arnold-Leut, after their founder Dr. Eberhard Arnold who organized a communal church in Germany in 1920.[14] For a period of time in the 1930s and 1940s, the Arnold-Leut were accepted by the other conferences as being Hutterian Brethren, but this association was broken when the traditional Hutterites judged the Arnold-Leut as being too evangelical and liberal. The relationship was reestablished in the 1970s, however, and the Arnold-Leut were associated with the Schmied-Leut conference. In 1990, however, the Darius-Leut and Lehrer-Leut broke fellowship with the Arnold-Leut and by implication with the Schmied-Leut on the basis of ten points of fundamental disagreement with Arnold-Leut theology and practice.[15] Subsequently, as outlined in the *Lakeside* case, the Schmied-Leut had a schism, with one group remaining in fellowship with the Arnold-Leut and the other group rejecting that relationship.

Aside from the Arnold-Leut, there are then three separate groups of Hutterites who have much in common but also have some differences in terms of rules of conduct. In 1950 the three groups came together and formalized a Constitution of the Hutterian Brethren Church and Rules as to Community of Property[16] and in 1951 the highest level of the church was incorporated in Canada by federal legislation.[17] The primary motivation for both the Constitution and the incorporation was the need for the three groups of people to cooperate on common issues involving the host society. Thus, there are three levels of the Hutterian Brethren Church: the colony level, the conference (Leut) level, and what might be called the constitutional level that includes all three conferences.

While each colony, once established, has economic independence, it should be noted that each colony is associated with the larger Leut for various temporal and spiritual matters. Each colony has two representatives (usually the first and second minister) who sit on the Leut council. There are a number of common Leut financial enterprises and a colony cannot split without Leut approval. Furthermore, the minister who heads up the colony is chosen by a process that involves ministers from throughout the Leut. The Leut itself is headed by a senior elder and there is a conference level council of ministers that has certain powers and responsibilities for the whole Leut.

At the colony level, the head of the colony is the minister and there are a number of other men who form the executive committee, or "witness brothers" as the term is used. There will often be a second minister appointed at some stage so that when the colony splits there will be a minister at hand for both the old and new colony. The next most important position to the first minister is the secretary or steward of the colony. While women are expected to be baptized and join the colony as members, they do not have a vote in terms of the decisions to be made at formal colony meetings.

The pattern of growth in the numbers of Hutterites is almost completely a matter of people being born Hutterite and eventually being baptized into formal membership. The numbers of people who were not born Hutterites, but joined a colony as adults is minuscule. The Hutterites just want to be left alone, they do not proselytize for converts in the host society. Rather than having any significant movement of converts from the host society joining a colony, there is a degree of defection, particularly among young unbaptized males who leave a colony and go into the host society for a time. However, studies indicate that the vast majority of these defectors return to the colony.[18] Most defectors want to taste the freedom in the "evil" world, but some defectors leave because they find a more vital personal spirituality in evangelical groups. These people are unlikely to return to the Hutterite colonies.[19]

Karl Peter makes the point that Hutterite society is not static. He claims that the worldview of Hutterites shifted fundamentally at some point from the early version where community of goods and living in community was a context in which the individual would struggle with selfish tendencies and achieve the psychological state of "gellassenheit," the overcoming of the flesh in a complete surrender of the self to God. The new version that developed, however, was that salvation was not an individual struggle of the conscience, but a gift, a guarantee that salvation was an individual's simply by that person's faithful living within the community of goods model. The colony was itself a portal of heaven where upon death the individual passed through the door into eternal life. Living in the world, in contrast to the colony, was living in an evil realm destined for eternal death. Thus at the colony level, salvation is secure and individuals have a "culture of work performance" where the performance of work is a major source of individual pride and satisfaction. Religion has become ritualized, while the survival of the colonies depends at the same time on a high level of economic rationality.[20]

Communal Property

The concept of communal property simply means that all property is church property. We can think of a whole Hutterite colony, including all the land, enterprises, housing units, common kitchen facility, machinery, and so forth as being a church, an "ark of salvation" set down in a "fallen" world. Hutterites live in a church, as compared to the modern secular-sacred division of life where we go to church occasionally. This communal property regime is grounded in Hutterian religious belief, most notably from Acts 2:44: "And all that believed were together, and had all things common."

It is noteworthy that this verse speaks of two matters: "being together" and "having all things common." One might argue that what really counts is living together, that is communal life. This living together is what is supported by community of property. Without community of property, people tend not to really live together in a meaningful way.

Aside from a few personal mementos that might fit into a hope chest, the individual Hutterite does not own anything. This renunciation of personal property should not be confused with personal deprivation, however. Some Christians may stress the renunciation of acquisitive impulses and embrace a lifestyle of material deprivation. This is not the current Hutterian practice that holds property in common so as to support a secure and healthy community life. Hutterite colonies are multi-million-dollar capitalist enterprises where the needs of the colonists are looked after from cradle to grave, and where the continual establishment of new colonies provides for the needs of the next generation. Furthermore, the various managers of enterprises may take a great deal of personal pride and psychic identification with the facilities and profits of the enterprise they head. All the property belongs to God, but stewardship involves expanding God's ark and even competing with other stewards to demonstrate one's worthiness.

One of the first concepts that law students learn is that property is not the physical thing but rather a metaphysical bundle of rights associated with the thing. This bundle can be divided up. Someone may have the right of possession and use while someone else may have the right of ownership. Just because Hutterites may not personally own property does not mean that they do not have property interests. They may have a rich bundle of usufructuary rights to colony property that makes them in reality much wealthier than many people in the host society.

How have the courts of the host society handled this issue of communal property? The issues that have come before the courts may be divided into two categories. First, community property has been attacked by external forces from the host society by way of discriminatory legislation,[21] discriminatory zoning practices,[22] "neutral" tax, and social welfare legislation that may not accommodate the communal way of life,[23] and confusion in the law as between giving colonies the status of religious organizations or treating them as mere business organizations.[24] Second, community of property has also been attacked as a result of internal disputes leading to claims for a share of the assets of a colony or claims to deny "ex-members" the continued use of property. It is into this second category that the *Lakeside* case falls (which is the subject of this chapter).

Unlike the Doukhobors and Mennonites, who originally were granted a large exclusive block of land for community settlement and then ran into internal and external conflict when those communitarian blocks of land reverted to individual ownership or when the exclusive area was opened up to other landowners outside the religious group,[25] the Hutterites simply bought blocks of land on the private market and held title to the land by way of trustees for the community or more commonly by setting up ownership of the land by a corporation. Ownership of land per se was not against Hutterian religious belief, so long as the ownership was collective.[26] Furthermore, while there was convenience in having Hutterite colonies close to each other, the fundamental Hutterite unit was the colony of approximately a hundred individuals, and these colonies could be spread out over many different municipalities.

In terms of the second category of litigation, arising from internal disputes rather than external threats from the host society, the prime issue is the alleged inequity of the Hutterian system of communal property as applied to departing or expelled members, who are not entitled to take a penny of colony assets with them, even though they may have contributed a lifetime of labor to the accumulation of those assets.[27]

The Lakeside Case

Round One

The dispute at Lakeside, a Schmied-Leut colony in Manitoba, goes back more than a decade ago when Daniel Hofer, Sr., the manager of the machine shop at the colony was engaged in inventing and manufacturing a hog feeder.[28] On behalf of Lakeside Colony he sought to obtain a patent on the invention, but before the invention was perfected, a patent was taken out by a different Hutterite colony in Manitoba using the same patent agents as Daniel Hofer, Sr., had hired on behalf of Lakeside. The colony that obtained the patent was Crystal Spring, headed by Rev. Jacob Kleinsasser, who was not just the head of that colony, but the senior elder for the whole Schmied-Leut Conference.[29] Daniel Hofer, Sr., claimed that his invention was stolen by Crystal Spring colony. After obtaining a patent, Crystal Spring started manufacturing the wet and dry hog feeder, which had the novelty of allowing the pig to choose to eat feed in a dry condition or a wet condition resulting in a faster weight gain and thus faster time to market. In addition to the profits made by Crystal Spring in manufacturing the feeder for sale to various hog producers, Crystal Spring made a deal with a company called C. and J. Jones whereby that company would not only market the hog feeders produced by the colony but would also have the patent assigned to it and sue various entities for patent infringement and split the proceeds of these infringement claims with Crystal Spring Colony. To understand the seriousness of Daniel Hofer, Sr.'s, allegation that one Hutterite colony, and the one headed by the senior elder at that, had stolen an invention from another colony and patented it for its own benefit, requires us to note that Lakeside colony was not a typical Hutterite colony. In the 1970s, Lakeside colony had gotten into various spiritual and financial difficulties, and to save the colony the Schmied-Leut conference had taken over the management of it. There were a number of outside overseers who acted as managers of Lakeside on behalf of the Schmied-Leut and under the supervisory authority of the senior elder, Jacob Kleinsasser.[30]

C. and J. Jones proceeded to make patent infringement claims against a number of manufacturers including quite a number of other Hutterite colonies. Despite the strict prohibition on Hutterites suing other Hutterites in civil court, through the front of C. and J. Jones, that is precisely, in effect, what the senior elder of the Schmied-Leut was doing. More damaging to the reputation of the senior elder was the fact that he did not tell the Hutterite colonies that Crystal Spring was sharing in the proceeds of patent infringement, or that the deal with C. and J. Jones was revokable. When Lakeside itself was faced with the demand to stop manufacturing the feeder, Daniel Hofer, Sr., refused, claiming that it was his invention all along. But the overseers of Lakeside colony accepted the Crystal Spring claim and negotiated a settlement of $10,000 for patent infringement and promised to stop manufacturing the device at Lakeside. This is when the rebellion on the part of Daniel Hofer, Sr., got into full gear.

Armed with the signatures of a majority of the ordinary members of Lakeside, Daniel Hofer, Sr., behind the backs of the overseers, put a stop order on the settlement check. The next day, December 21, 1987, was the date of the annual meeting at Lakeside. All but two of the male voting members were present at the meeting. The meeting focused on the refusal of Daniel Hofer, Sr., to stop manufacturing the feeder, and his claim that Crystal Spring had stolen his invention, and his action of putting a stop order on the check. The meeting was stormy and Daniel Hofer, Sr., refused to back down and obey the overseers. He was asked to leave the meeting at some stage and then the other members agreed that he should be put under church discipline for his defiance. The penalty would be a relatively mild form of shunning, namely that he should "eat in the bakehouse and sit in the hallway," until he repented. When Daniel Hofer, Sr., returned to the meeting and was told what the penalty was he rejected it. He considered that the overseers were in the pockets of Jacob Kleinsasser, and he asked for a higher court to consider his hog feeder claim. By higher court he meant a tribunal of Schmied-Leut ministers. Daniel Hofer, Sr., then left the meeting to go make more hog feeders.

After Daniel Hofer, Sr., left the meeting for the second time, the overseer president of Lakeside, Rev. Michael Wollmann of Springhill Colony, declared that Daniel Hofer, Sr., was out of the church. The members of Lakeside apparently agreed with this declaration although no formal vote was taken. According to the overseers, after Daniel Hofer, Sr., had refused to accept the mild punishment, his case immediately escalated into excommunication from the church. It was absolutely crucial at a colony, that once a decision had been made by a majority, the decision be accepted by all members whether they agreed or not. Furthermore, if a member did not accept the discipline of the church aimed at bringing him or her back into conformity, then the member was violating the vows of obedience made upon baptism.

After ten days for cooling off and faction formation, several further meetings took place at Lakeside on January 31, 1987. Between these meetings, the overseers of Lakeside went to visit the senior elder at Crystal Spring. The senior elder, who was by our standards of due process in a conflict of interest situation given that Daniel Hofer, Sr., was disputing the patent held by Crystal Spring, nevertheless not only denied the request of Daniel Hofer for a higher court within the church, he also sent a letter instructing the members of Lakeside that Daniel Hofer and anyone associated with his cause should be separated from Lakeside. At the end of the day the excommunication of Daniel Hofer, Sr., was expanded to include his two married sons. One son was the head of the hog operation on the colony, the other son worked in the machine shop. To make a long story short, eventually the number of persons associated with Daniel Hofer, Sr., increased to over one third of the total colony population.

Daniel Hofer, Sr., not only refused to back down on his allegation that his invention had been stolen and that Lakeside should be allowed to manufacture the device, he now took active steps to oust the overseers of the colony. For the pacifistic Hutterites, the dispute escalated into scandalous dimensions. There were two groups, the "dissenter" group and the "overseer" group, and with various enterprises in the hands of one or the other, there was a struggle for control. The police were called in when the dissenters tried to take hogs off to market and the overseers charged them with theft. Ultimately over the next several years there were a host of criminal charges laid as a result of physical fights, usually involving young unbaptized males from either side. Lakeside was in chaos.

Now what is unprecedented in the history of the Hutterian Brethren Church, is that in the face of this chaos, the church decided to go to the secular law courts and sue the dissenters so as to invoke the police power of the state to have them physically thrown off the colony.[31] The overseers on behalf of Lakeside Colony sued Daniel Hofer, Sr., and six other male defendants. Once the lawsuit started, a degree of control over Lakeside was made possible by interim court orders that drew lines between the two factions. Control over colony enterprises were taken out of the hands of the dissenters by court orders prohibiting them from entering various buildings. At the same time, they were allowed the use of a portion of the garage to carry on their own activities, and so forth.

What was not realized at the time of instituting the law suit was that this situation of having two factions at Lakeside shunning each other would last for many years as the case made its way through trial and two levels of appeal and then went into a second round. It was more than seven years later that the judgment in the second trial came out. Seven years in which the two sides continued to live apart on the same colony. The dissenters were not content to sit around and do nothing after being removed from various colony enterprises. They started a "colony within a colony" and undertook various new enterprises that were quite successful. The two sides took turns in food preparation, but ate separately. The skirmishes between the two sides continued through the seven years. Eventually even the children of the dissenters had to be taught in a separate German school on the colony.

After a lengthy trial in June, 1989, the judgment of Mr. Justice Ferg of the Manitoba Queen's Bench was delivered at the end of October 1989.[32] The decision came down squarely in favor of the overseer group. Daniel Hofer, whether he had any cause to complain about the hog feeder or not, had refused to abide by the decisions of the majority of the group and in refusing to accept punishment had in effect expelled himself from membership. The only judicial review of the expulsion that Justice Ferg entertained was that the court could ensure that the colony had properly followed its own internal norms in expelling the defendants.

Daniel Hofer, Sr., and those associated with him still refused to leave the colony; instead they appealed to the Manitoba Court of Appeal, which upheld the trial court decision in January, 1991.[33] However, the Court of Appeal was not content to simply judicially review the colony expulsion to see if it conformed to the internal norms of the Hutterite Church. The Court of Appeal imposed the requirements that those norms also had to conform to the rules of natural justice. While the majority of the court asserted that the norms followed in this case did conform to the rules of natural justice, there was a vigorous dissent from the late Mr. Justice O'Sullivan. Not only did he assert that the expulsions violated the rules of natural justice, he went on to claim that the court could review the merits of the decision and not just the process.

The defendants were granted leave to appeal to the Supreme Court of Canada, which ultimately delivered a lengthy judgment on October 29, 1992.[34] The Supreme Court of Canada applied the rules of natural justice to the disciplinary process of a Hutterite colony and ruled six to one that the dissenters were still members of Lakeside Colony. The actual result was hung on just one peg of the natural justice trinity of notice, opportunity to be heard, and an unbiased tribunal. Mr. Justice Gonthier for the majority stated that the defendants did not receive adequate notice that a decision was being considered as to their excommunication from membership.[35] Madam Justice McLachlin in dissent stated that while the rules of natural justice should indeed be imposed on the colony, those rules were flexible and contextual. As to notice, she concluded that the defendants always knew that their defiance would lead to expulsion and no formal notice in that context was necessary.[36]

While the defendants had successfully avoided expulsion by the Supreme Court's declaration that they were still members and had never been properly excommunicated, all the case meant in reality was that the overseer group had to start all over again with the expulsion of the defendants, this time following the rules of natural justice, which is what they proceeded to do.

Round Two

The dissenters were now members of the colony again in the eyes of the law. However, in the eyes of the overseer group the dissenters were not really members at all.[37] After the Supreme Court decision, colony enterprises were not returned to former managers. Full shunning continued. Indeed the overseer group now turned defeat into victory. They asserted that since the court had declared the dissenter group to be still members, all the assets of the dissenter group that had been built up over many years by the dissenters in running their own enterprises as a colony within a colony after they had been purportedly expelled in 1987 should now be turned over to Lakeside. This demand was made, however, without any offer of allowing the dissenters back into membership in fact or acceding to the request of Daniel Hofer, Sr., that if the original dispute was turned over to an impartial tribunal of Schmied-Leut ministers he would be bound by whatever decision they made. Daniel Hofer, Sr., refused to give an accounting of the dissenter's communal property until a proper adjudication of his original claims was forthcoming. In retrospect, however unfair, it would have been much better for the Hofer group if they had complied with the request for an accounting. Now the overseer group would claim a new ground for expulsion, namely the holding of "private property."

On the basis of his refusal to account for property accumulated after the original dispute, Daniel Hofer, Sr., and his brother Rev. Paul Hofer, and two sons of Daniel Hofer, Sr., were voted out of the colony again on December 11, 1992, which was a little more than a month after the Supreme Court had released its decision. This time, of course, there was formal notice, with lawyer's letters being hand delivered to the plates of the defendants as they ate. But the dissenter group would not leave the colony. Once again the overseers sued on behalf of Lakeside colony. This time, however, a whole new set of arguments were on the table, because the day before the vote at Lakeside, Jacob Keinsasser, the senior elder of the Schmied-Leut was allegedly removed from his position and the Schmied-Leut conference was in a schism.

Aside from the allegation that Crystal Spring had stolen Daniel Hofer, Sr.'s, invention, a number of other allegations against the senior elder had been made in the first round of litigation. Evidence was brought forward that Jacob Kleinsasser on behalf of Crystal Spring and another minister, Mike Waldner on behalf of two American colonies, had entered into a business arrangement in the early 1980s with two con men who proceeded to defraud the three colonies to the tune of several million dollars. Rather than getting low interest loans for the colonies, as originally agreed, the two con artists armed with broad powers of attorney and letters of credit from Kleinsasser and Waldner, bound the colonies to a host of questionable investments. Faced with various lawsuits as a result of these deals by the con men, Kleinsasser and Waldner formed a company in Atlanta that continued to manage some of these investments and subsequently lost even more money and was finally dissolved with a number of new lawsuits hanging over the corpse.[38]

When these financial matters came to the attention of other Schmied-Leut ministers, there were serious questions raised about the behavior of the senior elder. The allegations suggested that Kleinsasser had attempted to cover up the financial mess and had treated one of the American colonies in an inequitable way so as to advantage Crystal Spring. A related complaint that had also been raised in the first trial involved the Hutterian ownership of a hog killing plant in Neepawa, Manitoba. This plant was started by Springhill Colony, headed by Mike Wollmann, who was also the overseer president of Lakeside. After it began to lose millions of dollars, Jacob Kleinsasser, the senior elder, made an arrangement whereby all the colonies had to support the money losing plant by way of hog levies. The plant lost many millions more dollars.[39] Aside from the losses, however, the question for many of the Schmied-Leut ministers was whether the separatist Hutterites should own an enterprise that was not on a colony, was managed by non-Hutterites, and operated with unionized non-Hutterite workers.

Eventually a twelve-point indictment against Jacob Kleinsasser's leadership was formulated by the assistant senior elder, a Rev. Joseph Wipf from South Dakota.[40] As well as the various financial transactions noted above, and

Kleinsasser's Arnold-Leut connections,[41] questions were raised about the senior elder's mismanagement, and even personal ownership interest, involving various Schmied-Leut enterprises such as a credit company and an insurance company and a church trust fund.[42] There was also controversy over how the senior elder had handled various disputes at colonies, not only at Lakeside but also at Pine Creek, Rainbow, and Oak Bluff, just to name a few.[43] Various meetings of Schmied-Leut ministers took place dealing with this twelve-point indictment, culminating in a series of meetings at Starlite colony on December 9 and 10, 1992. After a great deal of discussion and after resolutely denying any wrongdoing, Kleinsasser finally asked all those who supported him to stand. The evidence clearly shows that more stayed seated than supported him. Nevertheless, just as Daniel Hofer, Sr., had not obeyed the majority of his colony, so now the senior elder did not obey the majority of the Schmied-Leut Conference. He did not step down and thus there was a schism in the conference.

The position of the majority who did not support Jacob Kleinsasser was that he had been voted out of office and they elected Joseph Wipf to be the new senior elder. The position of those who supported Jacob Kleinsasser was that the senior elder by Hutterian tradition was appointed for life and could not be removed by a vote. The anti-Kleinsasser forces were in the overall majority in terms of the whole Schmied-Leut conference, but in Manitoba they were in the minority. What is of great importance, however, is that it was the anti-Kleinsasser group that was recognized as the "true church" by the other two Leuts.

The anti-Kleinsasser majority of colonies would in time be called the "Reaffirmed" group in distinction to the "Kleinsasser" group of colonies. The Lehrer and Darius Leuts had broken fellowship with the Schmied-Leut over the Arnold-Leut association and other issues, but now that the majority of Schmied-Leut had removed the senior elder, a new union was made possible. A new Constitution of the Hutterian Brethren Church was drafted in 1993 and a Reaffirmation Document was sent to all the colonies, including those aligned with Jacob Kleinsasser, inviting them to reaffirm their allegiance to the church and sign on with the new constitution.[44] The Lakeside overseers threw the Reaffirmation Document into the garbage. The end result was that the Reaffirmed majority of the Schmied-Leut constituted part of the Hutterian Brethren Church along with the other two Leuts, while the Kleinsasser colonies incorporated their own conference in Manitoba. They were no longer part of the Hutterian Brethren Church.

Thus in the second round of Lakeside litigation, as well as natural justice arguments about a biased tribunal, the defense to the expulsion asserted that the overseers were no longer members of the Hutterian Brethren Church as required by Lakeside's own Articles of Association, and therefore they had no authority to sue of behalf of Lakeside. Furthermore, the counter-claim in the second round asserted that Lakeside colony belonged to the Hutterian Brethren Church, and should go to those members who were will-ing to sign the reaffirmation document. Of course, the Hofer group was quite willing to sign while the overseer group was not. Alternatively, the counter-claim asserted that the colony should be proportionately split between the two groups.

What made the second round in Lakeside interesting was that not only were there colonies aligned with the Reaffirmed group and colonies aligned with the Kleinsasser group, there were others that were internally divided, sometimes resulting in severe schisms within them.[45] The Lakeside adjudica-tion might serve as a precedent for how "dissenters" on other colonies could be treated. Could the majority simply expel the minority with no assets of the colony? Should colony assets be proportionally split when the colony was in a schism? Or should all the assets go to the minority, if that minority was in fact the "true" church according to Hutterian doctrine?

Given the schism within the conference and a law suit for over $300,000 by Daniel Hofer's law firm against the colony and the church to pay for the legal fees of the defendants, there were negotiations to settle the Lakeside case. Daniel Hofer, Sr., and his group could leave the colony and take the assets they had accumulated since 1987 with them. But the overseer group refused to have the colony divided proportionately. Daniel Hofer, Sr., was willing to leave Lakeside but only if the Reaffirmed conference would rec-ognize the new colony that would be formed by his group. Here is where negotiations broke down. The Reaffirmed ministers told Daniel Hofer that he should repent and make peace at Lakeside first. Daniel Hofer, Sr., wanted to know what he should repent of. To leave Lakeside without reconciliation with the church was folly. The dispute was not really about property at all, but about church membership. The colony could give the Hofer group a million dollars but it would not have mattered. The problem in essence was eternal salvation, not rights to communal property.

The trial in the second round of litigation took place in November and December, 1993. One dramatic moment was that during cross-examination of Daniel Hofer, Sr., on the topic of the wrongfulness of bringing lawsuits against him, he was questioned about the counterclaim and admitted that if the coun-terclaim was like going to law instead of being simply defense suggestions as to how to resolve the case, then he should drop the counterclaim. Indeed, after a recess that involved a conference between the defendant's lawyers and the group, the counterclaim was dropped as being against the religious con-victions of the defendants.

Mr. Justice DeGraves of the Manitoba Queen's Bench issued his judge-ment on March 21, 1994. He granted to the plaintiffs what they sought, namely an order enforceable by the state to kick the defendants off the colony with only the shirts on their backs, and take the various assets that they had accumulated since 1987 when they were treated as nonmembers and turn them over to Lakeside colony. Mr. Justice DeGraves viewed the holding of property by the Hofer group as a violation of community of property. Nowhere did he deal with the counterargument that the Hofer group believed in community of property just as much as any other Hutterites. They were simply running separate enterprises on the same colony in the context of a schism within the colony. The group repeatedly said that the property belonged to the church and would be put back into the common pot once reconciliation was achieved or an impartial tribunal in the church heard the case whatever the decision might be. The irony in terms of property was that the effect of winning the victory in the Supreme Court of Canada put the defendants in a worse position. Had they left the colony in 1987 and started up their own enterprises they would now have considerable assets. Because the court declared them to be still members of the colony, all of these assets were now in the hands of Lakeside and the dissenter group was subject to being thrown off the colony with nothing. More important, though, the defendants appeared to have no ark of salvation available to them.

On the issue of authority to sue, Mr. Justice DeGraves did find that the senior elder had been removed, and the new Constitution of the Church was valid, but the whole reaffirmation process took place after Hofer's group had been excommunicated and did not effect the continued authority of Lakeside to discipline its own members. In effect, he was turning the colony over to the schismatics.

Commentary

On one level, the denial of assets to departing or expelled members involves merely a matter of contract enforcement. When Hutterites as adults join the church they sign Articles of Association that explicitly include the promise to leave empty-handed should they depart or be expelled. Adults who do not join the church, but continue to live on the colony, are governed by a kind of implied consent to the same Articles of Association. Hutterites never really owned any property of the colony at any time, so why should they get any of the property when they leave?

On another level, however, the courts must be seen as upholding the community of property regime as a matter of freedom of religion. After all, the courts could declare contracts void as being against public policy. Furthermore, the courts could refuse to uphold improvident contracts on equitable or restitutionary grounds, especially when the voluntariness of such agreements are open to question. Hutterites are socialized from birth into joining the colony way of life. They cannot be married until they are baptized and join the church. Why should they necessarily be held to an associational contract made, often decades ago? Despite these arguments the courts have consistently refused to give departing or expelled members a share of the assets.

My position on this matter is that the courts are correct as a matter of freedom of religion to uphold the community of property regime despite its harsh consequences. To uphold the rights of groups sometimes means that the courts will have to overlook what in the wider society would be violations of individual civil rights. However, I would argue that there are two very different claims that need to be distinguished.

One is a claim by a person or a group of people who have left the Hutterite faith and who now want a personal share of the property. That is, there is a claim that some portion of church property should be converted to private property. In an earlier Manitoba case that went all the way up to the Supreme Court of Canada, some Hutterites left the faith and joined the Radio Church of God headquartered in Pasadena, California that produced the magazine, "The Plain Truth." After being excommunicated from the colony, these individuals sued the colony for a share of the assets. Their claim was denied at all levels.[46] In a related reported case in the United States of a nonmember living on the colony and then claiming wages for the work he did on the colony over many years the claim was also denied.[47]

Here, however, there is also a dispute over church property itself. Should the property go to one group or the other? In this second category there is no claim that church property should become private property, but rather there is a dispute within the church in a schismatic situation. Because the courts in *Lakeside* did not deal with the second category classification of the case they never turned to the well-developed law on church property disputes.[48] There was an earlier Hutterite case from Alberta in which the court did classify the dispute, perhaps wrongly, as a matter of church property rather than as a matter of a personal claim. The court ordered a proportionate division of the assets.[49] There is also a story about a second Alberta case categorized in this way, but there is no reported decision available.[50]

What must be conceded is that cases such as *Lakeside* are hard to classify in terms of the two categories I have drawn. What is also true is that it is a lot easier for the court to assert that a person or group has been excommunicated and therefore they are out of the church, so the court does not have to get into the theological morass of establishing which group may or may not be closer to the church for which, absent explicit norms, the property is held in trust.[51] However, if the courts are going to take jurisdiction in the first place,[52] these issues should not be avoided, as I believe they were in the *Lakeside* case.

Conclusion

After Daniel Hofer, Sr., understood that Lakeside Colony was going to expel the group for a second time, despite the Supreme Court decision in his favor, he wrote a letter on December 3, 1992 to the overseers. He ended it in this way:

> P.S. I advised our very upset members effected by your despicable acts to do like Isaac did (Genesis 26:21) and try to be patient until the church investigates said matters, and hold onto and live according to the teachings of Christ Jesus.[53]

As it turned out, Daniel Hofer, Sr., was quite prophetic when he cited Genesis 26:21. The story involves two failures before the victory. Genesis 26:19–22 reads:

> Isaac's servants dug in the valley and discovered a well of fresh water there. But the herdsmen of Gerar quarrelled with Isaac's herdsmen and said, "The water is ours!" So he named the well Esek (dispute), because they disputed with him. Then they dug another well, but they quarrelled over that one also; so he named it Sitnah (opposition). He moved on from there and dug another well, and no one quarrelled over it. He named it Rehoboth (room), saying, "Now the Lord has given us room and we will flourish in the land."

Daniel Hofer, Sr.'s, group of about forty-five people spent their first winter in 1995–1996 on a new colony they established near Beausejour, Manitoba.[54] Rehoboth would be a good name for the new colony. During the time when the trial court decision of Mr. Justice DeGraves was being prepared for an appeal, and during the time that a court case was being forced on both sides in the *Rock Lake* litigation,[55] the Reaffirmed conference accepted the Hofer group, after much negotiations between the groups, as being reconciled with the church. Now they could leave Lakeside without leaving the church. Apparently, they were able to take the assets they had accumulated since 1987 with them, but Lakeside itself was not divided. Rather, various Reaffirmed colonies aided the Hofer group in the purchase of land and equipment for the new colony. Lakeside colony, I presume, is at peace once more, nine years after Daniel Hofer, Sr., refused to stop manufacturing hog feeders. But the cost of going to law was enormous, not just in terms of the considerable legal fees. Largely as a result of the issues exposed in the litigation, the whole Schmied-Leut conference was torn apart by schism. Furthermore, the precedent has now been set that colonies must look to the external norms of natural justice in their decision-making processes, rather than just following their own internal religious custom. Do we applaud this as a small step by the state in protecting members of a religious group from being mistreated by the group, or do we see a slippery slope leading to increased state interference with the autonomy of religious groups, even if we think Daniel Hofer, Sr., deserved better treatment?

Notes

1. *Lakeside Colony of Hutterian Brethren v. Hofer* (1989) 63 D.L.R. (4th) 473 (Man. Q.B.); (1991) 77 D.L.R. (4th) 202 (Man. C.A.); (1992) 97 D.L.R. (4th) 17 (S.C.C.).

2. This invocation of the police power through civil litigation against "ex-members" might be seen as highly problematic for a group whose faith includes nonresistance and the specific injunction against civil litigation found in 1 Corinthians 6. However, this issue is not discussed in this chapter.

3. The second round of litigation proceeded to trial: *Lakeside v. Hofer* (1994) 93 Man. R. (2d) 161 (Man. Q.B.).

4. See M. Ogilvie, "Ecclesiastical Law—Jurisdiction of Civil Courts—Governing Documents of Religious Organizations—Natural Justice: *Lakeside Colony v. Hofer,*" *Canadian Bar Review,* 72 (1993): pp. 238–254.

5. See Huband J.A. of the Manitoba C.A. at 235, where he calls the regime, "manifestly inequitable."

6. Much of the early history of the Hutterites has been preserved in the writings of various sixteenth- and seventeenth-century Hutterite chronicles. These have been gathered together and translated into English. See, *The Chronicle of the Hutterian Brethren,* vol. 1 (Rifton, NY: Plough Publishing, 1987). This work contains approximately 800 pages of Hutterian writing to 1665.

7. Peter Rideman, *Confession of Faith* (Rifton, NY: Plough Publishing, 1970). Originally published in 1545.

8. See Guy F. Hershberger (ed.), *The Recovery of the Anabaptist Vision* (Scottdale: Mennonite Publishing House, 1957). I am aware that the historiography of Anabaptism includes the notion that the movement included various competing visions. See "The Anabaptist Vision: Historical Perspectives," *Conrad Grebel Review,* 12:3 (1994).

9. See Donald B. Kraybill, *The Riddle of Amish Culture* (Baltimore: Johns Hopkins University Press, 1989).

10. For an account of Hutterites in North America, I rely primarily on four main sources: Victor Peters, *All Things Common: The Hutterian Way of Life* (New York: Harper and Row, 1971); John A. Hostetler, *Hutterite Society* (Baltimore: Johns

Hopkins University Press, 1974); Karl A. Peter, *The Dynamics of Hutterite Society: An Analytical Approach* (Edmonton: University of Alberta Press, 1987); John Hofer, *The History of the Hutterites* (Altona: Friesen and Sons, 1988, rev. ed.).

11. My estimate from dated list of colonies provided in Hofer, *History*. This estimate is likely on the low side.

12. See John Ryan, *The Agricultural Economy of Manitoba Hutterite Colonies* (Toronto: McClelland and Stewart, 1977).

13. A map and list of colonies in Manitoba with phone numbers, created and printed for Emco Supply, lists ninety colonies in Manitoba in 1993.

14. See *Eberhard Arnold: A Testimony of Church-Community from His Life and Writings* (Rifton, NY: Plough Publishing, 1964).

15. Letter to "Society of Brothers who call themselves Hutterian Brethren." On file with author.

16. On file with author.

17. *Act to Incorporate the Hutterian Brethren Church*, S.C. 1951, c. 77.

18. See Karl A. Peter, *Dynamics*, ch. 3

19. For an account of some of the controversy surrounding evangelical movements within the Hutterian community, see Rod Janzen, *Terry Miller: The Pacifist Politician: From Hutterite Colony to State Capital* (Freeman, SD: Pine Hill Press, 1986).

20. See Karl A. Peter, *Dynamics*, Ch. 2.

21. The legislative restrictions from Alberta on communal ownership were upheld in *Walter v. A.G. of Alberta* (1969) 3 D.L.R. (3d) 1 (S.C.C.). For an excellent account, see William Janzen, ch. 4, pp. 60–84. See also, David Flint, *The Hutterites: A Study in Prejudice* (Toronto: Oxford University Press, 1975); Douglas Sanders, "The Hutterites: A Case Study in Minority Rights," *Canadian Bar Review*, 42 (1964): pp. 225–242. Discriminatory legislative restrictions in South Dakota related to removal of rights of incorporation as communals, rather than rights of land purchase per se. See *Chamberlain v. Hutterishe Bruder Gemeinde* (1922) 191 N.W. 635 (S.D.S.C.); *South Dakota v. Spink Hutterian Brethren* (1958) 90 N.W. 2d 365 (S.D.S.C.).

22. See *R. v. Vanguard Hutterian Brethren* [1979] 6 W.W.R. 335 (Sask. D.C.); *Hutterian Brethren Church of Eagle Creek v. Eagle 376* [1983] 2 W.W.R. 438 (Sask. C.A.); *Hutterian Brethren Church of Starland v. Starland* [1991] A.J. No. 495 (Alta C.A.); *Hutterian Brethren Church of Starland v. Standard M.D.* (1993) 9 Alta. L. R. (3d) 1 (C.A.); *Hutterian Brethren Church of Starland v. Starland M.D.* [1994] A.J. No. 276 (Alta. C.A.).

23. On the taxation issues, see: *Wipf v. The Queen* [1976] C.T.C. 57 (S.C.C) affirming [1975] F.C. 162 (Fed. C.A.); *Hutterian Brethren Church v. The Queen* [1980] C.T.C 1 (Fed C.A.) affirming [1979] D.T.C. 5052 (Fed. T. C.).

24. *Barickman Hutterian Mutual Corp. v. Nault* [1939] 2 D.L.R. 225 (S.C.C.).

25. See Willian Janzen, *Limits*, Chs. 2 and 3 regarding Mennonite and Doukhobor Land Reserves.

26. For the concept of ownership itself leading to conflict with religious belief, see McLaren on the Doukhobors in this volume.

27. Indeed, twice the Manitoba legislature has had bills in debate that would force the colonies to give assets to departed members. Both of these bills were defeated. See William Janzen, *Limits*, pp. 63–64, 67.

28. The outline of the facts in the Lakeside case are taken from *Lakeside Colony v. Hofer*, Case on Appeal to the S.C.C., which is a 12 vol. collection of the transcript of the trial and selected exhibits. On file with the author.

29. Jacob Kleinsasser was elected senior elder of the Schmied-Leut in 1978. He was also elected the senior elder of the whole Hutterian Brethren Church in 1980.

30. That the senior elder was involved in other colony oversights including Pine Creek and Rainbow colonies is outlined in Brian Preston. "Jacob's Ladder," *Saturday Night*, April 1992, pp. 30–38; 76–80.

31. A complete survey of reported decisions involving Hutterites in Canada and the United States bears out this claim. It was often asserted by the plaintiffs that the earlier Manitoba case of *Hofer v. Hofer* (1970) 73 W.W.R. 644 (S.C.C.) was a precedent, but in that case it was not the colony that initiated the law suit, but rather the ex-members. The closest case is the Alberta case of *Hofer v. Waldner* [1921] 1 W.W.R. 177 (Alta. S.C.T. Div.). Even there the church or the colony did not initiate a law suit to expel members, but rather some members under church discipline sued.

32. *Lakeside v. Hofer* (1989) 63 D.L.R. (4th) 473 (Man. Q.B.).

33. *Lakeside v. Hofer* (1991) 77 D.L.R. (4th) 202 (Man. C.A.).

34. *Lakeside v. Hofer* (1992) 97 D.L.R. (4th) 17 (S.C.C.).

35. Ibid., pp. 36; 55–56.

36. Ibid., pp. 59–62.

37. The brief overview of the facts in the second round are taken from notes at the second trial. The author was at the counsel table with the defendant's lawyer throughout the second round, but took no part in the proceedings.

38. The details of the various transactions involving the senior elder can be found in a manuscript written by a banker, I. Donald Gibb, "Summary of Transactions Involving Rosedale, Mike Waldner, Millbrook, Kleinsasser, Crystal Spring (From 1982 to the Present)." This manuscript of over one hundred pages of narrative plus exhibits of several more hundred pages was widely circulated among Schmied-Leut colonies in 1992. The Gibb manuscript is on file with the author.

39. Sid Wolchock, "Legal Matters and Documents for Consideration by the Hutterian Brethren" (1993) estimates that the plant lost 20 million of Hutterian money at the date of his writing. Wolchock manuscript on file with author.

40. Exhibit 58, Second Trial. On file with author.

41. Before he became senior elder, Kleinsasser was instrumental in getting the Arnold-Leut back into the Hutterian fellowship.

42. These matters are documented in Wolchock, "Legal Matters."

43. See Preston, "Jacob's Ladder" for an outline of various other disputes at colonies and the allegation of Kleinsasser's dictatorial style in regard to them.

44. Reaffirmation Document, Exhibit 30, Second Trial; Constitution of 1993, Exhibit A, Second Trial. Both on File with Author.

45. See, for example, the subsequent Rock Lake litigation where the colony was Reaffirmed, but the minority Kleinsasser supporters tried to take colony assets and build a new colony. *Precision Feeds Ltd. v. Rock Lake Colony Ltd.* (1993) 93 Man. R. (2d) 1; 10; 13 (Q.B.); *Precision Feeds Ltd. v. Rock Lake Colony Ltd.* (1994) 92 Man. R. (2d) 292 (C.A.); *Precision Feeds Ltd. v. Rock Lake Colony Ltd.* [1994] M.J. No. 450 and No. 703 (Man. Q.B.).

46. *Hofer v. Hofer* (1966) 59 D.L.R. (2d) 723 (Man. Q.B); (1967) 65 D.L.R. (2d) 607 (Man. C.A.); (1970) 73 W.W.R. 644 (S.C.C.).

47. *Hofer v. Bon Homme Hutterian Brethren* (1961) 109 N.W. 2d 258 (S.D.S.C).

48. For an excellent overview, see M. H. Ogilvie, "Church Property Disputes: Some Organizing Principles," *University of Toronto Law Journal*, 42 (1992): pp. 377–400.

49. *Hofer v. Waldner* [1921] 1 W.W.R. 177 (Alta. S.C.T.D.).

50. See Michael Holzach, *The Forgotten People* (Sioux Falls: Ex Machina Publishing, 1993. Originally published in 1980 in German). Holzach tells a story on pp. 182–83 about a dispute at the Big Bend colony and the disfellowship of the preacher who refused to leave with his followers. Holzach asserts that as a result of litigation, the dissenting group did get colony assets to form the new colony of Monarch which was not in fellowship with the wider Lehrer-Leut conference. I can find no reported case confirming this story, however.

51. See Ogilvie, "Church Property Disputes."

52. The American courts would not take jurisdiction over some cases that the Canadian courts accept. For example, in a case arising from the Schmied-Leut schism the court refused jurisdiction on the ground of the anti-establishment prohibition of excessive court entanglement with doctrinal matters. See *Wollman v. Poinsett Hutterian Brethren and Clarmont Hutterian Brethren* (1994) 844 F. Supp. 539 (S.D.D.C.).

53. Letter of Hofer, Exhibit 17, Second Trial. On file with author.

54. Information from Donald Douglas, lawyer for the Hofer group, Feb. 20, 1996.

55. Supra, n. 54.

Chapter 8

The Doukhobor Belief in Individual Faith and Conscience and the Demands of the Secular State

John McLaren

> The Doukhobors are what they are today because of their religion. Though many have abandoned or adapted their belief, it nevertheless shaped and continues to shape their history.[1]
>
> —F.M. Mealing, *A Survey of Doukhobor Religion, History, and Folklife*

Conflict among the Pines

On a shelf of land below the Doukhobor village of Crestova in the West Kootenay ranges of southeastern British Columbia lies the New Settlement. The community of some sixty families lives in plywood-sheathed bungalows set among a thick pine grove with one narrow road winding through it. At the entrance to the settlement, which is marked by a fork in the road, stands a group of people below a sign. The sign reads:

> This land is the Mother of us all and like the air we breath is a gift of God for all inhabitants.
>
> It should not *be* bought, or sold, or be bartered with.
>
> Placing Boundaries and stakes upon Mother Earth is exploiting it.
>
> All mankind are children of God, free to enjoy the land through love and harmony with all creation.

These people who want to know the identity and purpose of any stranger visiting the settlement are the Sons of Freedom Communal Doukhobors

(SFCD). Representing just over half the sixty families in their community they have recently been in dispute with the provincial government, as well as with some of the other Doukhobor families within their midst. The bone of contention is land and their relation to it.[1]

The members of the SFCD argue that their faith does not permit them to own land that is God's and God's alone, nor to pay taxes to the state. Moreover, it is their wish that in tune with their customs and traditions they live and work communally, an objective that they believe will be subverted by the individual ownership of land.

The Doukhobor Faith: Tradition and Experience

The Doukhobors are one of several radical sects that grew out of the schism (*Raskol*) in the Russian Orthodox Church in the late seventeenth century. The dissenters broke away in reaction to the steps initiated in the 1660s by Archbishop Nikon to reform the church's liturgy, institutionalize its priesthood, and identify more closely the interests of church and Crown. One group of schismatics entirely disavowed a priesthood and opposed any compact between faithful Christians and the state. In their faith beliefs, they stressed pacifism, the spirit of God working within human beings, and the need for individuals to follow the dictates of religious conscience.[2]

By the last two decades of the eighteenth century, one segment of this larger group were recognized in official circles as significant enough in size and potential influence to warrant identification as a particular sect of heretics—*Dukhobortsi* or wrestlers against the spirit. Under this name, they were subjected to episodic persecution, including the enforced splitting of families, removal of their children, beatings, imprisonment, exile, forfeiture of goods, and even death.[3]

Central to the faith tradition of the Doukhobors as it emerged from the haze of their early history is the strong assertion that God or the divine spark resides in every human being.[4] It follows that each individual has a relationship with God, whereby that person is responsible to him for his or her beliefs and conduct, and that it is God who rules consciences. As God exists in everyone, it follows that all are bound to have respect and love for each other, to treat one another as equals, and to avoid giving offense or, worse still, to injure or kill one another. Simply put, to harm another human being is to harm God.

The life and experience of Jesus Christ is also internalized in the experience of each human being who loves and has God within. Christ is the exemplar of the divine purpose. By accepting him at work within each individual, alongside God and the Holy Spirit, everyone has the capacity to live godly and virtuous lives, and to translate their faith into good works. For the Doukhobors this is the true test of Christian commitment.

The immediacy and authenticity of the individual's ability to recognize the divine inspiration and example was translated at a social and economic level into strong pressure for communal organization of life and labor.[5] Living out faith in the community in this way built on the tradition of the Russian peasant village (*mir*) and the practice of holding and working land in common, without any claim to owning it.[6] The power of the message in spiritual terms, however, meant a commitment to cooperation and an intensity of purpose making for communalist endeavor and success, only matched by the Mennonite colonies in southern Russia.[7]

The Doukhobors had no truck with either the institutions or ritual trappings of orthodox religion. The priests of the Russian Orthodox faith they charged with corruption and compromising with Mammon. As early as the late eighteenth century, in the teachings of Pobirohkin, the Doukhobors were persuaded that their faith was not of the book—the Bible, which was viewed as the product of fallible human interpretation. For them spiritual inspiration came from the "Living Book"—the inner manifestations of faith contained in an oral tradition of catechisms and psalms shared within families and the community at large and handed down through successive generations.[8] These representations of the faith met the needs of folk who spurned formal education and were largely illiterate.

Despite the anarchic and individualistic elements in the theology and belief patterns of the Doukhobors, they became committed to a tradition of strong semidivine leadership within the group. In time leadership took on hereditary form.[9] Acceptance of this form of authority probably stemmed from pragmatic concern that the group needed direction from a respected helmsman in times of stress and persecution, and from the belief that some individuals stood out in the community as exhibiting high virtue, living the Christian life to the full, whose example was to be emulated. It was a small jump from this sense of respect for leadership qualities to endowing the leader with Christ-like powers. The establishment of a singular authority was clearly encouraged by several of the early leaders, especially Ilarion Pobirokhin, the second identifiable historical leader of the sect, and Savely Kapustin who led it to the Crimea in 1801. The exercise of authority was charismatic, because of the belief of the faithful in the leader's divine presence and the need for that person to balance the egalitarian and collective impulses of his people with his own directions, inspirations, and insights. This was achieved by a combination of practical politics, mystical revelations, and prophesies. Among a people so dedicated to the notion of the divine spirit within and a felt personal relationship with God without reference to biblical authority or ecclesiastical institutions, the appeal of mysticism and prophesy was strong.[10]

These various ingredients of Doukhobor belief systems and political and social organization were ultimately to be honed and emphasized in the latter decades of the nineteenth century under the leader who followed them to Canada, Peter Verigin the Lordly. The experiences of the group throughout that century, however, were to demonstrate both the strengths and weaknesses in the extensive merging of the sacred and secular that the Doukhobor faith demanded, and the uneasy tension between anarchy, egalitarianism, and charismatic leadership that marked their religopolitical system.

The Doukhobors continued to be subject episodically to persecution by the Tsarist state, aided and abetted by the Orthodox hierarchy. This pattern of repression, together with their removal on two occasions to populate frontier areas, the first in the Sea of Azov area of the Crimea and the second in the Transcaucasus, was to accentuate both a determined, if fatalistic, attitude toward suffering for their faith.[11] It was also to lodge in the collective psyche an exilic myth in which a new land free of persecution and graced with God's bounty might open up to them.

The century was also marked by periods of calm and prosperity for the Doukhobor settlements. The evidence is that the success or failure of the community to deal with persecution on the one hand, or material prosperity on the other, was directly related to the effectiveness and strength of the leadership exercised. Where authority was effectively exercised such as under Kapustin, or the female leader, Lukeria Kalmykov (1864–1886), the group was able to survive migration, to resist fragmentation along wealth lines, and to keep at bay or even cooperate with the state.[12] By contrast during periods of drift and uncertainty, as there was during the reigns of the ineffectual immediate successors to Kapustin, fault lines emerged, there was backsliding by certain individuals from the faith into materialism and the state was tempted to intrude once again into their affairs.[13]

Ironically, the most turbulent period experienced by the Doukhobors in Russia ran from 1886 to the departure of 7,500 of them to Canada in 1899. During this time they were ruled by an astute, charismatic leader, but one whose power was limited because he could only exercise it from a distance. It was also a period of developing social and political turmoil within Russia as a whole. The community had split over the succession of Peter Vasilievich Verigin (the Lordly) to Lukeria Kalmykov. He had been groomed by her as her successor, but was rejected by a faction led by her brother. Verigin, having received the approbation of a majority of Doukhobors was in short order exiled by the Tsarist authorities to Siberia.[14] From that location the leader exercised inspired and effective long-distance control over his flock, communicating his own inspirations as well as weaving into his interpretations of the faith the opinions of Count Leo Tolstoy on Christian life and witness.[15] Among other directives, Verigin ordered abstention from meat eating, alcoholic drink, and smoking and later even sexual intercourse. Moreover, he emphasized both the communal ideal of life and work and the group's commitment to pacifism.[16] However, because of his situation as a political prisoner, Verigin's power and effectiveness were limited to dictating the corporate life of his flock. He was not able to respond in any diplomatic or mediative way to the broader tensions occurring within Russian government and society.

With the accession of Tsar Nicholas II in 1894, a new round of pressure to comply with the dictates of the state was applied to the Doukhobors and other dissenters, including military conscription. When young Doukhobor men refused to serve on the instructions of their leader they were subjected to harsh punishment by the military. After Verigin's followers generally engaged in a symbolic protest against war and violence by collectively burning their arms in 1895, persecution of the sect recurred in earnest. The repression included the forced dispersal of families to other regions, exile of leaders and continuing imprisonment and punishment of conscientious objectors. The result was a period of great hardship and privation for many of the faithful.[17]

Tolstoy, who felt a particular responsibility for this group, which in his mind practiced the purist form of Christianity, campaigned vigorously against the persecution.[18] He ultimately made an impassioned plea for the Doukhobors to leave Russia. In making an international issue of their plight he was assisted by both English Tolstoyans and Quakers. The campaign struck a responsive chord with the Tsarina, and the authorities relented and indicated their willingness to let Verigin's followers out of the country.[19]

During 1898, after Prince Peter Kropotkin had helped pave the way, negotiations were initiated by a mixed delegation of Tolstoyans and Doukhobors with the government of Sir Wilfred Laurier for the community to move to Canada. The Canadian government was anxious to fill up the prairies with reliable and robust agriculturalists. The Doukhobors were offered exemption from military service.[20] Moreover some, albeit hazy, concessions were suggested that would permit the immigrants to hold and work land in common, under the "hamlet clause" in the *Dominion Lands Act*.[21]

The New Home in Canada and Canadian Values

The Doukhobors came to Canada as communalist, pacifist Christians for whom religion and life were largely indistinguishable. They possessed a hostility toward, or at least profound distrust of, government and the exercise of state power and felt a strong commitment to put God before earthly authority. Their experience was of a predominantly agrarian, preindustrial society ruled by autocrats. The negative attitude that they exhibited toward both government and ecclesiastical authority had hardened with their recent mistreatment in Russia.[22]

Canada at the turn of the century was a modern industrializing state committed to increasing material wealth by encouraging individual initiative and enterprise, and the creation and protection of markets.[23] There were those in government and powerful elements of the business community who were becoming increasingly distrustful of forces within Canadian society who argued for communitarian or "socialistic" notions of obligation, and for the sharing of wealth. If the advocates of collectivism were recent immigrants they were viewed with a particularly jaundiced eye.[24]

The country was governed by a legal system which, subject to federalism, was highly centralized and had elevated the "rule of law" to a position of both institutional and rhetorical supremacy.[25] Among other demands, the "rule" required that the law be obeyed by all, from the highest to the lowest in the land, without exception. The law that governed property reflected the commodification of land and its economic value, laying great stress on individual ownership and exclusive possession.[26]

Canadian social policy was directed toward preaching the inherent merits and application of Canadian (British) values and morality to all residents of the country. This meant increasing pressure for non-English-speaking immigrants to assimilate and foreswear their ethnic cultures.[27]

In the religious realm there was a separation of the sacred and secular in the sense that life was not seen by most Canadians who called themselves Christians as a pervasive and intense religious or spiritual experience. Religion in Canada was largely organized institutionally around hierarchies, infrastructures, and bricks and mortar.[28] Faith focused on biblical authority, church tradition, and authority and liturgy, or a combination of these elements. Although some churches were dedicated to building a more virtuous society generally, the appropriate role was seen as one of pressuring the state to practice virtue and criticizing it if it did not. This process took place inside not outside the state.[29]

Within the agenda of the social gospel and the social purists who were dedicated to social as well as spiritual renewal there were strong racist, nativist, and classist strains. This often made for a "gospel" of criticism of and the forcing of conformity on those deemed to be ethnically inferior and religiously unorthodox and immature.[30]

Given this cultural divide, it is not surprising that friction would occur between the Doukhobor and non-Doukhobor communities. Unlike the experience of several other non-English-speaking European immigrant groups, however, the political and social stresses were not relaxed until many decades later, and only after a spiral of tension and bad blood that haunts many of those of Doukhobor origin in Canada to this day.

Religion, Culture, and Law and the Land Conflict

The original hazy understanding over land tenure involving the application of the "hamlet clause" to Doukobor colonies left uncertainty as to how homestead rights would be perfected.[31] The homestead law demanded registration for homesteads by individuals, and the perfecting of title only after the swearing of the oath of allegiance. No clear record existed as to whether concessions had been made by the government on these legal requirements in 1898.[32]

In the earliest period of Doukhobor settlement from 1899 to 1902 the leader, Verigin the Lordly, was still in exile Siberia. It was a time of uncertainty for the community as they came to terms with the challenge of starting from scratch in a new home. An increasing minority of families, many of whom had been the wealthiest in Russia determined that they would farm individually and take the benefit of some state services, especially education.[33] This movement away from communal life produced reaction from the traditionalists who were afraid of the community breaking up and losing its historic religious and cultural identity and underpinnings.[34]

Despite these tensions within, the communal ideal was kept alive from afar by both Verigin and Tolstoy,[35] and by a visit in 1900 by Alexander Bodyansky, an extreme follower of the Count who preached uncompromising communalism and resistance to both the homestead law and census taking.[36] These pressures resonated with the zealot minority in Saskatchewan. They set loose their animals; trashed implements, goods, and clothing made from animal products; and started on a pilgrimage in search of the new land in the early fall of 1902.[37]

The opposing trends toward both individualism and zealotry were reversed by the arrival of Verigin from Russia toward the end of 1902. The leader quickly reestablished authority and institutionalized the communal ideal in the Christian Community of Universal Brotherhood—the spiritual as well as the economic embodiment of the Doukhobor presence in Canada. The result was the establishment of a well-managed, increasingly well-financed, communal model of farming and production embracing the various colonies.[38]

The zealots continued their pilgrimages traveling between the colonies to preach the traditional ways and values and prevent any backsliding or accommodation by Verigin with the state, especially on the land issue. The first nude march occurred in May 1903, probably as an act of faith, showing man to God and nature.[39] When the shocked reaction of the authorities and non-Doukhobor community was made manifest to the marchers by North West Mounted Police officers and several outraged burghers of Yorkton, the practice of stripping off clothes individually and collectively quickly took on the character of protest by impulse.[40]

The land issue came to a head when Ottawa demanded that patents be perfected in the normal way by the swearing of the oath of allegiance on pain of losing homestead rights, and proceeded to take back "unoccupied" blocks of land made available under the "hamlet clause" and to redistribute them to non-Doukhobor settlers and speculators. The change in government policy on the issue was assisted by a highly biased and ethnocentric report prepared by the Rev. John McDougall, a former Methodist missionary to the Indians, who found no good reason for giving the Doukhobors special privileges in land holding.[41] This action on the part of the federal government was considered by the Doukhobors their first great betrayal in Canada—a willful revocation of promises solemnly made and a deceit that strengthened the view of some of the immigrants that no government was to be trusted.[42]

Although there is no doubt about government duplicity in dealing with the Doukhobor land issue in Saskatchewan, these events are also explicable in terms of a clash of belief systems about the relationship between land and those working it. In the Canadian mind land was a commodity designed for the succor of and exploitation by individuals or corporations. Power over it was limited only in the sense that it might be subject to renewed control by some other legal person with a superior right over it, or where it was being used for illegal or immoral purposes. Ranged against this individualistic, market-oriented view of land use was the Doukhobor article of faith that the land belonged to God. It was open to humankind to use and share in an economic and spiritual community, but not for individuals or groups to own or to claim as an exclusive possession. It was, moreover, subject to the obligation of responsible stewardship and respect for its productive capacity while use was being made of it. Both philosophies recognized land's productive potential, but the former ignored its value as a common resource and its use for collaborative effort, while the latter related its husbandry directly to a lifestyle and theology that made no distinction between the economic or social and the religious being.

The reversal of undertakings by Ottawa on land in Saskatchewan was not the last problem associated with Doukhobor land holding in Canada. For the majority of the immigrants who followed Verigin to southeastern British Columbia to build a new community in the wake of these sad events, the land issue seemed to have been settled. The tracts acquired by the leader in the West Kootenay ranges were held by him for the community in fee simple and ultimately registered in the name of the CCUB as a corporation.[43] Ostensibly, then, the community seemed secure, with a perfectly conventional, unassailable title to the land that it occupied.

These lands in the neighborhood of Castlegar and along the Slocan Valley were worked communally by the Doukhobor villages. Their inhabitants lived in communal houses accommodating several families and shared facilities for both social and religious observances.[44] The faithful at large came together for both communal and religious purposes in the village meeting or *sobranya*. The communalism practiced was, however, viewed with a jaundiced eye by elements of the non-Doukhobor population many of whom who were racist and ill-disposed to strangers who did not fit their model of the ideal Canadian, British, or American settler. The Doukhobor mode of social organization was seen as culturally bizarre. It was also branded as economically subversive, in particular as the CCUB endeavored to be self-sufficient and, where supplies and foodstuffs were needed, bought wholesale.[45]

The particular brand of communalism practised by Verigin and his followers was also problematic for some Doukhobors. The Independents normally went their own way, purchasing or leasing land in the normal way. The price was that they lost the services provided by and for the community. The traditionalist and ascetic Sons of Freedom, as the zealots became known, were clearly not happy with the degree of material wealth engendered by the economic operations of the community and the eroding spiritual commitment of its managers, as they saw it. Moreover, they reacted strongly to attempts by the provincial government to force compliance with the law. In the early 1920s frustration over the attempts of the provincial authorities to compel school attendance resulted in a rash of school burnings in the Kootenays.[46] In due course many of the zealot families were thrown off community land by Verigin the Lordly's son, Peter Petrovich, after he assumed the leadership of the Canadian Doukhobors in 1927. This was his response to a campaign of nude protests and renewed school burnings by the radicals designed to protest the leader's embracing public education for Doukhobor children.[47]

From 1929 the Sons of Freedom became effectively nomads and squatters, often living in tent communities wherever they could find waste, unoccupied land. Ultimately they were allowed to resettle on community land by their orthodox brethren after an extended spell in jail between 1932 and 1935.[48]

Ultimately, all CCUB land was forfeited in the late 1930s, a result of debts incurred during the Great Depression and in part related to the unstable administration of the corporation's business during the leadership of Peter Petrovich Verigin.[49] The farmers' exemption under debt relief legislation in British Columbia was denied by the Supreme Court of Canada without any serious consideration of the significance of religion in the Doukhobors's relationship with land. The CCUB, the jurists concluded, was a limited company engaged in a variety of commercial ventures and not a group of farmers. The farming was done by individual Doukhobors who held the land as tenants.[50] Meanwhile, the provincial government that could have loaned the CCUB the money to pay off the creditors but was basically unsympathetic to the Doukhobors and their communal lifestyle, stood by while the foreclosures by the mortgagees took effect. However, worried about the disorder it feared would follow a wholesale removal of the community Doukhobors from their land, Victoria settled the debts, the land reverted to the Crown and Doukhobor families were allowed to remain as its tenants. This was, of course, a status calculated to make them particularly uncomfortable, given their beliefs about land and its use. The loss of communal lands in British Columbia was considered by the Doukhobors to be the second great betrayal by Canadian authorities.[51]

The majority of community Doukhobors, left without a leader by the death of the younger Verigin in 1939, bereft of productive community structures and having many of their number working in the non-Doukhobor economy, reluctantly accepted the realities of their situation. By contrast the Sons of Freedom were now increasingly of the view that they were the only Doukhobors ordained and able to stand up to Mammon.[52] However, they split among themselves over who was their leader and became increasingly introspective and prone to interpreting events and statements in mystical ways by ascribing inverted meanings to them.

The complicated Freedomite mind-set and continuing insensitivity of British Columbia governments toward the Doukhobors and their culture (including lumping all of them indiscriminately together) resulted in an ongoing series of protests and depredations by the Sons from 1944 on. These outbursts included group or mass nudity, the burnings of premises (often, but not exclusively, their own or those of other Doukhobors) and in due course bombings of both Doukhobor ikons, such as Verigin the Lordly's tomb, and public facilities, including power plants, bridges, and rail lines.[53]

In the late 1950s, the government in Victoria, which was finally coming around to the idea that concessions to Doukhobor culture needed to be made on its part to bring peace to the Kootenays, resolved to settle the land issue. On the basis of an inquiry by Judge Lord of Vancouver, it began a process of surveying former community lands and selling them back to community members in fee simple at reduced prices.[54] A more imaginative and sensitive plan to have the Union of Spiritual Communities of Christ (USSC), the new incarnation of the community Doukhobors, hold the land in trust was shelved when it was challenged by non-Doukhobor interests.[55] Many Doukhobor families, like it or not, were now fully governed by the conventional system of land ownership and possession, and thus assimilated in terms of property rights.

This "deal" with government was not acceptable to Freedomite families who, having burned their own homes, often lived as squatters on vacant land, or took on the role of nomads. In 1962 a mass march was organized by several Freedomite women to the Mountain Prison in Agassiz in 1962 to show solidarity with their imprisoned menfolk.[56] In the process some Sons of

Freedom families resettled in the Fraser Valley and even in the Vancouver area. With the resulting dispersal of the zealot population and a more general weakening of resolve, the number of protests and depredations decreased.

By 1971, with the pending release of many Freedomite men from jail, negotiations opened for their resettlement on condition that they kept the peace. Land in the New Settlement was set aside by the Crown and conveyed to four "representatives" of the community for habitation and use by the released prisoners and their families. The agreement was in force until the mid-1980s when Stephan Sorokin, the spiritual leader of the Sons of Freedom, died and the land soon reverted to the government for nonpayment of taxes. It was at this point that the government sought to pressure the families in the settlement to purchase plots of land in fee simple, a move that created a reaction among the traditionalists in the community and led to resistance to attempts to survey and replot the land in 1995, arrests of the protesters and ultimately negotiations to secure a peaceful and lasting resolution of the problems.[57]

Throughout the vagaries of the Doukhobor experience with land use in Canada, the belief that land was held of God and thus not reducible to secular, legal rights was maintained, although it clearly weakened once first the community and later individuals felt compelled to hold land according to the demands of the dominant legal system. However, neither the government nor the legal system seemed willing to contemplate constructing a regime of land holding that might accommodate Doukhobor beliefs and sensitivities. This was so even though there were examples in the history of English law of the development of regimes to meet the scruples of communities (most notably religious ones) unable to accept title to land and unwilling to pay taxes to the Crown.[58] Instead, as time went on, the strategy developed of breaking the communal system of the Doukhobors and the value system that lay behind it. The Freedomites held out the longest against any compromise with the state on the land issue, reflecting a deep commitment to traditional Doukhobor theology and tradition. Recent events at the New Settlement indicate that this is still unfinished business for that group.

Explanations

The Doukhobors were not unique in running into discrimination and pressures to conform to Canadian values and law in Canada. Other religious communalists such as the strict Mennonites and Hutterites had similar experiences.

In Protestant English Canada cultural and linguistic pluralism was not welcomed, nor were religious communities that despised orthodoxy in religion and sought to preach a faith that stressed individual conscience as the guide to conduct and the life of the community as a religious experience. Such people were seen as immature and untrustworthy as citizens, given to "unreasoning" challenges to the accepted political, social, and legal order.

During much of the present century, the pressures for conformity by non-English-speaking immigrants was strong outside Quebec. By education in particular, immigrant children would be compelled to learn English, forget their mother tongue, and recognize the need to respect Canadian law and institutions.[59] There was rarely any systematic attempt to learn about or understand the political and cultural milieu from which non-Anglo-Protestant migrants came. This was clearly evident with the Doukhobors where there was only a handful of Canadians, such as James Mavor and J. S. Woodsworth, willing to inform themselves about the immigrants' history and tribulations and how it affected their view of society. For the rest stereotypes about Slavs in general as uneducated peasants and about the Doukhobors in particular as deranged, perverse, and deviant people provided the basis for sweeping, unfavorable judgments by many Canadians.

In Canada the law traditionally protected religious diversity and confession and conscience within limited boundaries. Those parameters reflected the early history of Canada in which for strategic reasons the Roman Catholic population of Quebec was accorded early a significant measure of religious freedom.[60] Within Protestant Canada, not without a struggle, the claims of mainstream sects to equality in their dealings with the state was recognized by 1850.[61] All of these faith traditions were accorded both recognition and respectability by government and law. There was far less comfort then, as now, with groups whose credo seemed to challenge the basic suppositions about the liberal, capitalist state and the subordinate or compliant nature of religion within it.[62] Clear delineation in both policy statements and the jurisprudence that certain functions are those of the state, for example, the control and management of land and education, has ruled out their location within the religious or spiritual realms and so worked against acceptance of religion as life. As one British Columbia judge, faced with the argument that to take Freedomite children into care for truancy, over the objections of their parents, constituted interference with their religious freedom, put it.

> I, for my part cannot feel that in this case there is any religious element involved in the true legal sense . . . I absolutely reject the contention that any group of tenets that some sect decides to proclaim form part of its religion thereby necessarily takes on a religious colour. . . .
> [Treating education as a matter of faith and conscience] involves the claim that a religious sect may make rules for the conduct of any part of human activity and that these rules thereby become for all the world a part of that sect's religion. This cannot be so.[63]

There has been a clear feeling within the dominant culture that groups that challenge the separation of the sacred and secular (particularly if done openly and vigorously) are somehow not respectable in religious terms, and are being extreme in their demands.

The problems of the Doukhobors were also associated with their religopolitical system. They were introspective because of their history, often assuming a "chosen people" frame of mind that gave little consideration to those who did not share their version of the faith. Anarchic elements in their approach to politics and law together with the individualistic notion of conscience and the suffering of their Russian experience made them prickly and difficult to deal with individually and collectively, as well as prone to division and fragmentation within. The countervail to their anarchic tendencies in the principle of semidivine, hereditary leadership was problematic too.[64] Charismatic qualities were required in the leader to keep the group together and contented, which meant that the leader and his policies were often subject to communal approval, and sometimes challenge. This caused great frustration in the non-Doukhobor community, which sometimes found it difficult to get a straight answer from the leader, or were faced with what seemed to be a *volte face*.[65] When authority was nonexistent or weak, the pressures for fission within the group became extreme resulting in what can only be described as disarray.[66]

The Doukhobors, as a result of their experiences, were justifiably distrustful of the dominant political, social, and economic culture and often paranoid about compromising with it. For the more zealous, the answer was a retreat into the past and asceticism. For many Doukhobors, the way to fight back was with strong words, which combined colorful elements of their faith with left-wing political discourse reflecting their belief in themselves as among the poor of the earth.[67] The more extreme flourishes of Doukhobor rhetoric, especially those emanating from the Sons of Freedom, were not calculated to win friends or calm nerves in the dominant community.[68] Indeed, the fact that the Doukhobors were Russian communalists and proud of it meant that in certain circles they were tarred with brush of Bolshevism and viewed as potentially subversive.[69]

Conclusion

In February 1996, a memorandum of agreement worked out with representatives of the British Columbia government by negotiators acting on behalf of the SFCD was approved and signed by the relevant ministers of the Crown.[70] This opened the way to the creation of a land regime in the New Settlement, using an intermediate trust, which the Franciscans of thirteenth-century England would have understood and appreciated.[71] It will accommodate the desire of the residents to use the land, but to foreswear ownership as a matter of religious conscience. The announcement of this memorandum followed in the wake of an agreement between the Nisga'a of the Nass Valley in Northern British Columbia, Victoria and Ottawa that will provide a land settlement and grant self-government to this First Nations group. In both instances, communal notions of life and property and recognition of a spiritual connection with the earth as the nurturer of humankind have received tentative legitimacy by the dominant political and legal system. One might be forgiven for hoping that Canadians are finally beginning to recognize the reality of cultural and religious pluralism within their midst and the need for the law to take account of and respect it. The sad irony for the Doukhobors is that for most of the descendants of the 7,500 who arrived on Canadian shores in 1899, assimilative forces may have proved too strong and legal creativity may have arrived too late for these recent developments to have much meaning. Meanwhile, in the New Settlement, there is cautious optimism that what for some has been a lifetime of struggle is almost over.

Notes

1. See *Castlegar Sun*, August 24, 1994, for details of the dispute. The description of the New Settlement are from my own observations during a visit on November 11, 1995.

2. On the earliest history of the Doukhobors, see Koozma Tarasoff, *Plakun Trava: The Doukhobors* (Grand Forks, BC: Mir Publishing, 1982), pp. 1–3; George Woodcock and Ivan Avakumovic, *The Doukhobors* (Toronto: McClelland & Stewart, 1977), pp. 17–34. Eli Popoff, *Stories from Doukhobor History* (Grand Forks, BC: Union of Spiritual Communities of Christ, 1992). On the history of the evolution of their religious beliefs, see F. M. Mealing, *A Survey of Doukhobor, Religion, History and Folklife* (Castlegar, BC: Kootenay Doukhobor Historical Society/Cotinneh Books, 1975).

3. For early examples of persecution of individual Doukhobors for their faith, see Popoff, *Stories*, pp. 13–25. Tarasoff (p. 3) reports the removal of children under ten years of age from their families in order that they be brought up in the Orthodox faith.

4. See Vladimir Bonch-Bruevich (ed.), *The Book of Life of the Doukhobors* (Saskatoon: University of Saskatchewan, 1978, trans. by Victor Buyniak), pp. xvii–xxxix and 1–11; John P. Stoochnoff, *Toil and the Peaceful Life: Doukhobors as They Are* (Calgary: Liberty Press, 1971), pp. 19–24; Mealing, *Survey*, pp. 5–9.

5. The development of communal living seems to have happened when the Doukhobors were moved to the Crimean area of Russia in 1801 under the relatively

benign policies of Tsar Alexander I toward the sectaries, and established colonies there, see Popoff, pp. 43–44. On the link between Doukhobor religious faith and communal living and architecture, see Donald Gale and Paul Koroscil, "Doukhobor Settlements: Experiments in Idealism," *Canadian Ethnic Studies* 9 (1977): p. 53.

6. Tarasoff, p. 6.

7. The pattern of Doukhobor settlement in the Milky Waters region may well have been affected by the Mennonite communities already flourishing there, ibid., p. 7.

8. See Bonch-Bruevich, *The Living Book* for an encyclopedic collection of catechisms and psalms. On their interpretation, see Mealing, pp. 41–64 and "On Doukhobor Psalms," *Canadian Literature*, no. 120, Spring 1989.

9. Tarasoff, pp. 3, 6–8.

10. On the character of charismatic authority, which seems to fit the Doukhobor situation very well, see Max Weber, *Economy and Society: An Outline of Interpretative Sociology* (New York: Bedminster Press, 1968), vol. 1, pp. 215–16, 244; vol. 3, pp. 1114–15.

11. Mealing, *A Survey*, pp. 7–8.

12. Tarasoff, pp. 6–10, 13–14; Nicholas B. Breyfogle, "Building Doukhoboria: Religious Culture, Social Identity and Russian Colonization in Transcaucasia, 1845–1895," *Canadian Ethnic Studies* 27.3 (1995): pp. 24–51.

13. Tarasoff, p. 10.

14. Popoff, p. 68 indicates that Verigin was the victim of a conspiracy between Alesha Zubkov, a former close confidante of Lukeria, who refused to accept him as leader, and the district police.

15. For examples of the fascinating correspondence between the two men, see Lidia Gromova-Opul'skaya and Andrew Donskov (eds.), *Leo Tolstoy—Peter Verigin Correspondence* (New York: Legas, 1995). See also Josh Sanborn, "Pacifist Politics: Tolstoy and the Doukhobors, 1895–99," *Canadian Journal of Ethnic Studies* 27.3 (1995): pp. 52–71.

16. Woodcock and Avakumovic, pp. 89–92.

17. The details of this period of tribulation for Verigin's followers are graphically described in a book by one of Count Tolstoy's followers, see Vladimir Tchertkoff, *Christian Martyrdom in Russia: Persecution of the Doukhobors* (Castlegar, BC: Spirit Wrestlers Association, 1993, reprint of 1900 original).

18. See the copy of letter from Tolstoy to the commander of the Ekaterinograd Penal Battalion, November 1, 1896 in Stoochnoff, pp. 57–59, and his "Conclusion" to Tchertkoff's book, pp. 50–53.

19. For the remarkable direct plea of Peter Verigin to the Empress Alexandra Feodorovna, dated November 1, 1896, see Stoochnoff, pp. 63–65.

20. See excerpt from a Report of the Committee of the Privy Council, December 6, 1898, in Stoochnoff, pp. 76–77. The exemption had previously been allowed by Order-in-Council to Mennonite and other pacifist immigrants, see William Janzen, *The Limits of Liberty: The Experience of Mennonite, Hutterite and Doukhobor Communities in Canada* (Toronto: University of Toronto Press, 1990), pp. 164–66.

21. Revised Statutes of Canada, ch. 31, s.37. For documentation, see Steve Lapshinoff, *Documentary Report on Doukhobor Lands in Saskatchewan* (Krestova, BC, 1989, unpublished), pp. 3–50. See also, Jeremy Adelman, "Early Doukhobor Experience on the Canadian Prairies," *Journal of Canadian Studies* 25 (1990–1991): 111, pp. 113–14.

22. This fact seems to have been recognized in press reports at the time of arrival of the Doukhobors in Canada in 1899, see excerpt from the *Halifax Morning Chronicle* in Stoochnoff, pp. 78–78. On the basics of Doukhobor belief at this time, see Lapshinoff, *Saskatchewan*, pp. 185–86—"Rules of Life of the CCUB," December 1896.

23. R. Craig Brown and Ramsay Cook, *Canada 1896–1921: A Nation Transformed* (Toronto: McClelland & Stewart, 1974), pp. 83–107.

24. Howard Palmer, *Patterns of Prejudice: A History of Nativism in Alberta* (Toronto: McClelland & Stewart, 1982), pp. 17–47.

25. Louis Knafla, "From Oral to Written Memory: The Common Law Tradition in Western Canada," in L. Knafla (ed.), *Law and Justice in a New Land: Essays in Western Canadian Legal History* (Calgary: Carswell Co., 1986), 31, pp. 64–68; John McLaren, "The Early British Columbia Supreme Court and the "Chinese Question": Echoes of the Rule of Law," *Manitoba Law Journal* 20 (1991): 107, pp. 125–47.

26. R. Cail, *Land, Man and the Law: The Disposal of Crown Lands in British Columbia, 1871–1913* (Vancouver: UBC Press, 1974).

27. See James S. Woodsworth, *Strangers at Our Gates* (Toronto: University of Toronto Press, 1972, reprint of 1909 original); James Anderson, *The Education of the New Canadian: A Treatise on Canada's Greatest Education Problem* (London: J. M. Dent, 1918); Neil Sutherland, *Children in English Canadian Society: Framing the Twentieth-Century Consensus* (Toronto: University of Toronto Press, 1976).

28. William Westfall, *Two Worlds: The Protestant Culture of Nineteenth-Century Ontario* (Kingston and Montreal: McGill-Queens University Press, 1989).

29. See Richard Allen, *The Social Passion: Religion and Social Reform in Canada 1914–28* (Toronto: University of Toronto Press, 1979), at 3–17; Carol Bacchi, *Liberation Deferred? The Ideas of English-Canadian Suffragists, 1877–1918* (Toronto: University of Toronto Press, 1983); Brian Fraser, *The Social Uplifters: Presbyterian Progressives and the Social Gospel in Canada, 1875–1915* (Waterloo, ONT.: Wilfred Laurier University Press, 1988).

30. Woodsworth, supra note 27.

31. Janzen, pp. 36–38. The "understanding" on communal farming was confirmed by a letter from Clifford Sifton, Minister of the Interior to the delegates from the Doukhobors of Thunder Hill Colony, February 15, 1902 in L. Strakovsky (ed.), *Doukhobor Claims for Compensation* (CCUB pamphlet, n.d.), pp. 4–6; Lapshinoff, *Saskatchewan*, pp. 214–16.

32. Adelman, pp. 113–14.

33. Woodcock and Avakumovic, pp. 159–60; James Wright, *Slava Bohu: The Story of the Doukhobors* (New York: Farrar & Rinehart, 1940), at pp. 142–44.

34. Wright, pp. 144–55; Lapshinoff, *Saskatchewan*, pp. 51–69, 199–203.

35. See Tarasoff, p. 69 for discussion of Verigin's correspondence; and the text of a letter from Tolstoy to the Doukhobors in Canada, February 27, 1900, in Stoochnoff, pp. 79–84.

36. Woodcock and Avakumovic, pp. 168–71; Lapshinoff, *Saskatchewan*, pp. 51–69, 199–203.

37. Woodcock and Avakumovic, pp. 177–81.

38. Ibid., pp. 198–204. See also Gale and Koroscil, pp. 62–64 on communal living in the Saskatchewan Doukhobor colonies.

39. J. Colin Yerbury, "The 'Sons of Freedom' Doukhobors and the Canadian State," *Canadian Ethnic Studies* 16 (1984): 45, p. 53.

40. Adelman, p. 120. For a discussion of the psychology that may have been at work here, see Shirley Ardener, "Arson, Nudity and Bombs among the Canadian Doukhobors: A Question of Identity," in G. Breakwell (ed.), *Threatened Identities* (London: John Wiley & Sons, 1983), 239, pp. 250–52.

41. Ibid., pp. 121–25. For McDougall's report and Ottawa's response, see Lapshinoff, *Saskatchewan*, pp. 117–52.

42. For a reasonably measured statement of this type, see letter from M. W. Cazakoff, Manager CCUB to Dr. W. J. Roche, Minister of the Interior, March 23, 1914 in L. Strakovsky, *Doukhobor Claims for Compensation* (CCUB pamphlet, n.d.), pp. 12–15.

43. Tarasoff, pp. 99–116. For documents relating to incorporation, see Steve Lapshinoff, *Documentary Report on Doukhobor Lands in British Columbia* (Krestova, BC, 1990, unpublished), pp. 35–46.

44. Gale and Koroscil, pp. 64–68.

45. Woodcock and Avakumovic, pp. 244–45. The unreasoning attitude of elements of the non-Doukhobor population was noted by William Blakemore in his Royal Commission Report of 1912—*Report of Royal Commission on Matters Relating to the Doukhobor Sect in the Province of British Columbia*, British Columbia, *Sessional Papers*, 1913, T64–65.

46. See John McLaren, "Creating 'Slaves of Satan' or 'New Canadians'? The Law, Education, and the Socialization of Doukhobor Children, 1911–1935" in Hamar Foster and John McLaren (eds.), *Essays in the History of Canadian Law*, vol. 6, *British Columbia and the Yukon* (Toronto: Osgoode Society, 1995), 352.

47. Woodcock and Avakumovic, pp. 313–16; Lapshinoff, *British Columbia*, pp. 105–09.

48. Yerbury, p. 57.

49. Woodcock and Avakumovic, pp. 305–06; Lapshinoff, *British Columbia*, pp. 137–207.

50. *Christian Community of Universal Brotherhood v. National Trust Ltd.* [1941] S.C.R. 601. The court specifically distinguished the case of Hutterite corporations by suggesting that the latter were primarily engaged in farming and that individual Hutterites had no rights to land. They were in the position of employees of the corporation, see Rinfret J. pp. 620–21. A Hutterite colony had been classified as a farmer for debt relief purposes by the court in *Barickman Hutterian Brotherhood v. Nault* [1939] S.C.R. 223.

51. Tarasoff, pp. 152–53.

52. Yerbury, pp. 58–59.

53. For the one significant attempt to bring calm reason to bear on the relations of Doukhobors and non-Doukhobors in the early 1950s, see Harry Hawthorn (ed.), *The Doukhobors of British Columbia* (Vancouver: J. M. Dent, 1955).

54. Judge Arthur Lord, *Doukhobor Lands Allotment Inquiry, Fifth Interim Report*, November 16, 1958. See also Tarasoff, pp. 166–68.

55. Tarasoff, p. 168.

56. Yerbury, p. 63.

57. See text supra pp. 117–18 and fn. 1.

58. See, for example, the use of the trust device to insulate the Franciscan order from feudal incidents because they were not permitted to own land. Having the land held by others was permissible since they were able to accept hospitality. John Baker, *An Introduction to the English Legal History*, 3rd ed. (London: Butterworths, 1990), p. 284.

59. See, for example, Anderson, *The Education of the New Canadian*.

60. On the politics of the Quebec Act of 1774, see Hilda Neatby, *Quebec: The Revolutionary Age, 1760–1791* (Toronto: McClelland & Stewart, 1966), pp. 125–41.

61. See Gerald Craig, *Upper Canada: The Formative Years, 1748–1841* (Toronto: McClelland & Stewart, 1963), pp. 273–72.

62. For a pungent critique of the marginalization of religious belief in the United States today, which has resonance in Canada, see Stephen Carter, *The Culture*

of Disbelief: How American Law and Politics Trivialize Religious Devotion (New York: Basic Books, 1993).

63. Sidney Smith J.A., in *Perepolkin v. Superintendent of Child Welfare (No. 2)* (1957), 23 W.W.R. 592 (BCCA), pp. 599–600.

64. On the Doukhobor leadership tradition more generally, see John McLaren, "Wrestling Spirits: The Strange Case of Peter Verigin II," *Canadian Ethnic Studies* 27.3 (1995): pp. 95–130.

65. McLaren, "Creating 'Slaves of Satan,' " pp. 353–54.

66. See Kathleen Bradbury, *Factionalism in the Doukhobor Movement* (University of Calgary, M.A. Thesis, Anthropology, 1976).

67. See, for example, BCARS, GR 441 Premier Oliver Papers, vol. 246, File 13, letter from W. Sherstibitoff, Director, CCUB to Premier John Oliver, April 16, 1925.

68. See the example mentioned in Woodcock and Avakumovic, pp. 313–14.

69. For an example of this simple-minded association of the Doukhobors and international communism, see McLaren, "Wrestling Spirits," pp. 101–02.

70. The SFCD were not willing to negotiate with government directly, but were represented by several non-Doukhobor individuals from the Kootenays and Victoria possessing empathy for them and their beliefs.

71. On the use of the trust to accommodate the religious scruples of the Franciscan Order in England, see Stephen W. Devine, "The Franciscan Friars, Feoffment to Uses and Canonical Theories of Property Enjoyment before 1535," *Journal of Legal History* 10 (1989), p. 1.

Chapter 9

The Law and Reconstituted Christianity:
The Case of the Mormons[1]

Carol Weisbrod

For every constitution there is an epic, for each decalogue
a scripture . . .
—Robert Cover, The Supreme Court 1982 term;
Foreword; Nomos and Narrative, 97 *Harvard Law
Review* 4 (1983)

Introduction

On January 4, 1896, the Mormon-dominated territory of Utah was proclaimed a state by President Grover Cleveland. An Enabling Act passed by Congress (1894)[2] authorizing Utah's constitutional convention and mandating certain constitutional provisions, had resulted in a constitution approved by Utah voters in 1895.

Utah was admitted to membership in the Union under a state constitution providing for religious freedom and the rejection of polygamy. The polygamy language read: "Perfect toleration of religious sentiment shall be secured, and that no inhabitant of said State shall ever be molested in person or property on account of his or her mode of religious worship: *Provided,* that polygamous or plural marriages are forever prohibited."[3] The state constitution also provided that no church would ever take control of the state: "There shall be no union of church and state, nor shall any church dominate the state or interfere with its functions."[4]

These two provisions highlight those aspects of the domestic and political aspects of the doctrine and culture of the Latter-Day Saints that troubled its neighbors.[5]

This chapter deals with these textual provisions as a reconstitution of Mormonism in its relation to the state of Utah and to the larger federal state, the United States. Part I of the chapter reviews the unsuccessful efforts of nineteenth-century Mormons to reach an accommodation with the United States government on the issue of polygamy (through the free exercise clause argument litigated and rejected in *Reynolds v. United States*) and concludes with the new constitution. Part II considers the twentieth-century history of polygamy and the modern association of the Mormon Church with traditional family structures. The third part of the chapter discusses aspects of reconstitution relating to church-state relations in a situation of disestablishment, under an approach to constitutionalism that moves beyond the idea of the Constitution as text to the idea of a working framework of religious groups in the modern state.

Part I: The Mormon Empire

The major nineteenth-century narrative of the Mormon encounters with the American legal system over the issue of polygamy begins in 1852, when the Mormons announced publicly that they were practicing plural marriage,[6] and ends in 1890 when the triumph of the federal government was formally acknowledged by the Mormon Church. It includes the trek to the Great Salt Lake Basin, a history of which George Bernard Shaw observed that it was "one of the most extraordinary episodes in the white settlement of the world."[7] The move to the west was, as Brigham Young made plain, a move out of the United States.[8]

The early history remains central to the Mormon understanding of their relationship to the American story. Elder Dallin H. Oaks, representing the Church of Jesus Christ of Latter-Day Saints, recalled that history in testimony submitted to the U.S. Congress in 1992: "I know of no other major religious group in America that has endured anything comparable to the officially sanctioned persecution that was imposed upon members of my church by Federal, State and local government officials," he said. "In the nineteenth century, our members were literally driven from State to State, sometimes by direct Government action, and finally expelled from the existing borders of the United States."[9]

But the federal presence was not to be eliminated. In 1850, Utah became a territory, subject to the authority of the American Congress. The Republican Party platform of 1856 included a reference to polygamy as a twin relic of barbarism; slavery, of course, the other.[10] The campaign against polygamy waited for the end of the Civil War, and then it began in earnest.

A critical moment in the narrative occurred in 1879, when the Supreme Court decided *Reynolds v. United States*, which litigated a federal statute, the Morrill Act,[11] passed in 1862 to deal with bigamy in the territories. This was a test case involving George Reynolds of Utah, secretary to Brigham Young. Reynolds's central argument in the Supreme Court was that his conviction for bigamy could not stand because polygamy was an exercise of rights protected under the religious liberty guarantees of the first amendment, directly operative in the territories. His rights, he said, were violated by the congressional action.[12] Reynolds requested the trial court to instruct the jury that if it found from the evidence that he was married "in pursuance of and in conformity with what he believed at the time to be a religious duty, that the verdict must be not guilty."[13] This request was refused.

Chief Justice Waite, writing for the Supreme Court on the subsequent appeal, considered the jury instruction. The issue was whether religious belief could justify an act made criminal by federal statute.[14] The Court rejected Reynolds's claim that the religious practice of polygamy was constitutionally protected. The trial judge had instructed the jury that:

> if the defendant, under the influence of a religious belief that it was right—under an inspiration, if you please, that it was right,—deliberately married a second time, having a first wife living, the want of consciousness of evil intent—the want of understanding on his part that he was committing a crime—did not excuse him; but the law inexorably in such case implies the criminal intent.[15]

Congress, the Supreme Court said, could not pass a law for the territories that would prohibit the free exercise of religion, but the antibigamy act was not within the congressional prohibition. The Court found the Morrill Act within the legislative power of Congress, since Congress was "left free to reach actions which were in violation of social duties or subversive of good order."[16] The Court then asked whether those who made the practice of polygamy a part of their religious belief were excepted from the operation of the statute,[17] and concluded that they were not.

The statute was upheld by the Supreme Court. Reynolds himself served nineteen months in jail and on his release married a third time.[18]

In 1865, Francis Lieber suggested that it might be appropriate to consider, among various amendments to the American Constitution, one declaring polygamy and polyandry a crime.[19] Presumably, he did this in part because he understood that if Utah, then a territory, were to be admitted to the union as a state, it would be very difficult to move legally against the alternative marriage form of the Latter-Day Saints (LDS). Marriage and divorce were in the control of the states, and not the federal government.[20] Without a constitutional provision to limit the behavior of the new state, Utah was free to adopt such provisions as it would regarding marriage and divorce.[21] Like many in his time, Lieber saw polygamy and theocracy as linked.

Polygamy was legally defeated in nineteenth-century America at roughly the same time that a large-scale pattern based on divorce and subsequent remarriage—"serial" polygamy, as its opponents called it, was becoming familiar. It is almost as though Mormon polygamy, the clear case, the one on which everyone could agree, was handled with particular harshness exactly because the issue of divorce, equally an attack on the basic conception of monogamous marriage for life, was a case on which a widespread societal consensus no longer existed.[22] But whether or not one accepts this relationship between the two issues, another relationship, a contrast, seems beyond dispute. While the forces of organized religion would have counted their campaign against Mormon polygamy a success, their campaign against lax divorce laws was, with a few exceptions, a failure.

The difficulty of proving plural marriage in Utah—because of the secrecy of the ceremony—was behind a second case under the 1862 statute. *Miles v. United States* (1880), reversed a bigamy conviction based on testimony of an (admitted) second wife on the grounds that under Utah law, until the first marriage was shown, the second wife was the lawful wife and could not testify against her husband.[23] Partly because polygamy was so difficult to prove, several other congressional enactments followed the original antibigamy statutes. The last of these, which involved a disincorporation of the Mormon Church and confiscation of its property, resulted in a formal declaration (September 25, 1890) by Wilson Woodruff, President of the Mormon Church under which the Mormon Church officially abandoned polygamy.[24]

Despite the declaration, hostility to the Mormon institution continued. In *Church of Jesus Christ of Latter-Day Saints v. United States* (1889) the Supreme Court said that polygamy was "a return to barbarism . . ."[25] Justice Stephen J. Field in *Davis v. Beason* (1890) stated that bigamy and polygamy are crimes, tending "to destroy the purity of the marriage relation, to disturb the peace of families, to degrade woman and to debase man." By contrast to *Davis v. Beason*, the rhetoric of *Reynolds* may be seen as moderate.[26]

The Mormon attempt to defend the group in constitutional litigation was, thus, not successful. Perhaps, however, one should stress the significance of the fact that the attempt was made at all. It is not to be assumed that religious groups will feel free under their own rules to invoke rights under the state system. They may refuse to interact in this way with state legal systems and insist that such an interaction would corrupt their own institutions. But the Mormons' sense that they were also a part of the larger system was revealed not only by their use of test case litigation as a defense strategy but also by their repeated applications for statehood and their general approach to the American Constitution as divinely inspired.[27]

The campaign against polygamy was, of course, directed at perceived immorality.[28] But it was also directed at an institution whose importance went beyond the sins of individuals. The real point was that marriage and the family were linked to an understanding of the state. The Court in the *Reynolds* case presented a discussion of marriage as a foundation of society that continues to be of considerable importance.

> Marriage, while from its very nature a sacred obligation, is nevertheless, in most civilized nations, a civil contract, and usually regulated by law. Upon it society may be said to be built, and out of its fruits spring social relations and social obligations and duties, with which government is necessarily required to deal. In fact, according as monogamous or polygamous marriages are allowed, do we find the principles on which the government of the people, to a greater or less extent, rests. Professor Lieber says, polygamy leads to the patriarchal principle, and [*sic*] which, when applied to large communities, fetters the people in stationary despotism, while that principle cannot long exist in connection with monogamy.

The decision in the *Reynolds* case has been read in the twentieth century as a statement that "found in polygamy the seed of destruction of a democratic society" and that viewed polygamy as "highly injurious to its female adherents."[29] *Reynolds* sustained a lower court instruction to the jury referring to "pure-minded women," "innocent children," and "innocent victims of this delusion."[30] But while the decision refers to the odiousness of polygamy, the *Reynolds* opinion does not detail the injuries to the innocent victims or other evils of the institution. Rather, the court was content to leave the issue with the observation that "Polygamy has always been odious among the northern and western nations of Europe, and, until the establishment of the Mormon Church, was almost exclusively a feature of the life of Asiatic and African People."

Chief Justice Waite referred to the opinion as his "sermon on the religion of polygamy."[31] John Noonan has suggested that Waite "sounded precisely like his contemporary, Pope Leo XIII."[32] When he noted that the forms of marriage are basic to society and of critical significance to governmental institutions, Justice Waite cited Professor Francis Lieber's thesis that polygamy leads to the patriarchal principle, and that this principle might fetter those people adhering to it in stationary despotism. Francis Lieber (d. 1872), a German émigré who achieved considerable distinction as a publicist in America,[33] was deeply interested in the forms of marriage and in the connections between the state and marriage. *Reynolds v. United States* constitutes an endorsement of Lieber's views on marriage. It was an invocation of one of the serious intellectual names of the age in connection with a cause he had long defended, and it is possible that Chief Justice Waite did not detail the dangers of polygamy because he assumed that in relying on the opinion of Professor Lieber he had done all that was required. In *Political Ethics* Lieber wrote: "The family cannot exist without marriage, nor can it develop its highest importance, it would seem, without monogamy.[34] Lieber detailed his conception of monogamy and its significance in an unsigned article published in *Putnam's Monthly* in 1855. Monogamy, he said,

> is one of the primordial elements out of which all law proceeds, or which the law steps in to recognize and protect. . . . Wedlock, or monogamic marriage, . . . is one of the frames of our thoughts, and moulds of our feelings; it is a psychological condition of our jural consciousness, of our liberty, of our literature, of our aspirations, of our religious convictions, and of our domestic being and family relation, the foundation of all that is called polity.[35]

The link to Christianity is explicit in later Mormon cases. Thus, the Supreme Court said in *Mormon Church v. United States* (1889) that polygamy was "contrary to the spirit of Christianity and of the civilization which Christianity has produced in the Western World" and again, "[b]igamy and polygamy are crimes by the laws of all civilized and Christian countries . . ." It may be noted that Justice Field was not even willing to call the advocacy of polygamy "a tenet of religion."

In fact, Lieber's provision on polygamy did not come into the federal Constitution. The Mormon Church was pressured by other means into giving up polygamy, and the later history of Utah as a state reveals not a commitment to the restoration of polygamy but rather a fairly intense commitment to a traditional version of monogamy. The church excommunicates those currently practicing polygamy.[36]

Part II: The State of Utah

Utah is understood to have a special role among the American states. It is described as the "different"[37] state by historians, because of its intense and well-known religious background, and many of its characteristics are viewed as special. Thus Utah, whose population is 70 percent Mormon,[38] is seen as committed to family life, temperance, clean living, and the traditional work ethic.

It has been suggested that "one need only look, in the 1980s, at the size of the Mormon family, at the Mormons' health code, at their participation in a churchwide welfare system, and at contemporary politics in Utah to see that Latter-Day Saints continue to be a "peculiar people."[39] The list of differences continues: "Despite their educational status and relative affluence, the Mormon birth rate is now twice the national average. The LDS death rate and the low incidence of a variety of diseases appear to be linked to their now strict adherence to the "Word of Wisdom" which, among other things, proscribes tobacco and prescribes temperance." Additionally, "Regular assignments on welfare projects ranging from picking oranges to canning meats keeps the communitarian spirit alive in a sea of individualism." Finally, it has been noted that "majority opinions [in Utah] on welfare statism, right-to-work, feminism, liquor-by-the-drink, right to life, anti-Communism, the MX missile, and the equal rights amendment reflect "the still powerful influence of the Mormon Church when the leadership obliquely or directly defines a Mormon position."[40]

J. D. Williams, in discussing Mormon theories of separation of church and state, noted that: "Whenever one church claims the membership (in fact or nominally) of 72 percent of the people of a state, as the Mormon Church does in Utah, its doctrines and practices are certain to have a pervasive influence on the folkways of the state." This will be true, he said, whatever the church does. "[E]ven if it never took a stand on a political question, the Mormon church would still significantly influence the metes and bounds of the political struggle in Utah." This list includes: "Sale of liquor by the drink, taxation of church welfare properties (farms, clothing mills, etc.), pari-mutuel betting and legalized gambling are all probably among the political questions which lie 'beyond the pale' in Utah because of the folkways of its predominant Mormon population."[41] Cheryl Preston identifies the differences in terms of higher education and more traditional family patterns.[42]

In this instance, however, one can say that the family values with which the Mormon Church is associated in 1996 are for the most part the same family values articulated by the Christian nation in 1896: heterosexual monogamy, family stability, large families,[43] and traditional family structures.

Reynolds itself continues to be reaffirmed. As recently as 1985, the Tenth Circuit reaffirmed the case in *Potter v. Murray City*.[44] At another level, however, in the child custody case, *Sanderson v. Tryon* in 1987 the Utah Supreme Court noted that "polygamous practices should only be considered as one among many other factors regarding the children's best interests."[45]

In the nineteenth-century, polygamy was associated both with the Mormons and with the literary if not fictional versions of Islamic and Middle Eastern polygamy. Today, we also associate polygamy with Muslim immigrants, excommunicated Mormon fundamentalists, and, sometimes with individual figures, as when Berthold Brecht is described as a polygamist.[46] But public defenses of polygamy have begun to appear, and there have been certain indications that nineteenth-century polygamy, at least, is not to be altogether condemned. Thus, a Utah judge recently wrote, "I cannot say, as the main opinion seems to imply, that polygamy is *morally* wrong. It is neither morally nor legally wrong in Turkey and elsewhere. It is questionable whether it was morally or legally wrong in Utah Territory in the nineteenth century, and I like to think, at least, that my great-grandfather was not only a law-abiding citizen, but was not immoral according the mores of his time. Whether it is moral, or legal, depends in most part upon time, place and circumstance."[47] In 1991 the plural wife, Elizabeth Joseph, wrote an op-ed piece in the *New York Times* defending contemporary polygamy as allowing a larger variety of choices for women. This can be taken as an indication of change in the current discussion.[48] Where defenses of polygamy had previously been available through, for example, the material of Joseph Musser,[49] one can now refer to a sympathetic discussion published in the *New York Times*.

Utah's commitment to monogamy continues, however, reflected by two quite recent legal events, the first a case upholding Utah's adultery statute,[50] the second the statute passed by Utah in an attempt to block any attempt to ask Utah to recognize homosexual marriages which may (or may not) be performed in Hawaii,[51] by indicating that the strong policy of the state of Utah favors heterosexual marriage. The statute provides that marriages between persons of the same sex are "prohibited and declared void."[52]

The possibility of looking at Mormon history in terms of two snap shots, or to suggest a contrast between the Mormons then and now is not, of course, new. Indeed, it is fairly standard to make that contrast, stressing a transformation of Mormon life after the turn of the century as an aspect of the assimilation and Americanization of Mormonism.[53] But another kind of analysis may add something to an account focused either in separatism or assimilation (from the point of view of the group) or rejection leading to acceptance (from the point of view of the state).[54] Such an analysis focuses on two modes of interaction between church and state, distinguished by universalist or particularistic objectives.

Part III: Another View of Reconstitution

One problem for a modern liberal state is how to acknowledge the group presence. Religious opinions are not merely background preferences, to be seen as forming voter opinion in the same way that all other background preferences form opinion. Churches have institutional relations with other groups, political and religious, and accept that a group awareness is needed for analysis of these relations.[55] The modern state of Utah, a state within the United States, is an interesting case study.

The reconstitution of Mormonism and Utah after 1896 begins with a rejection of church control of state politics. The Utah Supreme Court recently noted that "the Mormon majority at the 1895 convention acted deliberately to distance itself from any suggestion that the new government of Utah could justifiably be viewed as theocratic."[56] Utah had "struggled for statehood for nearly fifty years,"[57] and the church had been threatened with destruction and forced to abandon polygamy. The court concluded that "the Church, following the Manifesto of 1890, had worked to convince Congress of the sincerity of its renunciation of polygamy and of its intent to forswear control of civil affairs."[58] Thus, "statehood was obtained, but at a high cost."[59]

The narrative of the change from the nineteenth century to the twentieth century has been analyzed by historians and sociologists, sometimes in terms of early sectarianism followed by later assimilation. Recently, Armand Mauss discussed the change in terms of assimilation followed by a current period of retrenchment.[60]

Much of this analysis draws on the familiar typology of Ernest Troeltsch, relating to churches and sects.

> The church is that type of organization which is overwhelmingly conservative, which to a certain extent accepts the secular order, and dominates the masses; in principle, therefore, it is universal, i.e., it desires to cover the whole life of humanity. The sects, on the other hand, are comparatively small groups; they aspire after personal inward perfection, and they aim at a direct personal fellowship between the members of each group. From the very beginning, therefore, they are forced to organize themselves in small groups, and to renounce the idea of dominating the world. Their attitude towards the world, the State, and Society may be indifferent, tolerant, or hostile, since they have no desire to control and incorporate these forms of social life; on the contrary, they tend to avoid them; their aim is usually either to tolerate their presence alongside of their own body, or even to replace these social institutions, by their own society.[61]

One distinction in Troeltsch related to attitudes toward a larger unit, the church seeking cooperation, the sect seeking separation. Mauss can thus observe that the Mormons are more churchlike in Utah and less churchlike in other parts of the country or, indeed, the world.

The scheme described here as Mode I and Mode II is quite similar to church-sect analysis in many ways, but it does not focus, as the church-sect idea often does, on transformation over time in a single institution or form of organization. Rather, it looks at the way in which that institution relates to a larger unit, even taking the religious institution itself as constant (counterfactually, of course). Mode I and Mode II are labels given to two strategies of religious institutions in dealing with the state, the first involving a cooption of the state, the second an attempt to carve out space within the state for a religious life. Size and socioeconomic status have no defining relevance, and religious institutions may use both strategies at the same time. Applying these ideas to the history of the Mormons, before and after statehood, involves a different idea of constitutionalism from the one used up to now. The first two parts of this chapter focused on the "words on parchment" definition of constitutionalism.[62] The present part uses more the idea of constitutionalism as a way of being, a framework, or a set of folkways, rather than emphasizing language or the interpretation of language.[63]

One can see Mode I and II not as necessarily involving a shift from one to the other but rather as two approaches often in combination. A Mode I picture of Mormon behavior would emphasize its attempts to persuade state or federal governments that particular values should be adopted as universal. A Mode II picture would stress ways in which the LDS Church seeks to make room for its own values within a larger system, state or federal. A Mode I relationship focuses on engagement; a Mode II relationship focuses, in the end, on disengagement, though engagement to some degree may be necessary to reach disengagement.

To illustrate: The state of Utah is a state in a federal union. Utah is dominantly but not entirely made up of one religious group, a fact that has large consequences and that distinguishes the Mormon situation from that of other contemporary American religious groups. It is natural, even inevitable, Mauss notes, that the Mormons should attempt to dominate the policies of the state.[64] This effort might be seen in terms of a Mode I, parallel to the relationship evident in the nineteenth century, long after formal disestablishment, between Christian denominations and the federal government. The *Reynolds* case contains a reflection of this national Mode I relationship in the Court's analysis of the Christian nature of marriage. *Reynolds* can also illustrate a Mode II effort (the Mormon attempt to create space for its marriage institution) and another Mode I approach—by the Mormons—seeking an acknowledgment by the state of the importance of religious liberty, which was in effect prior to the argument on religiously founded polygamy.

Modern Utah also can reveal Mode II relationships, as religions that are not part of the Mormon Church attempt to create space for themselves. Here the example might be the excommunicated Mormon fundamentalists seeking recognition for polygamy (despite its illegality) through litigation over custody or adoption. This space is created not through an exemption like the one sought in *Reynolds*, but rather by a general—Mode I —rule broad enough to validate their activities. Thus: "polygamous or non polygamous families may adopt."

In relation to the federal government, the Mormon Church continues to engage in both Mode I and Mode II strategies. Examples of Mode I are the effort to defeat the Equal Rights Amendment or the MX missile program. An example of Mode II would be a use of the special exemption for religious groups in the federal statutes against discrimination.[65] Mode I and II are, again, operating together.

The recent Supreme Court case, *Bishop v. Amos*[66] illustrates Mode I and Mode II in operation in the modern setting. In 1964 Congress passed an act forbidding employment discrimination and added a limited exemption for churches with reference to religiously connected work. In 1972, that exemption was broadened so that religious groups could discriminate, in effect, even where the work was secular by general standards. Senator Ervin explained that "the amendment would exempt religious corporations, associations, and societies from the application of this act insofar as the right to employ people of any religion they see fit is concerned. That is the only effect of this amendment."[67] This is Mode II objective—autonomy for churches—achieved by a Mode I recognition of the exemption by the state. The exemption was upheld against a challenge to a Mormon Church employer's use of the exemption to "discriminate" against an employee who could not get a "temple recommend."[68]

Whatever may have been true in the past, a church attempting to create its own world in terms of family and eduction will necessarily involve itself in the structuring of the state environment. Whether it chooses Mode I or Mode II stances, or in what sequence or combination depends on the circumstances, but it seems clear that even in Utah, even in a "sovereign state," a religious group cannot control its environment in the way that was possible in the nineteenth century. This is increasingly true also in sovereign national states.[69] The constitutionalism of federal-state relationships and the constitutionalism of church-state relationships, frameworks including the ideas of the world in constitutional documents, make that sort of isolation fundamentally impossible.

These observations are not about changes in the characteristics of institutions, for example, churches becoming sects over time. That all churches are in a way sects is a given of the American legal situation. The effort is to describe the strategies that institutions adopt in working with and within larger units. The two larger units considered here were the federated state and the federal government, both with reference to a church, the Latter-Day Saints, which is in fact strong in many states and indeed many countries.

The attempt was to see the case of the Mormon Church not as simply representing *the church* standing against *the state,* but also to see the church overlapping and penetrating the state in the form of religious ideas in the consciousness of individual voters or religious affiliations of state officials, constrained then by both their official roles and their religious consciences.

Conclusion

The chapter has drawn on a distinction suggested in earlier work in which a "Mode I" interaction between religion and government is seen as one in which a religion hopes to universalize its values acting through the state; and a "Mode II" interaction is seen as one in which a religion seeks room for its own practices, attempting to preserve its own singularity without attempting a universal application of that standard. Modes I and II were seen as working in combination. Religious groups were taken as standing apart from the state, as powerful, in theory, as the state. The present discussion serves both as a continuation of that inquiry. It focuses on the Mormons and the state of Utah in a federal system, emphasizing issues relating to family law, and treating the reconstitution of a theocracy. Central to the discussion is the problem of internal groups in the nation.

The interactive strategies described involve either using political power to achieve particular state issues as universal objectives, or using arguments based on religious status to achieve protection and recognition by the state for particularistic goals, often autonomy. This Mode II objective is achieved often by a religious liberty argument that is in effect a Mode I argument, since the church seeks to have the state recognize religious liberty as a universal value. The modern history of the Mormon Church reveals clear instances of the use of these strategies, as well as one case, the problem of polygamy itself, where the Mode I policy reflects both the official position of the church and also certain ambivalence within the Mormon culture, so that as a matter of state law polygamy is both illegal and to some limited extent acknowledged.[70]

Addressing the popularity of the Zane Grey book, *Riders of the Purple Sage* (1912), Loren Grey wrote, "Perhaps it is because the practice of polygamy which the Mormon church repudiated long ago, but which endures among rebel sects scattered over many parts of the world—still holds a somewhat morbid fascination for many people all over the Christian world."[71] Whatever the reason, Grey's story of the Mormons is still told.

In a 1996 film version of Zane Grey's story,[72] the Mormon aspect of the background is largely excised. Some will recognize the nineteenth-century Mormons from the Utah settings, the strict obedience to group discipline, and the suggestion of polygamous arrangements among the group.[73] Others may think the sect a group out of time and place, believers from another planet. The 1996 *Riders* pursues the opposite approach from the 1940 Zanuck production of *Brigham Young*, which was very positive toward the Mormons and very quiet on the polygamy question.[74] The 1996 *Riders* is hard on the religious group and hard on polygamy, but suppresses the identification with the

Latter-Day Saints. Both films raise the issue of the group and the larger society. Both approaches reveal the tensions regarding the question.

When Brigham Young announced the removal of the Latter-Day Saints to Utah, he said that "the exodus of the nation of the only true Israel from these United States to a far distant region of the west, where bigotry, intolerance and insatiable oppression lose their power over them—forms a new epoch, not only in the history of the church, but of this nation."[75] The effort here has been to consider the constitutional framework of that new epoch.

Notes

1. This essay draws on Carol Weisbrod and Pamela Sheingorn, "Reynolds v. United States: Nineteenth-Century Forms of Marriage and the Status of Women," 10 *Connecticut Law Review* 828 (1978), and uses analytic categories discussed in Carol Weisbrod, "Family, Church and State: An Essay on Constitutionalism and Religious Authority," *Journal of Family Law* 26 (1987): 741.

2. Enabling Act, ch. 138, 28 Stat. 107 (1894).

3. UTAH CONST. art. I, section 4. Enabling Act, ch. 138, 28 Stat. 107, section 3 (1894).

4. UTAH CONST. art. I, section 4. On the history of church-state separation in Utah, see *Society of Separationists v. Whitehead*, 870 P.2d 916 (Utah 1993).

The American Constitution contains both an antiestablishment and a free exercise clause. Some constitutions create religious liberty with only a free exercise clause in effect. On such an approach, see R. Kay, "The Canadian Constitution and the Dangers of Establishment," *DePaul Law Review* 42 (1992): 361.

5. We can also see the official solution adopted in the form of constitutional provisions, words on parchment which, as Walter H. Hamilton wrote long ago, we trust to bind government. See Richard S. Kay's discussion of Hamilton's line in "American Constitutionalism," Larry Alexander (ed.), *Constitutionalism: A Philosophical Foundation* (Cambridge: Cambridge University Press, 1998). Also see Hamilton's distrust of the words on parchment approach in "The Path of Due Process of Law," Conyers Read (ed.), *The Constitution Reconsidered* (Morningside Heights: Columbia University Press, 1938), pp. 167–90.

6. The revelation of polygamy to Joseph Smith is dated 1843. Smith was murdered in Carthage, Illinois, in 1844. On America as Israel, see Conrad Cherry, *God's New Israel: Religious Interpretations of American Destiny* (Englewood Cliffs, NJ: Prentice-Hall, 1971).

7. George Bernard Shaw, *The Political Madhouse in America and Nearer Home: A lecture by Bernard Shaw* (London: Constable, 1939) p. 32.

8. See Brigham Young's "Exodus Announced, October 8, 1845," in Edwin S. Gaustad (ed.), *A Documentary History of Religion in America to the Civil War* (Grand Rapids: William B. Eerdmans Publishing Company, 1982) pp. 359–60: "The exodus of the nation of the only true Israel from these United States to a far distant region of the west."

9. Dallin Oaks, Testimony on Religious Freedom Restoration Act. Hearings before the subcommittee on civil and constitutional rights of the committee on the Judiciary House of Representatives 102nd Congress, 2nd Session on H.R., 2797 (Religious Freedom Restoration Act of 1991) May 13–14, 1992, p. 23.

10. For discussions of nineteenth-century Mormonism and anti-Mormonism, see Lawrence Foster, *Religion and Sexuality: The Shakers, the Mormons, and the Oneida Community* (New York: Oxford University Press, 1981).

11. Morrill Act, Ch. 126, 12 Stat. 501 (1862). The Act provided that "every person having a husband or wife living, who shall marry any other person, whether married or single, in a territory of the United States, or other place over which the United States [has] jurisdiction . . . shall . . . be adjudged guilty of bigamy."

12. The fact that Utah was a territory was critical to the litigation, since Congress, and not the states, was bound by the first amendment. It was only much later that the first amendment was understood to bind the state through "incorporation" in the Fourteenth Amendment.

13. *Reynolds v. United States*, 98 U.S. 145 (1878), at p. 162.

14. Ibid.

15. Ibid., p. 162.

16. Ibid., p. 164.

17. Ibid., p. 166.

18. Ray Jay Davis, "Plural Marriage and Religious Freedom: The Impact of *Reynolds v. United States*," *Arizona Law Review* 15 (1973): 287, p. 291.

19. See Carol Weisbrod, "On the Breakup of Oneida," *Connecticut Law Review* 14 (1982): 4.

20. See recently Anne C. Dailey, "Federalism and Families," *University of Pennsylvania Law Review* 143 (1995): 1787.

21. On federalization of family law, see Judith Resnik, " 'Naturally' without Gender: Women, Jurisdiction, and the Federal Courts," *New York University Law Review* 66 (1991): 1682. For a judicial discussion of Latter-Day Saint doctrines of marriage and divorce without emphasis on the polygamy issue, see *Hilton v. Roylance*, 25 Utah 129 (1902).

22. That consensus has broken down still further.

23. *Miles v. United States*, 103 U.S. 304 (1880).

24. See Edwin Firmage and R. Collin Mangrum, *Zion in the Courts: A Legal History of the Church of Jesus Christ of Latter-Day Saints: 1830–1900* (Urbana: University of Illinois Press, 1988). Carmon Hardy in *Solemn Covenant: the Mormon Polygamous Passage* (Urbana: University of Illinois Press, 1992) argues that, even after the Woodruff manifesto, leaders of the Mormon Church continued to sanction polygamous marriages while publicly denying their existence.

25. This case has been viewed by several as the closest thing to a federal disestablishment of a religion that the United States has seen. See J. D. Williams, "Separation of Church and State in Mormon Theory and Practice," *Dialogue*, vol. 1, no. 2 (1966): p. 38.

26. See Leo Pfeffer, *Church, State and Freedom* (Boston: The Beacon Press, 1953, 1967) noting that the conflict was between Old Testament and New Testament forms of marriage.

27. See Richard Bushman, "Inspired Constitution" in Mark Cannon et al. (eds.), *What Is the Proper Role of the Latter-Day Saint with Respect to the Constitution? Brigham Young Studies*, 4 (1962): pp. 151–77, at p. 158.

28. In litigation over the conviction of a polygamist under the Mann Act in the 1940s, the issue of polygamy was again discussed by a Justice of the U.S. Supreme Court. Justice William O. Douglas, writing the majority opinion in *Cleveland v. United States*, 329 U.S. 14 (1946), upheld the application of the Mann Act to the interstate transportation of a plural wife. Douglas said that "[t]he establishment or maintenance of polygamous households is a notorious example of promiscuity." Ibid. p. 19.

29. *People v. Woody*, 61 Cal. 2d 716, (S.C.,1964), pp. 724–25.

30. *Reynolds*, pp. 167–68.

31. B. Trimble, *Chief Justice Waite: Defender of the Public Interest* (Princeton: Princeton University Press, 1938) p. 244 n. 18.

32. John Noonan, "The Family and the Supreme Court," *Catholic University Law Review* 23 (1973) 255. In the *Reynolds* opinion, Chief Justice Waite quoted language used by Thomas Jefferson in a letter to the Danbury Connecticut Baptists. Jefferson had referred to the "wall of separation" between church and state.

33. See recently Aviam Soifer, "Contributions: Facts, Things, and the Orphans of Girard College: Francis Lieber, Protopragmatist," *Cardozo Law Review* 16 (1995): 2305.

34. See Francis Lieber, *Manual of Political Ethics, designed chiefly for the use of colleges and students of law* (Philadelphia: J. B. Lippincott, 1876).

35. Lieber, "The Mormons: Shall Utah Be Admitted into the Union?" 5 *Putnam's Monthly* 225, 234 (1855).

36. Ken Driggs, "After the Manifesto: Modern Polygamy and Fundamentalist Mormons," *Journal of Church and State* (1990): pp. 367–89, at p. 388.

37. Frank Jonas, *Politics in the American West* (Salt Lake City: University of Utah Press, 1969.) Especially Jonas, "The Different State," pp. 327–79. The Mormon majority in Utah constitutes the major population of the state. Such a majority could, of course, also exist in a town. See description of Mormon town(s) in Alberta, Brigham Card, et al., The *Mormon Presence in Canada* (Logan: Utah State University Press, 1990), p. 275.

38. It is often said that Mormons refer to non-Mormons as Gentiles (so that in Utah, Jews are called Gentiles). But see Mauss "Mormon Semitism and Anti-Semitism," *Sociological Analysis* 29 (1968): pp. 11–27.

39. Grant Underwood, "Revisioning Mormon History," *Pacific Historical Review* (1986): p. 413.

40. Richard Poll, quoted by Underwood. *Pacific Historical Review*, (1986): p. 413. The Mormons opposed an MX missile base in Utah.

41. Williams, p. 38.

42. Cheryl B. Preston, "Joining Traditional Values and Feminist Legal Scholarship," *Journal of Legal Education* 43 (1993): p. 514.

43. Timothy Egan, "Utah's Claim to Fame: No. 1 in a Family Way," *New York Times* (April 23, 1995).

44. *Potter v. Murray City*, 760 F.2d 1065 (10th Cir. 1985). See also *Barlow v. Blackburn*, 798 P.2d 1360 (Ariz. C.A. 1990).

45. *Sanderson v. Tryon*, 739 P.2d 623 (Utah S.C. 1987). See also *Matter of Adoption of Waiting*, 157 Utah Adv. Rep. 26, 808 P.2d 1083 (Utah S.C. 1991).

46. Esselin, *Berthold Brecht: A Choice of Evils,* 4th ed. (London: Methuen Ltd. 1985, 1993) xii.

47. Judge Henriod, in *In re State in Interest of Black*, 3 Utah 2d 315, 283 P.2d 887 (Utah 1955).

48. Elizabeth Joseph, "My Husband's Nine Wives," the *New York Times* (May 23, 1991).

49. J. Musser, *Celestial Marriage* (1940–1970). Musser had five wives and twenty children. See Driggs, "After the Manifesto: Modern Polygamy and Fundamentalist Mormons," *Journal of Church and State*, 32 (1990): p. 382. See Martha Sonntag Bradley, "Joseph W. Musser: Dissenter or Fearless Crusader for Truth," in Roser Launius and Linda Thatcher *Differing Visions: Dissenters in Mormon History* (Urbana: University of Illinois Press, 1994).

50. *Oliverson v. West Valley City*, 875 F. Supp. 1465 (D. Utah 1995). The adultery statute litigation, a statement of a commitment to traditional monogamous forms, is perhaps somewhat complicated by the fact that Mormon doctrine assumes the potential for plural marriages in the next world.

51. *Ninia Baehr v. John C. Lewin*, 74 Haw. 530, 852 P.2d 44 (Haw. S.C. 1993).

52. UTAH CODE ANN. section 30-1-2(5) (1893).

53. Generally, A. Mauss, *The Angel and the Beehive: The Mormon Struggle with Assimilation* (Urbana: University of Illinois Press, 1994).

54. As Leo Pfeffer once noted, "marginal religion" is not a legal category in the United States. Irving Zaretsky (ed.), "The Legitimation of Marginal Religions in the United States," *Religious Movements in Contemporary America* (Princeton, New Jersey: Princeton University Press, 1974), p. 9.

55. See generally Aviam Soifer, *Law and the Company We Keep* (Cambridge, MA: Harvard University Press, 1995).

56. *Society of Separatists v. Whitehead*, 870 P.2d 916 (Utah S.C. 1993), pp. 935–936 (upholding opening prayer in council meetings).

57. Ibid., p. 936.

58. Ibid.

59. Ibid.

60. Mauss, p. 85. Mauss identified five areas in which the modern Mormon church is concentrating on sectlike behavior, as an aspect of retrenchment. The church is particularly interested in: continuing revelation, missions, temples and genealogical research, family renewal, and religious education.

61. Ernst Troeltsch, *The Social Teaching of the Christian Churches* (New York: The MacMillan Company, 1931).

62. See discussion in Brent Corcoran, (ed.), *Multiply and Replenish: Mormon Essays in Sex and Family* (Salt Lake City: Signature Books, 1994).

63. See Weisbrod, "Family Church State" on Llewellyn, and Hamilton on folkways and constitutionalism.

64. Mauss therefore turns his attention to the relations between the Mormons and the federal government (p. 109).

65. Through the Religious Freedom Restoration Act 42 U.S.C. Chapter 21B.

66. *Corporation of Presiding Bishop v. Amos et al.*, 483 U.S. 327 (1987).

67. See 118 *Congressional Record* 4503 (1972). Senator Ervin continued, "In other words, this amendment is to take the political hands of Caesar off of the institutions of God, where they have no place to be."

68. On temple recommend, see LDS brief in *Bishop v. Amos*, p. 4.

69. See Mark Janis, Richard Kay, and Anthony Bradley, *European Human Rights Law* (Oxford: Oxford University Press, 1995).

70. On the complexity of legal messages, see Carol Weisbrod, "On the Expressive Functions of Family Law," *University of California at Davis Law Review*, 22 (1989): p. 991.

71. Loren Grey, Foreword by Zane Grey, *Riders of the Purple Sage* (Lincoln: University of Nebraska Press, 1994). He suggests that "this may be the result of their frustration over the puritanical dogma which pervades most Christian religions even today, and which still stifles so powerfully in many what we view as freedom of personal choice and sexual expression" (p. viii).

72. The plot concerns Jim Lassiter's attempt to find the Mormon abductors of his sister, Millie Erne.

73. One commentator referred to the group in the new film as the "not-Mormons." (Jim Molpus, "Press the Remote: Rider Remake Ruined by Mishmash Morality"), *The Nashville Banner*, January 19, 1996, p. c2.

74. See James D. Arc, "Darryl F. Zanuck's Brigham Young: A Film in Context," *B.Y.U. Studies*, 29(1), pp. 5–33.

75. Gaustad, *A Documentary History of Religion in America to the Civil War*, pp. 159–60.

Chapter 10

Anti-Semitism and the Growth of Rights Consciousness in Western Europe and North America

Phyllis M. Senese

Anti-Semitism thrived in western Europe and North America from the seventeenth to the twentieth century despite changing patterns in the relationships between the state, the law, and a consciousness of rights. While the conception of rights for Jews underwent considerable alteration over those centuries, it is essential to appreciate that change in a much longer historical context. The notion of rights of conscience for Jews derived only from an extension of such rights first to Protestant dissenters. Any transformation of state policy and of law with respect to Jews was, in fact, conditional. As a historically despised, defamed, and demonized minority, Jews (and all the rejected "others" of the West) had been expected for centuries to compromise, accommodate, and assimilate into the majority Christian community—ideally through persuasion, but by force if necessary—with no notion that they, *as Jews*, could conceivably lay claim to rights of any kind. Movement away from those age-old assumptions did occur but only after traditional concepts of the state and law in relation to religious privilege disintegrated in the wake of new and pragmatic thinking about individual rights and religious pluralism.

The initial stages of transforming the Jew into a reviled "other" began in the early second century C.E. with the creation and cultivation of a language of hatred directed against Jews by powerful segments of the emerging Christian community. Disparagement of Jews rested initially in large measure on notions of supercession and an imperative to convert Jews to Christianity. By insisting that Christianity had superceded Judaism, Christian theologians and commentators were convinced that any relationship between God and the once "chosen people" had ended—forever. The intensity of the supercessionist view grew out of a conviction that God had abandoned the Jews *because they deserved to be abandoned* and a certainty that Christianity alone was the one, true path to God. The continuing vitality of Judaism, even after the destruction of Jerusalem and the Temple by the Romans in 70 C.E., was regarded as an affront to Christian claims of supercession and cultivated a fear that the very existence of Jews and Judaism was a rebuke to Christian claims of an exclusive relationship with God. The survival and flourishing of Judaism and Jews over the centuries came to be regarded by many Christian commentators as a threat, a potential alternative, to Christianity. Conversion of the Jews, then, by any means, came to be understood as necessary proof of the validity of Christianity, a religious duty of great import, and was couched in an extravagant language of hatred. The words and ideas contained in this language of hatred were fundamentally anti-Semitic, setting the stage for centuries of persecutions and pogroms, paving the way to Auschwitz.[1]

With the union of the Christian Church and the Roman Empire in the fourth century, this anti-Semitic language and its imperative to reject, limit, and contain the Jews acquired the full force of the state to impose Christian conclusions about the Jews on the society, culture, and the laws of the Empire. This alliance of church and state transformed the demand to convert Jews from a specifically religious injunction to a justification based on the security and economic, social, and political stability of the state. By the eleventh and twelfth centuries, physical attacks on Jews had become part of an established pattern of persecution in Europe, "persecution became habitual":

> Deliberate and socially sanctioned violence began to be directed through established *governmental, judicial and social institutions*, against groups of people defined by general characteristics such as race, religion or way of life; and that membership of such groups in itself came to be regarded as justifying those attacks.[2]

For Jews, then, conversion represented little more than a continuation of anti-Semitism, intimidation, coercion, and persecution; for them conversion signified compulsion and not the free choice of a free will.

Over the centuries, Christendom and Europe came to be perceived as identical, ensuring that the state and the law were readily available to devise and enforce legal restrictions on Jews, restrictions flowing from Christian anti-Semitic assumptions about Jews. Real Jews vanished from public consciousness to be replaced by a mythological "figment of the [Christian] imagination."[3] Over time, in place after place in western Europe, in a kaleidoscope of circumstances, Jews found themselves subject to laws that limited their occupations, their ability to acquire land and real property, their places of worship, their public and private behavior, their relations with non-Jews, and legal precedents were established requiring Jews to submit to forced conversions, to live in ghettos, and to wear distinctive clothing or badges. Significantly, and with rare exceptions, the power of states and laws were *not* deployed to prevent or contain the ever-growing list of persecutions of Jews or of the crimes anti-Semites fabricated and ascribed to the Jews—deicide, the poisoning of wells during plague outbreaks, the massacre of Christian children for ritual purposes (the blood libel), and an eternal, international Jewish conspiracy to destroy Christendom. By the early modern period, western Europe had been "cleansed" of its Jewish population, with laws in place to punish any who dared to return. Significantly, the expulsion of the Jews from western Europe did little to dampen anti-Semitism—it flourished in the West in their absence. Biblical Israelites might command respect but real Jews were the children of Satan.[4] These accusations, embellished over time, remain the hallmark of anti-Semitism today, while the concept of laws to curtail hate are still in their infancy.

Christendom shattered in the immediate wake of the Reformation, splintering popular and legal assumptions about the relationship between church and state, between citizen and religion, between adherents of different faith traditions. After three centuries, the Reformation and the Enlightenment[5] would transform the legal and intellectual landscape of Europe in ways that few could possibly have imagined in 1520. At the outset, the disputes about religious faith and conscience unleashed across western Christendom had nothing to do with Jews. Quarrels between and among Christians were of concern to Jews only to the extent that the rising levels of emotion and violence that beset Christians might put Jewish communities in direct danger. Martin Luther's condemnation of Jews in 1543, after they had failed to meet his expectation that they would flock to Protestant Christianity, demonstrated to Jews that the upheavals in Christendom would not bring to an end their persecution by Christians. Predictably, as Jews did not meet Protestant expectations of quick conversion to new forms of Christianity, traditional anti-Semitic rhetoric and hatred of Jews continued unabated in many places in western Europe.

When the Reformation destroyed the illusion of a single cohesive Christendom, it became necessary to reformulate definitions of the unity of the state and the community. Over the centuries European states had emerged with ideas about authority, law, social order, and economic development that were tied explicitly to Christian principles. Patterns of persecution over the centuries of Jews (and all "others") rested on an assumption of an essential link between religious uniformity and social stability. But when Christianity ceased to be unified, the immediate anxieties were fundamental. Does authority to govern still come from God? If so, how ought Christian authority be justified and implemented in a context of growing Christian diversity exemplified too often by religious animosity, rivalry, and hostility even to the point of war? Could a Christian state and all its institutions survive and flourish in a condition of religious pluralism? If Luther were correct in insisting that the only authority to define true belief was individual conscience formed by individual reading and interpretation of scripture, what role continued to exist for the state? Or later when, repelled by the upheavals and revolts flowing from claims of individual conscience and a freedom to act on it, Luther called for a submission to state authority, was religion to be no longer a matter of conscience? Alternatively, was the solution offered by the Holy Roman Empire—*cuius regio eius religio*—a model for all Europe scrambling to maintain unity *in spite of* diversity? Or was Calvin's vision of localized, lay control of all society by "the elect of God" a viable alternative?

The Enlightenment impulses toward individual liberty, progress, democracy, and toleration completed the reorienting of western Europe. A general belief in progress, reason, science, and secular values (at least among intellectuals) led to calls for an equality of rights for all and an abolition of the privileges of the few. Glowing tributes to individual liberty and democratic government swept western Europe, as did a sense of the universalism of humanity under a natural law of right and reason that made it permissible (at least for some), to reinvent Jews in western Europe as a part of that universal humanity. New political structures began to emerge that were characterized by particular class interests, secular bureaucracies, and a highly centralized structure for decision making and control, in which *raison d'état* would come to carry a higher priority than religious tradition. The essential political question soon became one of establishing how to preserve civil peace in a state acknowledging that religious divisions among citizens had reached a new critical level. In the long run, this meant that in country after country there would come a time when citizenship would be divorced from religious affiliation even when Christian tradition, values, and assumptions were still deeply embedded in the fabric of state order and organization. The law would gain greater significance as the arbiter between the individual and the state. By the nineteenth century, Jews in many parts of western Europe found themselves emancipated politically, freed from occupational restrictions, living outside ghettoes, respected as intellectuals—and witnesses to the disintegration of their own communities into discordant fragments.

How this all came to pass assumes some comprehensible shape if the examples of England and France are considered. How these two countries approached the dilemmas created by the Reformation and then the Enlightenment offers an instructive perspective on anti-Semitism in the nineteenth and twentieth centuries. Old formulas about the nature of society and its relationship to God were modified into a secular, liberal individualism. The very concept of the individual, of the state of law, of religious conscience, and toleration were transformed. Individualism and freedom of religious conscience created conditions favorable to Jewish emancipation by the nineteenth century. However, the price Jews were expected to pay for this new status was extremely high: cultural extinction. While the experiences of Jews on the way to emancipation in Britain and France were quite different the result was the same: by comparison to previous centuries of direct persecution emancipation unleashed a more subtle but equally malign brand of anti-Semitism.

In the case of England, seventeenth-century political pragmatism helped create a new spirit of toleration and a willingness to reopen the country to Jewish settlement. If domestic peace were to be preserved after the religious and political upheavals of the sixteenth and early seventeenth century, a practical policy of toleration was essential. In the long run, acceptance of religious pluralism as a fact of political life opened a growing gap between public institutions and individual conscience.[6] Initially the tensions inherent in this dichotomy were largely ignored in favor of the illusion of public peace. The result, as exemplified by the Toleration Act of 1689, was to concede that religious diversity had become the norm in English society and at the same time limit toleration in a state organized on the principles of an established Church and specific Christian assumptions and values. In a context of religious pluralism, allegiance to the law and the state it represented suggests that it would be possible only if the state were nondenominational. In seventeenth century England, the power of the state and the law were judiciously manipulated to sustain an illusion of nondenominationalism as a facade for a well-established Church of England. At the same time, fundamental notions of citizenship and rights began to change as Dissenters demanded and won some legal recognition through the Toleration Act. The Act did not remove disabilities from Jews, Catholics, "ungodly" Christians, and other minorities. It did permit members of these excluded minorities to live freely in England, to acquire real property, to conduct their business affairs, and to maintain a worshiping community.[7] This initial limited approach was extended through the eighteenth and nineteenth centuries by legislative and judicial increments. Accommodation to this gradualism made it possible for religious minorities in England to be absorbed into British society. Eventually, a privilege for some Christians was extended as a natural right to all for an equality of conscience. This meant for Jews that the way cleared gradually for their full recognition by the state and the law as citizens equal to all others, with commensurate rights and protections. In fact, this transformation of law and attitude as far as Jews were concerned was so gradual and erratic that it was not until the late nineteenth century in Britain that Jews could be said to have achieved full legal equality.[8] Gradual pragmatism was a strategy to postpone the extension of rights to all, especially to Jews; it was a device for preserving the status quo of power and authority as long as possible while *appearing* to generate change. But securing removal of all legal disabilities and achieving various legal rights protecting religious belief, security of person and property, occupation, residency, citizenship, and education were in themselves no guarantee that anti-Semitism would disappear. As rights for Jews expanded, the intensity and spread of anti-Semitism increased significantly in late-nineteenth-century western Europe, including Britain and, by then, in North America too.

What the British case demonstrates is that a pragmatic approach to the question of religious diversity made it possible to create and perpetuate socially useful policies and practices that promised unity *out of* diversity if only in appearance. It all rested on a calculation that a little timely tinkering—for example, in the wording of oaths—would make it possible in practice to incorporate all citizens under one flag, one language, one monarch, even one God, no matter what the citizens might really believe. The presumption of unity *in* diversity was explicitly exported to Britain's North American colonies from the seventeenth century onward. In the American colonies, the pace of the emancipation of, and extension of a variety of rights to, Jews and other minorities occurred at a more rapid rate and with less public disruption than in Britain itself. Where Jews were part of early settlement patterns in colonial America, evidence of anti-Semitism remained relatively slight. Conversely, overt anti-Semitism was more readily apparent when Jews were among the latecomers to a specific place. In the long run, however, in colonial America, and later in the United States of America, old anti-Semitic stereotypes of Jews, and the language of hatred that shaped them, were transplanted across the Atlantic as part of the cultural baggage of British and European immigrants.[9]

By contrast, in France, reaction to the effects of the Reformation produced different conclusions. Religious conflict in the sixteenth century convinced those in power that religious diversity doomed the Christian order on which French government, law, and society rested. Unity under the crown was possible only in circumstances of religious homogeneity. For this reason, the religious compromises and pragmatism of the Edict of Nantes (1598) were revoked in 1689, through at great economic cost. That France itself might be forever stigmatized as inherently parochial, superstitious, backward, and unprogressive was considered irrelevant. What mattered most was complete religious uniformity to ensure domestic peace, social stability, and the centralizing thrust of Louis XIV's notions of royal rule. In the English case, the religious diversity of the early seventeenth century demanded toleration to preserve domestic peace. Under Louis XIV, Catholic homogeneity itself ensured internal peace in France thus removing the apparent need for any policy of religious toleration. While the revolutionary transformation of the balance of power between monarch and Parliament in England, which began in the seventeenth century, forced the issue of toleration and pragmatic politics, France would not begin to move in a comparable direction until its Revolution of 1789. In the English case the politics of diversity compelled the gradual extension of civil rights and freedom of religious conscience to Jews; in France official religious conformity slammed the door to emancipation firmly shut until the ancien régime was swept away.

French insistence on religious conformity was exported by law to the French colonies overseas. For example, as early as 1627, only Catholics were permitted to settle legally in New France; a regulation that remained unchanged until the end of French rule. No extension of settlement rights or of religious observance were ever granted to non-Catholics in New France. Those few Protestant or Jewish individuals who turned up in the colony occasionally and temporarily while on trade missions were usually ignored by officialdom as long as they remained discrete and unobtrusive. Although much of the trade between France and this colony in the eighteenth century was conducted by Jewish commercial companies and financial interests, prohibitions against their settlement in the colony were never relaxed.[10] This helped create in the colony a uniquely French North American society, called *Canadien,* accustomed to uniformity as a key element of its identity. Through their history as a French colony, the *Canadiens,* no less than colonial Americans, brought to North America a heritage that preserved a legacy of anti-Semitism. Only when Britain acquired New France in 1763, renaming it Québec, was access to the territory opened to Protestants and Jews and generally only those with no connections to France. In British North America, a pattern of accelerated Jewish emancipation ensued that was similar in speed to colonial America and for many of the same reasons.[11]

Traditional anti-Semitism that had crossed the Atlantic with English and French settlers was continuously reinforced from the eighteenth to the twentieth century by the continuity and expansion of anti-Semitic stereotypes and slurs against Jews in Europe, their constant transmission to North America and their adoption by Christian populations long conditioned to accept anti-Semitic rhetoric.[12] Just because a spirit of pragmatic toleration was coming into vogue did not curtail or eliminate anti-Semitic language, attitudes, habits, or actions. The 1711 posthumous publication of Johann Eisenmenger's diatribe *Das entdeckte Judenthum (Jewry Exposed)* offered the Enlightenment age a secularized compendium of "old Christian ideas about Jews and Judaism which were shared by the learned and unlearned."[13] *Philosophe* anticlericalism attacked Judaism and Jews as substitutes for Christianity and Christians. There would be little to distinguish Eisenmenger's and the *philosophes'* contributions to regenerating anti-Semitism from Edouard

Drumont's *La France juive* or the early-twentieth-century Russian concoction *The Protocols of the Elders of Zion*. The French Revolution too would contribute a new anti-Semitic stereotype: the Jew as subversive and revolutionary. Nineteenth-century anti-Semites would embellish old myths of Jewish affinity for wealth and the blood libel. Antisemitism proved adept at surviving and transforming its appearance but not its essence through the nineteenth century. Twentieth-century Europe and North America would inherit a cornucopia of anti-Semitism that was constantly refilled.

For France, the Revolution in 1789 finally produced a long-awaited opening for Jewish emancipation. The achievement of citizenship and civil rights was implemented in the early nineteenth century wherever Napoleonic France made its influence felt before 1815; the clock was often turned back after Napoleon's exile to St. Helena. In reality, full emancipation for Jews would not be achieved in France until 1831 and later in many other parts of western Europe. Jewish emancipation in France and the countries it directly influenced was riddled with essential ambiguities and an underlying dynamic of great menace to Jews. The contradictions may best be illustrated by the conclusion of le comte Stanislas Clermont-Tonnerre in 1789:

> il faut refuser tout aux Juifs comme nation et accorder tout aux Juifs comme *individus* . . . il faut qu'ils fassent dans l'État ni un corps politique, ni un Ordre; il faut qu'ils soient *individuellement* citoyens.[14]

Jews could make an important contribution to modern society but not through traditional Judaism: "Jews had to be made better before they could be acceptable."[15] Being "made better" in the eyes of many thinkers and politicians demanded of Jews numerous specific transformations that were intended to undermine and eventually destroy a Jewish identity. Jewish theology and all religious texts were to be jettisoned to retain only Jewish ethical precepts stripped of all religious content and context. The theological and intellectual integrity of Judaism had already been badly shaken by such Jewish rationalists as Baruch Spinoza and Moses Mendelssohn, leaving many younger eighteenth-century Jews religiously adrift. Young Jews in many parts of western Europe avidly embraced Enlightenment ideals, while many Enlightenment philosophers espoused "Jewish emancipation [as] the 'radical chic' of [the] day."[16] The consequences of the Enlightenment for traditional Judaism was its eventual shattering by those Jews who left it for the Jewish Reform movement (consciously imitative of many features of German Protestantism), for some denomination of Christianity or for a complete rejection of religion in favor of assimilation and secularism. To begin to be acceptable to modern ideals, Jews were to abandon traditional religious practices, rituals and way of life to facilitate their integration into, and disappearance in, the larger society.

Individualism was to be embraced both in theory and practice by Jews as part of being "made better." According to Enlightenment emancipators, for example, Jews needed to be named in the same way as everyone else: a given (Christian) name and surname or family name, not the traditional form of the daughter or son of a parent. Traditional Jewish names might suffice in a tight, closed community but not in a diverse, modern, bureaucratic society. Such a change would mean that where once Jewish community leaders negotiated with civil authorities on behalf of the whole community, individualized names would leave individual Jews isolated to respond to bureaucratic demands for civic registration, taxation, and even military conscription where it existed in western Europe. Napoleon's "Frenchman of the Judaic persuasion" would be like every other individual in France. While in theory the Enlightenment preached toleration and freedom of conscience, many important thinkers of the period did not in fact extend that toleration to religious communities (be they Jewish, Christian, or Muslim) or to individuals wanting to remain strongly tied to religious communities. Individualism constituted a direct attack on Jewish identity.

Ironically, while individualism had become the touchstone of western society by 1800, a new collectivist perspective was emerging in response to the French Revolution—nationalism. The individual was to be resubmerged into a larger identity; not Christianity, not Catholicism nor Protestantism but the elusive, idealized nation. Nationalists argued in favor of a "national" identity based on a presumed commonality of descent, language, culture, territory, and a "national" rereading of history. Jews had no place in "national" history except as an "other." Increasingly in the nineteenth century, nationalism in various western countries singled out Jews as the "enemy" to be crushed at all costs. The Dreyfus *affaire,* which drew attention around the world to anti-Semitism, amply demonstrated the consequences for Jews of the rising tide of nationalism.[17] Beginning in the early nineteenth century, and well into the twentieth, nationalism showed that a separation between religious identity and civic emancipation was an illusion. Those, like Jews, who did not fit a vision of *national* identity, might be tolerated but never accepted as integral members of society; Jews in many places would once more find themselves vulnerable to demands for their expulsion. Nationalism returned political debate to the problem of reconciling unity *and* diversity while rejecting any idea of unity *in* diversity. Multiculturalism in a single state was a dream for the future. The uproar in many countries at the end of the twentieth century over the possibility of peaceful multiculturalism illustrates just how far that dream still is from reality.[18]

By the end of the eighteenth century, it was becoming increasingly clear to Jews that their civic emancipation entailed the destruction of their corporate identity. Judaism had survived the centuries of persecution by evolving tightly cohesive, contained communities. All life was organized communally, not merely as a defensive posture, but in fulfillment of religious commandments that required the faith to be lived and observed in private and in the public life of the community. Traditionally, in good times and bad, Jewish communities had been permitted a high degree of autonomy in internal matters of religious orthodoxy, communal facilities, adjudication of disputes, and in establishing rules of daily conduct. The inseparability of public and private connections to religious tradition was the foundation of Jewish life in the Diaspora; an inseparability that had begun to disappear in Christianity in the wake of the Reformation and Enlightenment. Accepting emancipation on the terms of the French Revolution paved the way for attacks on Jewish communal existence as the antithesis of modern, secular individualism. So much disintegration of Jewish communities had already occurred by the late eighteenth century that, for many Jews, the temptation to claim individual emancipation as "an entrance ticket to European society" was irresistible. To remain a traditional Jew was possible only at great spiritual and economic cost and great personal risk in the face of rising anti-Semitism in the nineteenth century. One response by Jews to the growing spiritual crisis in their communities was the reinvigoration of Jewish messianism. From the late-seventeenth-century stories of the Messiah's coming swept through Jewish communities everywhere. For many the long-awaited Messiah would herald Jewish liberation and restoration to Eretz Israel.[19]

Significantly, Jewish messianism dovetailed neatly with a Christian messianism that had swept England in the seventeenth century and had grown to have an important influence in western Europe by the end of the eighteenth.[20] On the surface of it, Christian messianic assumptions and policies might appear to support Jewish emancipation and advance religious toleration. The price to be extracted from Jews *as Jews* for this brand of toleration was identical to all others: elimination.

In the English case, toleration was limited from the seventeenth to the twentieth century through the capture of the political, economic, and religious elites by a new strain of messianism. Throughout Christian history, a millenarian strain had surfaced periodically heralding the second coming of Jesus and the end days. Such a period was reintroduced into England by the Reformation. By the mid-1650s, English millenarian hopes were tied inextricably to the return of the Jews first to England and then to Palestine. The presence of Jews in England itself was to be welcomed and toleration was to be accorded them but *only* as a prelude to conversion. This English messianism insisted that it was England's providential role to gather and protect the Jews of the world to prepare the way for their conversion to Christianity, which would set in motion the prophecies about the return of Jesus to bring human history to a glorious end. England's reward for fulfilling this sacred duty would be economic preeminence and imperial triumph.[21] How were Jews to reach their homeland in Palestine? How would they survive once they got there? A typical answer came from rector Richard Beere of Lincolnshire in 1790:

> This island shall be among the first of the nation to convey you to your country . . . it is by England that Jacob must arise. For this much appears to have been pre-ordained . . . what a glory it must be to England to stay foremost among the nations on this great occasion . . . For whenever our Hebrew brethren shall come to be collected together . . . and again settled in their own land . . . [they] will stand in need of manufactured articles . . . especially woollens and linens . . . [they will] become a great people and will remain grateful to England for befriending them . . . [and will] do well to make her in particular their friend.[22]

Where once conversion was an instrument of state coercion and terror, by the late eighteenth century it became a tool of international policy and diplomatic maneuvering. At the beginning of the nineteenth century, many European and North American Christians became bewitched by the fervor surrounding millenarian prophecies about the imminence of "the last days." This anticipation created scores of societies dedicated to the conversion of Jews and influenced many politicians to devote themselves to helping Jews congregate as Jews in Eretz Israel. Once returned to their ancestral homeland, Jews were to be converted (peacefully and obviously with divine assistance) as the final preparation for the return of the Messiah. These people were Christian Zionists before Zionism influenced the Middle Eastern policies of many European governments. For example, missionizing flitted through British policy decisions about Palestine beginning in the 1840s, laying the foundation for heightened rivalry between Jews and Arabs that to this day contributes to continuing conflicts in the region. British policy makers assumed that if Jews everywhere were helped by Britain to return to Palestine, Jewish gratitude would translate into unconditional support of British interests and demands in the Middle East. From the British perspective, by the 1840s, conversion itself was of little importance; what mattered was to make sure that the French or Germans did not accomplish this first, thus reaping obvious international advantages for themselves at the expense of Britain. This British strategy was enthusiastically supported by many Christians in Canada and the United States. However, until after the Holocaust, no thought was ever given by many Christians to understanding that missionizing and conversion efforts were a subtle but essentially destructive form of anti-Semitism. While this form of anti-Semitism has largely died out, at least officially, in the mainstream Christian churches it lingers today in many fundamentalist Protestant circles.

Liberals, particularly in western Europe and North America, tended to assume that after 1800 the extension of legal rights to Jews would end anti-Semitism. In fact, the reverse occurred. As Jews gained rights and entrée into the full life of nineteenth-century society, they rapidly became prominent in the arts, sciences, politics, finance, and commerce. The more they succeeded, the more they all came under savage attack in the press, in political debates, in Christian religious circles, and especially by the new biological determinists spawned by social Darwinism. It quickly became a habit of political, social, and religious leaders in western Europe and North America to dismiss evidence of anti-Semitism as merely outdated relics or as examples of Jewish hysteria, thereby proving to themselves that stereotypes about Jews were correct. Not only did states turn a blind eye to anti-Semitism, in some instances, states actively perpetuated it. Portugal and Spain, for example, delayed any move toward emancipation until the twentieth century; Portugal in 1910 and in the case of Spain, not until after the death of Franco. In the late nineteenth century, the Canadian government unashamedly included anti-Semitic rhetoric in posters designed to recruit immigrants to populate the prairies. Until well after World War II, many governments in the west were willing to tolerate varying levels of anti-Semitism, to ignore or permit informal discriminatory practices that were becoming entrenched, and to bar the door to Jews fleeing Nazi Germany. In Canada and the United States, for instance, university admission quotas, establishing self-regulating professions that could and did exclude Jews from careers and advancement, and restrictive covenants in real estate, were all commonplace until relatively recently.

What this suggests is that anti-Semitism has had, and continues to have, a firm grip on many segments of the state, the law, and society in the western world. The novel eighteenth-century notion that all were created equal (at least those who were males and substantial property owners) has never rid itself of the contagion of anti-Semitism. For this reason, the entire western world is implicated in the destruction of European Jewry in the 1930s and 1940s. The sin of omission is as grave as the sin of commission. It has only been since the late 1940s that Christian scholars and theologians have turned to reexamine their own religious origins with a critical eye, excavating in the process the Christian roots of anti-Semitism, Christian culpability for its longevity, and Christian complicity in the Holocaust. They are only now inching slowly toward a long overdue *mea culpa.*

Notes

1. See Rosemary Radford Ruether, *Faith and Fratricide: The Theological Roots of Anti-Semitism* (New York: The Seabury Press, 1974); William Nicholls,

Christian Antisemitism: A History of Hate (London & Northvale, NJ: Jason Aronson, 1993).

2. R. I. Moore, *The Formation of a Persecuting Society: Power and Deviance in Western Europe, 950–1250* (Oxford: Blackwell, 1990), p. 5 emphasis in original; Jeffrey Richards, *Sex, Dissidence and Damnation: Minority Groups in the Middle Ages* (London and New York: Routledge, 1994), ch. 5.

3. Joshua Trachtenberg cited in David A. Katz, *Philo-Semitism and the Readmission of the Jews to England, 1603–1665* (Oxford: Clarendon Press, 1982), p. 4.

4. Moore, *Formation of a Persecuting Society*, pp. 27–45; Bernard Glassman, *Anti-Semitic Stereotypes without Jews: Images of Jews in England, 1290–1700* (Detroit: Wayne State University, 1975); Katz, *Philo-Semitism*, pp. 3–6; see also Elaine Pagels, *The Origin of Satan* (New York: Random House, 1995).

5. See the chapters in this book by Justin Champion and Martin Fitzpatrick.

6. For example, Jay Newman, *Foundations of Religious Tolerance* (Toronto: University of Toronto Press, 1982), ch. 7.

7. For example, Richard Burgess Barlow, *Citizenship and Conscience: A Study in the Theory and Practice of Religious Toleration in England during the Eighteenth Century* (Philadelphia: University of Pennsylvania Press, 1962), ch. 1.

8. H. S. Q. Henriques, *The Jews and the English Law* (1908; reprinted Clifton, NJ, Augustus M. Kelley Publishers, 1974), ch. 10.

9. See David A. Gerber, "Anti-Semitism and Jewish-Gentile Relations in American Historiography and the American Past," David A. Gerber (ed.), *Anti-Semitism in American History* (Urbana and Chicago: University of Illinois Press, 1986), pp. 3–56; Sheldon J. Godfrey and Judith C. Godfrey, *Search Out the Land: The Jews and the Growth of Equality in Colonial British America, 1740–1867* (Montreal and Kingston: McGill-Queen's University Press, 1995), chs. 3 and 4.

10. Jacques Langlais and David Rome, *Juifs et Québécois français 200 ans d'histoire commune* (Montreal: Fides, 1986), pp. 3–7; Denis Vaugeois, *Les Juifs et la Nouvelle France* (Trois Rivières: Boréal Express, 1968); Richard Menkis, "Antisemitism in Pre-Confederation Canada," Alan Davies, (ed.) *Antisemitism in Canada: History and Interpretation* (Waterloo: Wilfrid Laurier University Press, 1992), pp. 11–38.

11. Godfrey and Godfrey, *Search Out the Land*, chs. 6–16.

12. For example, in Davies, *Antisemitism in Canada*, see Michael Brown, "From Stereotype to Scapegoat: Anti-Jewish Sentiment in French Canada from Confederation to World War I," pp. 39–66; Gerald Tulchinsky, "Goldwin Smith Victorian Canadian Antisemite," pp. 67–92; Stephen Speisman, "Antisemitism in Ontario: The Twentieth Century," pp. 113–35; Pierre Anctil, "Interlude of Hostility: Judeo-Christian Relations in Quebec in the Interwar Period," pp. 135–66; Howard Palmer, "Politics, Religion and Antisemitism in Alberta, 1880–1950," pp. 167–96; and in Gerber, *Anti-*

Semitism in American History, see Jonathan D. Sarna, "The 'Mythical Jew' and the 'Jew Next Door' in Nineteenth-Century America," pp. 57–78; Ellen Schiff, "Shylock's *Mishpocheh:* Anti-Semitism on the American Stage," pp. 79–99; Robert Singerman, "The Jew as Racial Alien: The Genetic Component of American Anti-Semitism," pp. 103–28; David A. Gerber, "Cutting Out Shylock: Elite Anti-Semitism and the Quest for Moral Order in the Mid-Nineteenth-Century American Marketplace," pp. 201–32; Elinor Lerner, "American Feminism and the Jewish Question, 1890–1940," pp. 305–28.

13. John Edwards, *The Jews in Christian Europe, 1400–1700* (London and New York: Routledge, 1991), p. 169.

14. Patrick Girard, *Les Juifs de France de 1789 à 1869: de l'émancipation à l'égalité* (Paris: Calmann-Lévy, 1976), p. 51, emphasis added; pp. 21–94.

15. Nicholls, *Christian Antisemitism*, p. 290.

16. David Goldberg and John D. Rayner, *The Jewish People: Their History and Their Religion* (Harmondsworth: Penguin, 1989), p. 132.

17. For example, Phyllis M. Senese, "Antisemitic Dreyfusards: The Confused Western-Canadian Press," Davies, *Antisemitism in Canada*, pp. 93–112.

18. For example, Amy Gutman, ed., *Multiculturalism: Examining the Politics of Recognition* (Princeton: Princeton University Press, 1994).

19. For example, Paul Johnson, *A History of the Jews* (New York: Harper & Row, 1987), pp. 260–73; Martin Gilbert, *The Dent Atlas of Jewish History* (London: JM Dent, 1993), pp. 53–54.

20. For example, Mayir Vereté, "The Restoration of the Jews in English Protestant Thought, 1790–1840," *Middle Eastern Studies*, January 1972, pp. 3–50.

21. Ibid., Katz, *Philo-Semitism*, chs. 1–5.

22. Vereté, "Restoration," p. 38.

Chapter 11

The Struggle to Preserve Aboriginal Spiritual Teachings and Practices

*James [Sákéj] Youngblood Henderson**

Eurocentric religious and political leaders have by their law and policies sought to extinguish Aboriginal teachings and practices. Operating with a strong belief in European cultural superiority,[1] these leaders and the churches and governments that they represented, sought to destroy many Aboriginal consciousnesses, knowledge, languages, spiritual teachings and practices through colonialism and by engendering rampant intolerance.[2] Many complex motives explain the need to eliminate Aboriginal knowledge and spiritual teachings. Among the primary factors were the belief that Aboriginals followed the wrong, pagan religion and for their salvation needed to convert to Christianity, the only true religion.[3] In short, there was rejection of our humanity, our spirituality.

European Christians have been very successful in ruining the ecology of North America and suppressing Aboriginal consciousness, languages, and spiritual teachings.[4] They were "the civilized." Aboriginals were the unknown "others." Their God in His Gospel did not tell them about us or our lands, and this omission helped the rise of secular authority.[5] Christians argued that Aboriginal peoples were infidels, natural slaves or children, and backward savages, instead of being human and constituting nations. Although Pope Paul III declared in 1537 "Indians are truly men . . . they may and should, freely and legitimately, enjoy their liberty and the possession of their property,"[6] these teachings have been ineffective in preventing the brutal genocide and ethnocide of Aboriginal peoples and the ecological destruction of their land.[7]

This chapter is about the continuing struggle to protect and enhance Aboriginal spiritual teachings and practices. Faced with the magnitude and importance of the task in contemporary society, this chapter is only a modest and temporary bridge over the gap between worldviews that is involved. Conceptualizing the modern struggle for spiritual integrity for Aboriginal peoples requires a major rethinking of the operation of both divine order and secular law in Canadian society. Such reconceptualization also requires an understanding of the constitutional shield devised to limit the power and use of the existing interpretative monopolies of the divine order and secular law in Canada. From these perspectives, we may reach an understanding of how Aboriginal spirituality protects an ecology, a unique cognitive space, an endangered linguistic consciousness, and a way of life. This chapter is an invitation to an awareness of the cognitive struggle involved in preserving Aboriginal teaching and practices, and the role and relevance of law to that project. Inherent in this chapter is a request for reconfiguration of religious thought about Aboriginal spirituality and practices, and a request for new covenants between religious leaders and Aboriginal spiritual leaders.

Divine Order, Secular Law

Under their belief in a universal and personal God, European Christian denominations and their members strove to make Aboriginal people convert to them. Often these missionary initiatives crushed Aboriginal consciousness and languages, and engendered religious dissension within Aboriginal civilizations. These processes have left deep scars in the minds and hearts of the Aboriginal people.

Strife and oppression involving religious passion and dogma marked the history of early modern Europe. European aristocracies and states worked at devising structural remedies to limit religious passions and conflict. By the eighteenth century, the political principle emerged that, in order to maintain peace within state, religion could and should be separated from the state. On this view, religion was appropriately a matter of individual conscience. Government constraints on private choice of religious beliefs were progressively removed, thus affirming an inherent freedom to act on those beliefs. This principle lies at the root of freedom of religion in modern European and North American thought.

Yet, in the process of colonization, the secular state and dominant Christian denominations recombined to create a new era of religious wars, this time, against Aboriginal peoples around the world. The core element of the teachings of these transcendent faith traditions is that an anthropomorphic and personal God created the world according to His design. Because this God made the world, most Christian denominations believe that the world cannot fully share the sacred or divine nature of its Creator. At the same time, those faith traditions also believe that the functioning of the world reveals the cosmic order of the divine lawgiver, in other words, the idea of regularities.[8] They see these regularities of the cosmic order as *God's talk*—that describes what happens and establishes what ought to be. Prophets articulate the cosmic order or divine ideals. Unfortunately, because their God is considered divine, the faithful see His commands as universal and valid for all peoples. They believe that the divine order is a higher normative order that transcends human society, just as God transcends the world. The divine normative order is the reference point by which the faithful evaluate all peoples and is superior to the laws of human sovereigns or the customs of different peoples. To accept the cosmology of the transcendent religion and the related idea of higher law, most Christians must commit themselves to standards whose validity is universal and objective rather than a product of their own beliefs or desires.[9] The belief in the existence of standards of conduct given by God has contributed to the idea of universality in religion, generality in the rule of laws, and equality under the positive law.[10]

Semitic monotheism (represented by Judaism, Christianity, and Islam) asserts the central belief that all humans have an immortal soul made in the image of the personal God. This immortal soul is distinct from their earthly body, but is not necessarily separate. This belief also affirms a dichotomy between humans and the world. Moreover, these monotheistic religions also believe that God deals with humans and allows some of its members to live in His presence forever. At the same time, the faithful also assert that its members have essential equal worth derived from the fatherhood of a personal God. Out of this dichotomy is forged a theory of salvation,[11] and also the distinction between the elect and the damned. Therein lies the foundation of dialectical hierarchy and colonialism's promotion of differences between civilized and savage peoples.[12] The priesthood or learned men divined the will of God's and systematized the divine commandments that become the core of a sacred law of salvation.[13]

Invariably, some interpretations of divine law became blended with limitations on secular authority. As a system of beliefs and practices in modern states, divine law predominates over democratic forms of society. It expresses the true and right order, and provides a framework of legitimacy for the European notions of political and legal order.[14] That divine order is transformed into the "higher" universal standards. Its demands are partially articulated and sanctioned by elected legislators in the name of democratic processes. Additionally, this order sets boundaries to majoritarian choice. It establishes the principles and values that provide for both justification and critique of the law of the state. All Christian denominations adhere to the belief that there are entitlements and responsibilities that no secular law or political decision can disregard. Consequently, the beliefs of a divine order may be transferred into the ideology of secular legislatures. Moreover, in the absence of legislation or when interpreting it, impartial judges often apply a system of beliefs and practices, also derived from the divine order.

Canada is a legalistic nation, in the sense outlined above. The Canadian Charter of Rights and Freedoms recognizes both a divine order and the secular state subject to a rule of law.[15] The charter provides that "Canada is founded upon principles that recognizes the supremacy of God and the rule of law."[16] Both principles are pervasive and mystical beliefs. The rule of law is the distinguishing process of the Canadian legal system, but unlike the supremacy of God it cannot operate as a fundamental premise or as a source of constitutional legitimacy. In section 2(a) the charter provides "Everyone has the . . . freedom of conscience and religion."[17] While this constitutional right paradigm appears neutral, from an Aboriginal perspective, it is a eurocentric projection of its religious and political self-image.[18]

Freedom of conscience and religion under the charter is not absolute. Two overarching qualifications limit charter freedoms. The freedoms are subjected to some secular political control—"such reasonable limits prescribed by law as can be demonstrably justified in a free and democratic society" contained in section 1.[19] More important for this chapter is the second limitation. This limitation is independent of secular political control. The eurocentric divine order, freedom of conscience and religion, and secular law are limited by constitutional protections of aboriginal and treaty rights, the Aboriginal Shield.

The Aboriginal Shield

The Aboriginal Shield is contained in section 25 of the charter[20] and section 35 of the Constitution Act, 1982.[21] It is a structural remedy to religious intolerance directed at Aboriginal culture and spirituality and similar to the concept of separation of religion and the state. It seeks to protect Aboriginal people from any perpetration of Christian notions of a divine order and discriminatory secular laws. The purpose of these constitutional sections is to provide a comprehensive constitutional shield protecting aboriginal and treaty rights. The Aboriginal constitutional shield has the potential to end five centuries of persecution, moral judgementalism, and legal and religious welfare directed at Aboriginal teaching and beliefs. Aboriginal rights are found in the ancient base of the worldviews, languages, customary teachings and practices of Aboriginal people.[22] They are not founded on a Christian divine order or in artificial laws based on rule from above, democratic lawmaking, or majority intolerance.[23]

In the Constitution of Canada, the Aboriginal constitutional shield performs the traditional function of round hide shields that Aboriginal people carried as they traveled. These hide shields protected the holder from spiritual forces within an ecology, and were decorated according to their holder's visions. Similar to the visions painted on the hide shields, the black ink of the constitutional shield operates in Canadian law to protect the rights of Aboriginal peoples from the imported eurocentric notions of divine order, from fundamental individual freedoms, and from secular legal artifacts.

Section 25 of the charter provides special protection for Aboriginal rights from those located in the immigrants' creative imagination and social artifacts. It states that the charter does not affect Aboriginal rights and freedom.

> The guarantee in this Charter of certain rights and freedoms shall not be construed so as to abrogate or derogate from any aboriginal, treaty or other rights or freedoms that pertain to the aboriginal peoples of Canada.[24]

Thus, courts cannot interpret any of the individual freedoms in the charter as limiting Aboriginal spiritual teachings, observances or practices. Neither section 25 nor the rest of the charter lists these unique protected rights of the Aboriginal people. Instead, section 25 is an analytical device for protecting all of the "existing aboriginal and treaty rights of the aboriginal peoples of Canada" found in section 35 of the Constitution Act, 1982.[25] These aboriginal and treaty rights are sequestered from control by the invocation of reasonable limits prescribed by democratic law set out in section 1 of the charter, and from judicial intervention. They are, thus, part of the supreme law of Canada.[26]

These two sections are complementary, and they locate a constitutional home and shield for Aboriginal rights. They affirm Aboriginal rights as fundamental rights in the conscience of the nation. On the one hand, section 25 defines Aboriginal rights as an integral and legitimate part of the new constitutional order in Canada and explicitly protects these rights from the Eurocentric personal rights guarantees and freedom of religion, and from the religious rules or morality of the churches and their representatives.[27] On the other hand, section 35 protects these fundamental rights that are distinct from the secular and religious rights of the rest of the population in whose name legislation is enacted in a legislature or law applied by judges appointed to the courts.[28]

At the center of these constitutional rights is the ability of Aboriginal peoples to define their own contexts or ideas of existence, meaning, and spirituality surrounding the mystery of human life and to control their own thoughts and identity.

The existence of the Aboriginal Shield in constitutional law raises important challenges to eurocentric thought, institutions, and religions within Canada. It creates an important space for the preservation and enhancement of Aboriginal thought, teachings, and practices. It directly challenges the implicit operations of the Christian divine order in Canada. I will contextualize this challenge by raising three urgent concerns, each that requires a reconceptualization of reciprocal rights and responsibilities. First, the most problematic concern is protecting the environments that are the foundation of Aboriginal spirituality. Second is the protection of Aboriginal consciousness and language that expresses our teachings and practices. Third is the need for new covenants to establish a respectful relationship between eurocentric religions and Aboriginal peoples.

Protecting Sacred Ecologies

Most Aboriginal spiritual teaching and practices flow from ecological understandings rather than cosmology.[29] Ecology is not viewed as a mass noun. Aboriginal people believe ecology is a sacred living order, self-subsisting if not self-generating, and independent of human will. N. Scott Momaday, a Kiowa-Navajo writer, summarized this understanding:

> Sacred ground is ground that is invested with belief. Belief, at its root, exists independent of meaning. That is, expression and object may escape what we can perceive as definable meaning. The intrinsic power of sacred ground is often ineffable and abstract. I behold a particular sacred space, and I understand that it is in some way earned. It is consecrated, made holy with offerings—song and ceremony, joy and sorrow, the dedication of the mind and heart, offerings of life and death. The words "sacred" and "sacrifice" are related. And acts of sacrifice make sacred the earth. The indigenous people of the world know this as they know the sunrise and sunset.[30]

Aboriginal knowledge and wisdom were found in the ability to apprehend the hidden harmony of the changing ecologies and to create alliances with the transforming forces within it. These understandings inform Aboriginal consciousness, languages, and teachings.[31] These ecological habitants are considered a sacred realm, and they contain the keepers that taught Aboriginal ancestors the core of our spiritual teaching and practices.[32] The core belief of Aboriginal spirituality is that everything is alive and Aboriginals seek spirituality through intimate communion with the ecological biodiversity.[33] Such beliefs deny a distinction between the sacred and the profane, since all life processes are holy and sacred.

The relationships between land and the people, their kinship with the other living creatures that share the land, and with the spirit world have forged the most significant part of Aboriginal teachings, knowledge, language, and spirituality. They establish the belief that all these relationships are interrelated and are a sacred order.[34] Together they create the context of the sacred. Experiencing an ecology in which one lives is both a personal necessity and an integral part of the spiritual teachings and practices. This sacred order is not considered either a paradise or natural; it has to be renewed and sustained by humans.

Most religions have noted these unique relationships that exist between the land and aboriginal peoples. In his discussion of the rights of minorities, Pope John Paul II is the first pope to recognize the unrivaled unity among Aboriginal peoples. He stated:

> Certain people, especially those identified as native or indigenous, have always maintained a special relationship to their lands, a relationship connected with the group's very identity as a people having their own tribal, cultural, and religious traditions. When such indigenous peoples are deprived of their land they lose a vital element of their way of life and actually run the risk of disappearing as a people.[35]

The Pope's statement implied that Aboriginal peoples' right of life embraces an adequate land base to practice their religious freedoms.

A few countries have adopted procedures for the identification and protection of places of historical, cultural, or religious importance. They do not apply such laws consistently to spiritual sites of interest to Aboriginal peoples. Often they do not prevent the government itself from disposing of sites or developing them for other purposes. The U.S. Congress, for example, acknowledged that it has enacted laws designed for the conservation and preservation of natural species and resources without any consideration regarding the legal effect on Aboriginal religions. To remedy these infringements of freedom of religion and to protect the sacred places of Aboriginal people, under the First Amendment of the Constitution that guarantees freedom of religion, Congress enacted the American Indian Religious Freedom Act.[36] The act embodies an interpretative policy that declares:

> that henceforth it shall be the policy of the United States to protect and preserve for American Indians their inherent rights of freedom to believe, express, and exercise their traditional religions of American Indi-

ans, Eskimo, Aluet, and Native Hawaiians, including but not limited to access to sites, use and possession of sacred objects, and the freedom to worship through ceremonials and traditional rites.[37]

Consultations with native traditional religious leaders is required to decide appropriate religious culture rights and practices.

Many different sacred places exist as the Federal Agencies Task Force charged with consultation found.[38] They range from the familiar burial grounds to mythic, legendary, or petroglyphic places; from purification, healing, renewal of fertility places to sacred plant, rock, and animal places; and from medicine wheels and sun temples to vision and dreaming places. The Aboriginal belief in sacred ecologies is distinct from eurocentric religions. Often Eurocentric religions have sacred places where they build churches or buildings to confine the spirit, but this is the opposite of most Aboriginal worldviews. Most eurocentric "faith-centered" beliefs can be expressed everywhere and anywhere. Aboriginal worldviews based on ecologies have proved vulnerable to eurocentric religions and theories of progress.[39]

Protecting those ecologies, their biodiversity, and sacred status is an integral part of protecting Aboriginal spirituality and teachings. Properly understood, protecting the ecologies would give birth to a new proprietary category—sacred lands. The Supreme Court of Canada in *Guerin v. The Queen* has already held that Aboriginal interests in the land are a *sui generis* interest that is distinct from British property concepts.[40]

We need protection of the environment to end our grieving, and to generate a balance that can heal a dominated and oppressed spirituality and heal a country. To protect the environment is to protect Aboriginal worldviews, languages, identity, spiritual teaching, and practices. Enhancing the biodiversity of the ecologies is not only essential to self-preservation but also to the preservation of a sacred way of life.

Protecting and Enhancing Aboriginal Consciousnesses

Today, Aboriginal thought, language, and spirituality are nearing extinction. They are endangered consciousnesses. These consciousnesses are encased in and are manifested through Aboriginal linguistic structures. These structures are foreign to English-speakers. Language scholars estimate that Aboriginal peoples of America at the beginning of the cultural holocaust spoke more than 2,000 separate languages. Five hundred years later, only 500 Aboriginal languages are spoken in the Americas, with only 200 that are phonemically written. In North America, Christian missionaries and politicians extinguished or replaced about 67 percent of Aboriginal consciousness.

Often they replaced Aboriginal consciousness with English thought, language, and spirituality.[41] Most often this suppression of Aboriginal consciousness was accomplished by religious or public education. Both European Christian religious doctrine and secular thought contributed over the years to the curricula of public and separate education systems. Everywhere in Canada, through educational imperialism and physical and mental abuses, there was created a new consciousness among Aboriginal peoples.[42] Provincial and band education have continued to champion eurocentric thought and practices and the relentless and unreflective attack on Aboriginal consciousness, teachings, and practices, attempting in the process to metamorphose the young Aboriginal into a foreign consciousness. These efforts have created cognitive and religious dissension among Aboriginal youth.

Recent studies in Canada show the results of these initiatives. All fifty-three Aboriginal languages in Canada are critically endangered.[43] Only three Aboriginal languages in Canada have a chance of surviving into the next century with a sufficient number of proficient speakers to sustain them unless immediate remedial measures are taken by Canadian governments and other institutions, such as the churches, schools, and colleges. Despite the studies, neither governments nor other bodies are taking those measures, despite their complicity in the destruction of the Aboriginal languages. They still fail to grasp the integral significance of Aboriginal languages to spiritual teachings and practices that together form the basis of Aboriginal identity.

Essential to the protection of Aboriginal spiritual teachings and practices is protecting how they are transmitted to the next generation. Learning the existing teachings involves an intimate and endless talk with elders and relatives. Spiritual teachers conduct traditional teachings orally. This process takes patience and prudence. The Aboriginal view of spirituality is based on sounds, rather than written words. Aboriginal sounds embody an elegant way of explicating an ecological order composed of very complex systems of relationship enfolded in stories, songs, prayers, rituals and talks. These sounds inform a remarkable connection to a balanced livingness within a spiral of life and the power to renew livingness. Indeed, the sounds of songs and prayers have created certain ecologies, and continue to renew and balance them.[44] This gives them a great human responsibility in maintaining an ecosystem that is detached from any notion of the Christian divine order. These sounds are creative acts of caring. Thus, Aboriginal languages are indispensable and irreplaceable in Aboriginal consciousnesses, spiritual teachings, and ceremonies. With the loss of these languages, Aboriginal worldviews and spiritual teaching about a particular ecosystem also vanish.

Aboriginal spirituality, as it has appeared to non-Aboriginals, exists as distorted translations that must be corrected. Very few Europeans have ever mastered any of these Aboriginal languages, in part because of their difficult sounds and unfamiliar grammar systems. Most eurocentric writings have subdivided or fragmented Aboriginal consciousness and teachings into separate and artificial categories of eurocentric thought, impressing on them concepts and constructs such as "religion," "spiritual," "supernatural," "cultural," "artistic," "intellectual," or "legal." This terminology and its ideological base is the assumptive context of eurocentric thought, yet it is misleading and inappropriate when applied to Aboriginal worldviews and practices.

Eurocentric thought about Algonquian consciousness, for example, is derived from the missionaries, explorers, anthropologists, and linguists. These immigrants have little understanding of the sources of that consciousness[45] or the members of the linguistic group.[46] They usually derive the name of the linguistic category from Champlain's interpretation of *"Algounequins,"* as meaning the people of the place.[47] Many Aboriginal peoples in Canada have been arbitrarily placed in this linguistic category.[48]

Eurocentric translation of Algonquian teachings and practices has also abused and misinterpreted them. The core of the problem is that missionaries, anthropologists, and linguists have tried to understand Aboriginal languages within their own linguistic conventions. Their methodology was to impose foreign categories on Aboriginal knowledge, language, and teachings. Often, the missionaries were the first literate European observers of Aboriginal peoples. They were the first to interpret Aboriginal languages and teaching. They assumed a thing-concept of nature, what we often call the *noun-God consciousness.* The thing-concept consciousness of European language system is based on the biblical estrangement of man from nature. These systems teach one to be an impartial observer of nature in order to gain objective knowledge of an external realm of thing-objects. This creates a reality of two items only: the observer and the observed, which are respectively, the knower and the known, or the subject and the object.[49] For example, the English language is noun-oriented. It habitually classifies and categorizes the world into nouns to the dismay of Algonquian people who believe that everything moves in an interrelated and interdependent process. Algonquian sounds, by contrast, create a language that is more verb-oriented, that reflects a dominant polysynthetic consciousness, language, and order.[50] Our cognitive orientation is toward relationships, process, and flux rather than things. English verbs, however, *require* nouns to make complete thoughts or sentences. Such linguistic conventions and categories are alien to and dissonant with Algonquian consciousnesses.

Spirituality in Aboriginal thought revolves around the forces called "creativity" in English. Since Aboriginals connect everything and changing, creativity or spirituality is the matrix that holds everything together, their vision of creativity is distinct from Eurocentric thought. Algonquian people view the matrix as eternal, but in a continuous state of transformation. Mikmaq language structure, for example, affirms this view of the universe, building verb phrases with hundreds of prefixes and suffixes to choose from, to express the panorama. With this fluidity of verb phrases, every speaker can create new vocabulary "on the fly," custom-tailored sounds to meet the experience of the moment, to express the finest nuances of awareness. Through unique word-endings, Aboriginal language structures place emphasis on the established relationship. These are often divided by European linguistics into animate and the inanimate categories.

The missionaries attempted to match Algonquian spiritual teachings and practices to ideas of the Christian religion. Their purpose was to use Algonquian sounds to affirm Christian symbols and beliefs. Translators' beliefs determined the method and relevance of the Algonquian beliefs and their sounds. To affirm their belief in a universal noun-God who created the world, they manipulated eurocentric words for Algonquian sounds. One of the toughest tasks Aboriginal people had was explaining to Europeans who their noun-God was. Since the Europeans insisted that one God created all humans and that all humans just had different nouns, different names, which referred to the same person, eventually they discovered their God among Algonquian beliefs of powers residing in the ecology and "cultural heroes."[51] Usually the attempts to impose the existence of a transcendent God and God's talk on Algonquian thought have produced analogies that are false or distorted. This process of imposition is not benign: it arose from the strategies of a Christian denomination seeking to initiate hostile theological indoctrination processes. At best, these Christian efforts have been genuine acts of faith. Commonly, however, translations have constituted acts of spiritual and cultural appropriation. At worst, they have been part of an attempt to destroy the belief systems and language of entire groups of peoples. In any event, these efforts arise from mixed motives in which outsiders seek to understand incomprehensibility. The consequences of these motives have been tragic.

Let us briefly review the appropriation process. Aboriginal peoples often talk about forces of creativity rather than a personal or anthropomorphic creator.[52] They view the entire ecosystem as a flux or as a creator of flux. Human creativity is a great responsibility, for people need human creativity to see the patterns of change and to adjust to the flux. Thus, they have no categories of the sacred and the profane. Creativity energizes all life. It manifests the spiritual nature of all life. Indigenous languages in North America express the vastness of the realms and their processes through verbs of creativity, being, and becoming. The Hopis call these creative forces *a'ne himu* (really process or mighty something) said to be the realm of soft, unmanifested essence as opposed to hard manifested forms. Missionaries and ethnologists have often described the Lakota phrase *wakan anka*—"the Great Spirit" or their person God. In Lakota thought, *wakan* means sacred and *tanka* means vast or great; thus *wankantanka* symbolizes all sacred processes in the universe. If the sound must be translated, one should discuss it as *the most sacred* or *vast creative forces*.[53] Similarly, in Cherokee thought and linguistic structure, *unehleanvhi* represents the spiritual nature of the universe, but has been translated to mean the creator by eurocentric theology. Also, missionaries have imposed the idea of a personal God on other Aboriginal understandings of the flux. Thus, such terms as *Knich'kaminau* or *Niskam* (Míkmaq), *Gichi-manidoo* (Ojibwewin-Ikidowinan), *Ma'ura* (Winnebago), or *Máheóo* (Tsistsistas) was created to construct God.

These phrases are not analogous to a noun-God or supreme-God or Son-of-God concept associated with eurocentric theology or thought. They are more than simply divergent—they exist in an altogether different realm.[54] These differences provide distinctive foundations for ethics, personal decision making, and purposes. Among those who still think and speak in Aboriginal languages, their distinct and coherent worldview remains operative. In most Algonquian consciousness, however, the Europeans' interpretations of spirituality continue to be destructive to cognitive solidarity of Algonquian teachings and practices. Often Algonquian consciousness remains operative in many who do not speak Aboriginal languages but can understand them. And sometimes it remains in those who neither speak nor understand these language systems.

Learning English has not always disintegrated the implicit order of Aboriginal consciousness. In many cases, the learning process has been complementary, merely transforming Aboriginal consciousness within English consciousness. Most assimilated Aboriginals continue to passionately and intuitively seek to be in balance with the sacred processes and live in dignity with ecological integrity. This search is a manifestation of a traditional process that originally tied those Aboriginal teachings and practices together.

In the modern reformation of Algonquian spirituality, Aboriginal peoples often have to rely on European writings about their languages and beliefs. Young Algonquian people cannot assume that alien eurocentric languages translate Algonquian realms or beliefs faithfully.[55] Similarly, they cannot understand Algonquian spiritual ideas by attempting to match them up with their understanding of Christian ideas, since both the learning method and the alien languages create certain paradoxes, doubts, and confusion. That was, and is, the general process of cognitive imperialism.[56] It is important that we look beyond the available translations to the original ideas to see the multiple layers of meaning and subtle channels of communication. In the restoration, we have to be aware of the contagion inflicted on Algonquian languages and spiritual ideas. The dilemma is that Aboriginals cannot do this if they speak only European languages.

Necessity of New Religious Convenants

In the modern secular order, religions are viewed as a complex phenomenon that are the focus of serious study and consideration. Aboriginal spiritual teachings and practices, however, have not been considered as legitimate religions.[57]

Christian religious leaders often see Aboriginal spirituality as curious reflections of their personal God, but of little consequence. Christian religions were and continue to be exported to Aboriginal people as a superior commodity that it was and is deadly to refuse.[58] Their leaders transformed the divine order into a fierce religious export firmly controlled by cultural serial killers, intent on destroying and eradicating Aboriginal teachings and practices. Unfortunately, eurocentric academic disciplines and educational systems have been complicit with Christian domination and religious oppression. All of them contributed to the American cultural holocaust and cognitive imperialism. None of the dominant Christian denominations have accepted total responsibility for the cultural holocaust or attempted to compensate for the wrongs to Aboriginal peoples. Some denominations have offered a limited apology for past wrongs,[59] most continue their oppression of Aboriginal spirituality.

The new Constitution of Canada is designed to protect Aboriginal language, teaching, and practices from such abuses. Modern Aboriginals have the constitutional choice between Aboriginal and eurocentric religious and secular conscience. The Canadian constitution creates a protected sphere of inviolable Aboriginal conscience, belief, and practice from other religious freedoms and state powers. No other nation has enshrined such a choice for Aboriginal people.

Although these constitutional clauses surround and protect Aboriginal spirituality in Canada, however, they may not be sufficient to prevent the combined ideology of divine order and secular law from destroying important ecosystems or prevent Aboriginal languages from becoming extinct. Words on paper are not as powerful as the assumptive contexts, ideologies, and worldviews of non-Aboriginals.[60] Aboriginal peoples will continue to struggle with others to restore and enhance their relationship to the sacred ecologies in their own languages and spiritual traditions. The willingness and ability of the Canadian legal system to protect unfamiliar Aboriginal spiritual teachings and practices under the constitutional covenant is uncertain. Even if the legal system is responsive, we must weigh the meaning and cost of litigation against the value of an authentic conversation about the relationship between Aboriginal rights and eurocentric notions of freedom of religion.

Some Christian religious leaders have difficulty understanding Aboriginal teachings that lack the structure of religious hierarchy, community, and controlling text. Most Aboriginal teachings and practices do not appear to have a priesthood, any churches, any philosophy, any history, and any holy book. Aboriginal peoples encased all these elements in ecological contexts and their intractable languages. In the case of those who did have written texts, priests, and temples, as with the Mayans, Christian conquerors destroyed them.[61] In other cases, Christian denominations sought to create hierarchy and community within Aboriginal civilizations.

The advent culture of Christianity has not proved beneficial to Aboriginal peoples. Very few Aboriginal peoples survived the 500-year nightmare of genocide, ethnocide, ecological destruction and various shaming ceremonies required to prove that they were humans and entitled to human rights by Christian religions, nation-states, and colonial powers.[62] Where Aboriginal consciousness and teaching have survived, Aboriginal peoples have learned of their inferiority, and live with restless doubts about Aboriginal and Christian traditions. The survivors are no more than vestiges of the Aboriginal people. We remain a vulnerable, marginalized, abused, and disadvantaged people. We often blame ourselves or our ancestors for our terrible abuse or doubt our own capacity to rebuild our lives based on our traditional beliefs. Terrible ecological damage denies us a relationship with the environment. Poverty and racism confine our life choices to a reservation. Christian and eurocentric thought has deprived us of any firm sense of how we fit into the environment and society around us and we, therefore, suffer a consciousness of aversion. All too often, we feel homeless in nature and are left at a loss to judge and to justify the conduct of our own lives. We seem powerless to create a secular society that is nourishing or sustainable. All too often we exist as cultural blanks,[63] fragmented by our search for spirituality among a babble of squabbling teachings and promises by the churches and the state.

Faced with this legacy of the advent culture, the constitutional protection of Aboriginal teachings and practices raises hard questions about evangelization or propagation of religions. This issue is of little consequence to believers who seek to live out the committed life. Yet, relentless eurocentric evangelization is a huge obstacle to the healing of Aboriginal peoples. Evangelization raises the crucial issue of the relationship between Aboriginal teachings and practices. This issue has never been fully or adequately addressed by eurocentric religions. They presume it as a divine right, but evangelization has been forced on Aboriginal people.

Because of the Aboriginal Shield in Canadian constitutional law, no eurocentrism or other religions can coerce any Aboriginal person to affirm a specific religious belief or to manifest a specific religious practice for sectarian purposes. If necessary, Aboriginal people will raise their constitutional shield to create a "wall of separation" between eurocentric religions and

Aboriginal teachings and practices to ensure the exercise of their spirituality in Canada. Their only other choice is cognitive extinction.

Evangelization has harmed Aboriginal people. Because Canadian religious and spiritual leaders have not confronted and resolved this issue, it continues to hinder the Aboriginal struggle to heal the scars of oppression, renew our self-confidence, and recover our undeniable dignity. This is a difficult and complex issue that needs an authentic solution. I would suggest that other religions should suspend missionary activity among Aboriginal people, until an evangelization protocol or covenant has been achieved with the spiritual teachers and peoples of each Aboriginal community.

Aboriginal people have long been aware of the limitations of Christian religions. As early as 1777, a Cherokee commented about eurocentric thought:

> Much has been said of the want of what you term "civilization" among the Indians. Many proposals have been made to us to adopt your law, your religion, your manners and your customs. We do not see the propriety of such a reformation. We should be better pleased with beholding the good effects of these doctrines in your own practices than with hearing you talk about them or of reading your newspapers on such subjects.[64]

Aboriginal peoples are still waiting to see the "good effect" of religious doctrines in daily practice. We should not be expected to fulfill the spiritual needs of strangers.

Regardless of the actual legacy of Christian actions, Aboriginal spiritual teachings and Christian faiths can be complementary. Aboriginal consciousnesses and teachings has always been flexible. It has allowed each person a choice, without forcing absolute conformity to experiences or values. Aboriginal communities accept more diversity than most linguistic communities.[65] Christian compulsion has never driven Aboriginal thought in Canada to formally systematize its teachings or practices into a theology. Aboriginal thought, teachings, and practices have rejected the ideas of canonized, authoritative codifications, universal principles, or heresy. Aboriginal consciousness and languages have honored creativity and spiritual growth, and Aboriginal culture is tolerant of its members being traditional and Christian.[66] Once eurocentric and Christian thought accepts its teachings as local ideals instead of universal principles, and the ecology is respected as sacred, little substantial difference will exist in the teachings about living a decent life among most religions.

Some Aboriginal peoples have created such a complementary relationship between the two teachings, for example, the Mikmaq rites under the 1610 Concordat with the Holy See exempts them from canon law.[67] From a

Míkmaq perspective, for example, the teachings of the founders of monotheistic religions, Moses, Jesus Christ, and Mohammed, are part of *npuoinaq*, sacred thoughts—nothing more, nothing less.

Many Aboriginal spiritual teachers are seeking a new covenant with other religions on many issues, especially of a partnership in protecting and enhancing the environment and restoring Aboriginal consciousness and languages. Developing some concerted strategies for protecting Aboriginal teachings and practices by new convenants must begin. It is long overdue. Each religion must establish a new relationship with the various Aboriginal spiritual teachers and practitioners. They must grasp the teachings and practices according to sacred geography and Aboriginal thought.

Under the Aboriginal Shield there exists a new constitutional division between religions and secular law on the one hand and Aboriginal teachings and practices on the other. This is a new constitutional relationship, under which Aboriginal spiritual teachers and practitioners are asking for genuine respect for their teachings and practices. Other religious leaders must recognize the right of and need for Aboriginal teachers and practitioners to preserve and enhance their spiritual integrity. Aboriginal spiritual teachers and practitioners are asking for space and time to practice their freedom of belief. They are asking for the opportunity to nourish and spiritually heal some of their people, in privacy and with solidarity. At the same time, they are asking for a respectful dialogue with other religious leaders on how to create a sustainable covenant between the distinct worldviews and teachings.

Notes

*Guidance provided by *ababinilli, máheóo*, and *niskam*; although I assume full responsibility for interpretation. This chapter is written in an Algonquian version of English—an attempt to express indigenous thoughts within the limited framework of the structure of English thought. Special reverence is due to the elders who have continued the teachings of Aboriginal spirituality to the youth, despite domination and oppression.

1. J. M. Blaut, *The Colonizer's Model of The World: Geographical Diffusionism and Eurocentric History* (New York/London: The Guilford Press, 1993); S. Amin, *Eurocentrism* (New York: Monthly Review Press, 1988).

2. E. Dussel labels this process the "original sin" of the Americas in "Was America Discovered or Invaded," *Concillium*, 200 (1988): p. 130.

3. In the Christian tradition, the Pauline "natural man" has to become a "new creature" in order to be saved (1 Corinthians 2:14; 2 Corinthians 5:17). *R. v. Syliboy* [1929] 1 D.L.R. 307 (N.S. Co. Ct) (Míkmaq as uncivilized peoples); *Jack and Charlie v. The Queen* (1986) 21 D.L.R. (4th) 641 (S.C.C.) (Coast Salish's sacrament rejected).

4. R. Wright, *Stolen Continents* (New York: Viking, 1992).

5. L. Hanke, *Aristotle and the American Indians* (Chicago: Henry Regnery Company, 1959).

6. Paul III, Sublimis Deus, June 9, 1537 in F. A. MacNutt, *Bartholomew De Las Casas: His Life, His Apostolate, and His Writings* (New York and London: G. P. Putnam & Sons, 1909), pp. 430–31.

7. Currently, the battle is in international human rights. See R. L. Barsh, "Indigenous Peoples in the 1990s: From Object to Subject of International Law?" *Harvard Human Right Journal*, 7:1 (1994): 86, and R. J. Williams, *The American Indian in Western Legal Thought: The Discourse of Conquest* (Oxford: Oxford University Press, 1990).

8. H. Wolfson, *Philo* (Cambridge: Harvard University Press, 1968) vol. 2, pp. 439–60.

9. See F. L. Neumann, "Types of Natural Law," in H. Marcuse (ed.), *The Democratic and the Authoritarian State. Essays in Political and Legal Theory* (Glencoe: Free Press, 1957), pp. 69–91.

10. See P. Goodrich and Y. Hachamovitch, "Time Out of Mind: An introduction to the Semiotics of Common Law," in P. Fitzpatrick (ed.), *Dangerous Supplements: Resistance and Renewal in Jurisprudence* (London: Pluto Press, 1991), pp. 167, 174.

11. M. Weber, *Wirtshaft and Gesellschaft*, J. Winckelmann (ed.), (Tübingen: More, 1972), pp. 319–21. "Salvation" was an unexplored concept in Aboriginal thought which focused on what "is" rather than what "ought" to be.

12. See Blaut, pp. 1–50.

13. Examples are the Jewish *halakhad*, Roman canon law, Islamic *shari'a*, and Hindu *dharmas'ästra*.

14. French postmodern thinkers (Derrida, Foucault, Baudrillard, and Lyotard) argue that the Enlightenment did not secularize thought or render law or society or humans independent from the divine order. Instead law incorporated religious assumptions into its own categories as "white mythology." A. Carty, "Introduction: Post-Modern Law," in A Carty (ed.), *Post Modern Law: Enlightenment Revolution and the Death of Man* (Edinburgh: Edinburgh University Press, 1990); P. Fitzpatrick (ed.), *Dangerous Supplements: Resistance and Renewal in Jurisprudence*.

15. Part I of the Constitution Act, 1982, being Schedule B of the Canada Act 1982 (U.K.), 1982, c. 11. [hereafter called Charter].

16. Ibid. (Preamble.)

17. Ibid. See *R. v. Big M Drug Mart Ltd.* (1985) 18 C.C.C. (3d) 385 (SCC).

18. M. E. Turpel, "Aboriginal Peoples and the Canadian Charter: Interpretive Monopolies, Cultural Differences," in R. Devlin (ed.), *Canadian Perspectives on Legal Theory* (Toronto: Edmond Montgomery, 1991), pp. 506–17; P. Monture-Angus, *Thun-*

der in My Soul: A Mohawk Women Speaks (Halifax: Fernwood Publishing, 1995), pp. 131–52.

19. Charter, sec. 1.

20. Charter, supra note 15.

21. Part II of the Constitution Act, 1982; Schedule B of the Canada Act 1982 (U.K.), 1982, c. 11. The Aboriginal peoples of Canada includes the Indian, Inuit, and Métis peoples. In the Constitution Amendment Proclamation, 1983, these constitutional rights were explicitly "guaranteed equally to male and female persons." Sometimes the treaties affirm freedom of religion, for example, in the Treaty of 1726 with the Míkmaq, the imperial Crown promised them they would not be molested in "the exercise of their Religion, Provided the Missionary's Residing amongst them have Leave from this Government for Soe Doing," National Archives of Canada, Colonial Office Records GR 217, vol. 4, p. 82. This treaty was affirmed in subsequent treaties.

22. Section 22 of the charter makes it clear that the provision for English and French languages does not abrogate or derogate from any legal or customary right or privilege to other languages acquired or enjoyed before or after the charter. This section preserves Aboriginal languages through the operation of Aboriginal rights.

23. See *Sparrow v. The Queen* [1990] S.C.R 1075; [1990] 3 C.N.L.R. 178 (Aboriginal fishing rights). Aboriginal rights are fact intensive, that is, resting on understanding of fact.

24. Charter, sec. 25.

25. It is broader than rights defined in section 35. Some are defined rights such as the Royal Proclamation of 1763 and modern land claim settlements, while others are undeclared rights, see section 26 of the charter.

26. Section 52(1), ibid. ("The Constitution of Canada is the supreme law of Canada, and any law that is inconsistent with the provisions of the Constitution is, to the extent of the inconsistency, of no force or effect.")

27. Section 24(1) of the Charter provides for judicial intervention to protect Aboriginal rights that have been infringed or denied by either the federal government or provinces.

28. J. Y. Henderson, "Empowering Treaty Federalism," 58 *Saskatchewan Law Review*, 18 (1994): pp. 241–332.

29. See C. Vecsey and R. W. Venables, *American Indian Environments: Ecological Issues in Native American History* (Syracuse: Syracuse University Press, 1980); J. D. Hughes, *American Indian Ecology* (El Paso, Texas: Western Press, University of Texas, 1983).

30. Speech at "Cry of The Earth: The Legacy Of First Nations, the Prophesies of Turtle Island," November 22, 1993, United Nations, New York. See also L. Levy-Bruhl, *How Natives Think*, trans. Lilian A. Clare (New York: Washington Square Press, 1966), especially pp. 13, 25.

31. A typical experience in attempting to understand Aboriginal religions is described by Joseph E. Brown, *The Spiritual Legacy of the American Indian* (Labanon, PA: Pendle Hill, 1964) in the following turn: "In my first contacts with Black Elk, almost all he said was phrased in terms involving animals and natural phenomena. I naively would begin to talk about religious matters, until I finally realized that he was, in fact, explaining his religion," p. 16.

32. V. Deloria, Jr., *God Is Red* (New York: Grosset and Dunlap, 1973), p. 294; Chief John Snow, *The Mountains Are Our Sacred Places* (Toronto: Samuel Stevens, 1977).

33. See Federal Agencies Task Force, *American Indian Religious Freedom Act Report* (Washington, DC: U.S. Department of Interior, 1979), p. 52.

34. Among the Míkmaq, these accumulated experiences are represented by the sound *nestumou*. See, J. Y. Henderson, "Mikmaw Tenure in Atlantic Canada," *Dalhousie Law Journal*, 18(2)(1995): p. 196, see especially pp. 225–36.

35. John Paul II, *To Build Peace, Respect Minorities: World Day of Peace Statement*, December 8, 1988, in *Origins* 18 (1998): p. 466 and p. 478. John Paul stated that minorities have a fundamental right to "exist," to "preserve and develop their own culture" and to "religious freedom."

36. American Indian Religious Freedom Act (1978) 42 USC 1996. See also Native American Graves Protection and Repatriation Act of 1990 and the National Museum of the American Indian Act of 1991; S. O'Brien, "A Legal Analysis of the American Indian Religious Freedom Act," in C. Vecsey (ed.), *Handbook of American Indian Religious Freedom* (New York: Crossroads Publishing, 1991), pp. 27–43; E. Sewell, "The American Indian Religious Freedom Act," *Arizona Law Review*, 25 (1983): pp. 429–53.

37. Ibid.

38. *Federal Task Force Report*, p. 52. See also S. C. More, "Sacred Sites and Public Lands," in Vecsey, *Handbook* pp. 81–99; D. E. Walker, Jr. "Protection of American Indian Sacred Geography," in Vecsey, *Handbook* pp. 100–15.

39. Sewell, pp. 429–53.

40. *Guerin v. R.* [1984] 2 S.C.R. 335; *Canadian Pacific Ltd. v. Paul* [1988] S.C.R 678; *Delgamuukw v. British Columbia* [1993] 5 C.N.L.R. 1 (B.C.C.A.), p. 23 (MacFarlane J.A.), and pp. 262–64 (Hutcheon J.A.).

41. D. Champagne (ed.), *The Native North American Almanac* (Detroit: Gale Research Inc., 1994), p. 427. See Native American Language Act, [U.S.A.] P.L. 101–477, section 102(9) (1990).

42. See M. A. Battiste, "Micmac Literacy and Cognitive Assimilation," in *Indian Education in Canada: The Legacy* (Vancouver: University of British Columbia Press, 1986); M. Battiste and J. Barman (eds.), *First Nations Education in Canada The Circle Unfolds* (Vancouver: University of British Columbia Press, 1986); J. R.

Miller, *Shingwauk's Vision: A History of Native Residential Schools* (Toronto: University of Toronto Press, 1996).

43. See Assembly of First Nations, *Towards Rebirth of First Nations Languages* (Ottawa: AFN, 1992); House of Common Standing Committee on Aboriginal Affairs, *You Took My Talk: Aboriginal Literacy and Empowerment* (Ottawa: Queen Printer, 1990).

44. The Navajo ceremonial *hózhóójí* (blessingway) demonstrates the way in which the Navajo envision how thought and sounds of a *yattíii* (speaker) become manifest in the creation of the world and in the sustaining life.

45. The original meaning of the sound *Algonquian,* it is said by some Míkmaq elders, was derived from the distinct rock formation around the Great Lakes where an ancient ideographic script or rock drawings were carved. Some eurocentric linguists assert that the word is derived from Míkmaq term *alkoome* that referred to people who stand in the canoe and spear fish in the water or *állegonkin* which refers to the dancers or *el legom'kwin* (friends, allies). See P. Vessel, *The Algonkin Nation* (Arnprior, Ontario: Kichesippi Books, 1987), pp. 11–14.

46. In eurocentric linguistic traditions, this consciousness is called the "Macro-Algonkian Phylum." Typically, it is subdivided into two different branches: the Algic and the Gulf. C. F. and F. M. Voegelin, *Classification and Index of the World's Languages* (New York: Elsevier, 1977).

47. H. P. Biggar, *The Works of Samuel de Champlain* (Toronto: Champlain Society, 1922–1936) vol. 1, p. 105ff.

48. O. P. Dickason, *Canada's First Nations* (Edmonton, University of Alberta Press, 1992), pp. 63–67.

49. K. E. Von Maltzahn, *Nature as Landscape: Dwelling and Understanding* (Montreal and Kingston: McGill-Queen's University Press, 1994), pp. 3–6.

50. The sounds of the languages put a great emphasis on prefixes and suffixes and syntax around a "verb" structure to express meanings. There is no concept of a sentence, each sound serving that purpose. Previously, I have attempted to explain the relationship, in J. Y. Henderson, *Governing the Implicate Order* (Ottawa: Centre of Linguistic Rights, University of Ottawa, 1995), pp. 287–314.

51. See Åke Hultkrantz, "The Problem of Christian Influence on Northern Algonkian Eschatology," in *Belief and Worship in Native North America* (Syracuse: Syracuse University Press, 1981), pp. 187–211. No concept of Supreme Being was originally part of Northern Algonkian thought.

52. For example, in Míkmaq, Creator is called *Kisúlkw*, the Savior is *Kisúlkwl or Westaúlkw.* In Cree, to create is *osihiwew* or *ositchikew*, Creation is *osihiwewsin* or *ositchikewin*, and Creator is *osihiwew*, Fr. G. Beaudet, *Cree-English, English-Cree Dictionary* (Winnipeg: Wuerz Publishing, 1995), p. 122.

53. W. K. Powers, "The Plains," in I. E. Sullivan (ed.), *Native American Religions: North America* (New York: MacMillan Publishing, 1987), p. 23.

54. The process of maintaining Míkmaq consciousness is called *tlilnuo'lti'k*, and is distinguished from the process of maintaining their thought, sounds, or language, which is signified by the sound *tlinuita'sim*.

55. M. A. Reddy (ed.), *Statistical Record of Native North Americans* (Detroit, MI: Gale Research Inc., 1993), p. iii.

56. Battiste, "Micmac Literacy and Cognitive Assimilation," supra note 42.

57. See *Report of the United Nations Seminar on the Effects of Racism and Racial Discrimination on the Social and Economic Relations between Indigenous Peoples and States*, Commission on Human Rights, 45th Sess., U.N. Doc. E/CN.4/1989/22 (1989).

58. K. Rahner, "Towards a Fundamental Interpretation of Vatican II," *Theological Studies*, 40 (1979): p. 717.

59. For example, *Letter of Apology from Christian Churches of Seattle, Washington, of November 21, 1987* (Seattle: Native American Task Force on The Church Council of Greater Seattle); *An Apology to Aboriginal Peoples of Canada from the Presbyterian Church of Canada* (Winnipeg, Manitoba, November 17, 1995).

60. Canadian judges have proved resourceful in devising their own limitations to constitutional rights, see, for example, *The Queen v. Sparrow* [1990] 1 S.C.R. 1075.

61. For an exception, see M. Marshall and D. L. Schmidt (eds. and trans.), *Míkmaq Hieroglyphic Prayers: Reading in North America's First Indigenous Script* (Halifax: Nimbus Publishing, 1995). This is related to the other Algonquian writing script, rock art, and symbols.

62. M. Stogre, *That the World May Believe: The Development of Papal Social Thought on Aboriginal Rights* (Sherbrooke, QC: Éditions Paulines, 1992).

63. L. Little Bear, "What's Einstein Got to Do With It?" in R. Gosse, J. Y. Henderson, and R. Carter (eds.), *Continuing Poundmaker and Riel's Quest: Presentations Made at a Conference on Aboriginal Peoples and Justice* (Saskatoon: Purich Publishing, 1994), pp. 69–78, especially, pp. 74–75.

64. Old Tasse in N. S. Hill, Jr. (ed.), *Words of Power: Voices from Indian America* (Golden, Colorado: Fulcrum Publishing, 1994), p. 36.

65. Champagne (ed.), pp. 658–83.

66. Vecsey, *Handbook* pp. 12–15.

67. See Champagne (ed.), p. 472.

Chapter 12

Expansion and Constriction of Religion: The Paradox of the Indian Secular State

Robert D. Baird

India provides an interesting window for examining the relationship between religious conscience, the state, and law. It is a land in which ancient traditions live on alongside modernity. Some 80 percent of the 850 million Indians are classified as Hindus. So, although it is not a Hindu State, India has the world's largest population of "Hindus." Into a context in which the state traditionally protected and supported "Hinduism" or "Islam," depending on the rulers' convictions, India became an independent secular state with a constitution of her own choosing which embodied many of the modern human rights that grew out of the Enlightenment.

Traditional Hindu law was based on an assumed hierarchy of inequality that provided differing penalties not only for different crimes, but for difference of caste or gender of the one who committed the infraction. The Constitution of India, by contrast, mandates the expansion of rights, including religious rights, to all persons regardless of caste, gender or religion. Although the term *secular* was not inserted into the Preamble until the emergency of 1976, not only was India consistently designated a "Secular State,"[1] but by highlighting the concepts of *justice,* liberty, equality, and fraternity, The Constitution of India reads like a document with roots in enlightenment thought. The original preamble states the following:

WE, THE PEOPLE OF INDIA, having solemnly resolved to constitute India into a
SOVEREIGN DEMOCRATIC REPUBLIC and to secure to all its citizens:

JUSTICE, social, economic, and political;
LIBERTY of thought, expression, belief, faith and worship;
EQUALITY of status and opportunity; and to promote among them all
FRATERNITY assuring the dignity of the individual and the unity of
the Nation;
IN OUR CONSTITUENT ASSEMBLY this twenty-sixth day of
November, 1949, do
HEREBY ADOPT, ENACT, AND GIVE TO OURSELVES THIS CON-
STITUTION.

Articles 25 and 26 of this constitution grant all persons (not merely
citizens) entitlement to freely "profess, practice, and propagate religion."[2]
Religious institutions are granted the right to manage their own affairs in
matters of "religion." These rights are not unqualified, however. They are
subject to "public order, morality, and health," to regulating practices closely
related to "religion" that might be deemed "secular," and to the opening of
Hindu religious institutions, particularly temples, to all classes of Hindus.
Since persons previously identified as "untouchables" were systematically
excluded from the inner parts of temples on the grounds that they would
pollute the deity, and since the reason for that exclusion was considered
religious, this provision required a reformulation of religious practice. Although religiously, Sikhs, Buddhists, and Jains might be considered distinct
religions, as a matter of law, all are considered "Hindus."[3]
    Article 44 goes somewhat further in advising the future Parliament to
adopt a uniform civil code for all citizens regardless of religious tradition.
It reads, "The state shall endeavour to secure for the citizens a uniform civil
code throughout the territory of India."[4] Although this article is found in a
section titled "Directive Principles," and is not therefore judicable, one step
in the direction of a uniform civil code was taken with the passage of the
bills referred to as the "Hindu Code" in 1955–1956. Even though forty-six
years later, most Muslims still resist the implementation of a uniform civil
code, there is growing discussion by Hindus on the political right as well
as statements from the Supreme Court of India urging that this directive
principle be fulfilled.
    The ultimate arbiter of the meaning of constitutional provisions is the
Indian court system, culminating in the Supreme Court of India. I will
proceed by analyzing several Supreme Court cases that restrict religious
conscience by limiting actions that practitioners profess to be dictated by
their religion. I am here dealing with cases that constrict the sphere of
"religion." Of course, one may *believe* anything one wants unless beliefs
result in activity that runs counter to constitutional principles.

The Constriction of Religion

The Constitution of India not only grants freedom to profess, practice, and propagate "religion." It also defines an area of existence closely related to religion," namely "the secular," which is to be controlled and regulated by the state. Moreover, although a religious denomination has the right to "manage its own affairs in matters of religion," the Supreme Court has determined that a denomination does not have the power to determine the extent of the realm of "religion."[5]

It should come as no surprise to learn that economic matters connected with religious institutions are secular matters and can be regulated and even managed by government. In *Commissioner, Hindu Religious Endowments, Madras v. Sirur Mutt*,[6] it was conceded that the determination of what rituals were necessary in a temple was a "religious" determination, but that the scale of expenses, being economic, was "secular" and could be controlled by the government without interfering with religious freedom. Financial matters, and the acquiring and administering of property are "secular" matters. Hence, there is no interference with "religion" if a governmentally appointed commissioner oversees the daily affairs of the temple, for that is a "secular" matter.[7] When Sikhs contested governmental action legislating the method of representation on the board that manages their Gurdwaras, it was determined that the manner of representation was "secular" and could be determined by the state.[8] When an appeal regarding the extent of the Shri Jagannath Temple Act of 1954 reached the Supreme Court, the realm of the "secular" was broadened, thereby further constricting the realm of "religion."[9] It was argued that the Raja of Puri, who had exercised both religious and economic authority over the Shri Jagannath Temple, was deprived of his religious rights. Not only did the Supreme Court uphold the right of the state to regulate and oversee the daily affairs of the temple, it also found that the governmentally appointed committee had the power to determine what rites should be performed to conform to the "Record of Rights." It was held that such a determination was "secular." When the priests performed those rituals so mandated by the Committee, what they were doing was religious. This power of the Committee to mandate which rituals must be performed was not considered an interference with "religion" since it was intended to maintain religious integrity.

The priests of south Indian temples traditionally served hereditarily. In a desire to guarantee that priests would be qualified to perform the essential rites, The Tamil Nadu Hindu Religious and Charitable Endowments (Amendment) Act (1970) eliminated hereditary appointment of temple priests and allowed government considerable power in making such appointments. The petitioners argued that setting aside hereditary rights was an interference with religious freedom, and that if Saivites were appointed to Vaisnava temples or visa versa, the images would be polluted. The Supreme Court examined the relevant *Agamas* and conceded that such appointments would be polluting and would be inappropriate.[10] So long as Saivite priests were appointed to Saivite temples and Vaisnava priests to Vaisnava temples, the act of appointment was a "secular" act. It was "secular" since it was not essential to religious practice.

In the above cases, although religious denominations were given freedom to manage their own affairs in matter of "religion," they did not possess the power to determine the extent of the sphere of "religion." As a result, that sphere was constricted. Traditionally, the valuation of religion extended to every aspect of life. With the new categories of "religion" and the "secular," government had a means of constricting the sphere of "religion." There is one final illustration of this constriction.

Article 44 of The Constitution of India places a moral obligation on Parliament to enact a uniform civil code for all of India. At the time of independence, not only were Muslims and Hindus governed by differing laws regulating marriage, divorce, and inheritance, but there existed no unity on such matters, neither among all Hindus nor among all Muslims. Neither community was in favor of such a code since it of necessity involved the secularization of law.[11] *The Report of the Hindu Law Committee* reveals that the Hindu Law Committee, which traveled to population centers throughout India, found almost universal opposition to the codification of Hindu law by the state.[12] Representatives of various Hindu religious groups argued that Hindu law was religious and therefore outside the scope of governmental authority. Although Parliament was unsuccessful in passing a comprehensive "Hindu Code Bill," it did pass a series of bills in 1955–1966 that covered the same matters.[13] Not only were these bills intended for all "Hindus," and provided a "system" of law for such matters, but they also *reconfigured* Hindu law on modern principles. Some of the issues that were most objectionable were captured by the Shastra Dharma Prachar Sabha in a pamphlet titled *Why Hindu Code Bill Is Detestable.*[14]

> Yet these vicious bills are directed to (1) provide for intercaste marriage, (2) Sagotra marriage, (3) introduce divorce, (4) make bigamy punishable by law, and (5) give a married daughter share in her father's property. The bills go against fundamental principles of the Hindu Shastras, God's spoken words, on which the society is based.

These changes were nevertheless made, over a considerable chorus of protest. Questions of monogamy, divorce, and inheritance were considered by Parliament to be "secular" matters to be decided on principles of equality, rationality, science, and social utility.

Although there were those who, like Nehru, considered the passage of these bills as the first step toward a uniform civil code, in the intervening forty-six years, no further steps have been taken. Muslim law has remained untouched, permitting multiple wives, divorce by triple talak, and leaving inheritance largely within the domain of males. While the Bharatiya Janata Party (BJP) has again raised the issue of a uniform civil code, until now the Hindu majority has been reluctant to legislate for the Muslim minority. Muslims still resist with vigor the secularization of their civil law.

Nevertheless, the secularization of law is another area in which the sphere of "religion" has been constricted. The Constitution commands the State to regulate such matters. It has already done so for Hindus. The principle exists for doing the same for Muslims. Only an adverse political fallout and the threat of violence has inhibited the full implementation of Article 44. This much is indisputable: to the extent to which the state assumes jurisdiction for determining the content of family law, to that extent the realm of "religion" has been constricted.

Constrictions on Religion

Not only has the sphere of "religion" been constricted, but once that sphere has been determined by the Constitution and the courts, it becomes subject to constrictions of its own.

In one sense, the treatment of religious freedom in the courts has expanded the scope of religious expression for numerous Hindus. If all Hindus are to be admitted to temples and if women as well as men are to be treated equally before the law, that is surely an expansion of religious expression for many.

Nevertheless, the expansion of religious opportunities for certain segments of the "Hindu" population, has necessitated the constriction and reformulation of "religion" for others. We have already seen that this has taken place as a result of excluding certain activities from the sphere of "religion" and thereby opening it to governmental supervision and control. Even after the sphere of "religion" has been constricted, however, there are further constrictions imposed on that newly defined sphere.

These constrictions are largely the result of a conscious determination by the Constituent Assembly. All persons are granted the right freely to profess, practice, and propagate religion. But this is subject to "public order, morality and health." Therefore, if a Hindu festival procession intends to play religious music as it passes by a Mosque, and if, in the judgment of city officials, this might lead to violence, the permit may not be issued. Such free expression is subject to "public order." If the gathering of millions of Hindus at Allahabad to participate in the Kumbha Mela presents the threat of the spread of disease, government may set up inoculation barriers and other health facilities and impose a variety of other regulations. This is within its jurisdiction since the freedom of religious expression is subject to health. If legislatures pass bills making the dedication of devadasis illegal, that is within their jurisdiction since the prostitution connected with certain devadasi practices is considered immoral. And, freedom of religion is subject to "morality." This last category is most subject to change according to popular values at a given time and place. In addition to the above three qualifications on religious freedom, nothing can prevent the state from "providing for social welfare and reform or the throwing open of Hindu religious institutions of a public character to all classes and sections of Hindus."[15]

I now turn to several Supreme Court cases which placed further constrictions *on* "religion." In *Sri Venkataramana Devaru v. State of Mysore*,[16] the Gowda Saraswath Brahman sect contended that the Madras Temple Entry Authorization Act (1947), which opened their temple dedicated to Sri Venkataramana to all Hindus, was in violation of Article 26(b) of the Constitution. They held that participation in temple worship was a matter of "religion." Admitting the precedent that "religion" includes practices as well as beliefs, the court proceeded to determine whether or not exclusion of a person from a temple was a matter of "religion" according to "Hindu ceremonial law." The Court observed that, along with the growth of temple worship, there also grew a body of literature called *Agamas,* which offered instructions on temple construction, the placing of the deities, and degrees of participation. On one such text, the court commented as follows:

> In the Nirvachanapaddathi, it is said that Sivadwijas should worship in the Garbhagriham, Brahmins from the ante chamber or Sabah Mantabham, Kshatriyas, Vyasias [*sic*] and Sudras from the Mahamantabham, the dancer and musician from the Nrithamantabham east of the Mahamantabham, and the castes yet lower in scale should content themselves with the sight of the Gopurum.[17]

In a 1908 case, *Sankarakinga Nadam v. Raja Rajeswara Dorai*, it had been held by the Privy Council that trustees, who agreed to admit persons into the temple whom the *Agamas* did not permit, were guilty of breach of trust.[18] The court could not avoid the conclusion that the matter of temple entry was a matter located within the sphere of "religion."

> Thus under the ceremonial law pertaining to temples, who are entitled to enter into them for worship and where they are entitled to stand and

worship and how the worship is to be conducted are all matters of religion.[19]

But the issue did not end there. Article 25(2)(b) provided that nothing in the Article should prevent the state from making a law "providing for social welfare and reform or the throwing open of Hindu religious institutions or a public character to all classes and sections of Hindus."

The Supreme Court recounted the position of "Hindu social reformers" whose work culminated in Article 17, which abolished "untouchability." Some Indians had been denied access to roads and public institutions "purely on grounds of birth" and the court asserted that this was not defensible on "any sound democratic principle." The court concluded that there were two constitutional principles, Article 26(b) and 25(2)(b), which were in conflict. Moreover, they were also of equal authority. Appeal was made to the "rule of harmonious construction" whereby two conflicting provisions are interpreted so as to give effect to both. In an attempt to accommodate both provisions, the court opened the temple to all classes of Hindus, while preserving the right of the denomination to exclude the general public from certain specific religious services. The court felt it had given effect to both provisions since even after the limited exclusions, "what is left to the public of the right of worship is something substantial and not merely the husk of it."[20] While low-caste Hindus who had previously been excluded from temple worship and were to "content themselves with the sight of the Gopurum," were permitted entry and thereby given an expanded range of religious expression, traditional faith was constricted and had to be reformulated in the light of this Supreme Court judgment.

The nature of the freedom to propagate one's religion has been a matter of controversy in India for some time. The question of whether or not to include such a provision in the Constitution was thoroughly debated in the Constituent Assembly. Both Muslims and Christians have commonly considered propagation as an essential part of their religious faith. Hindus have been less inclined in this direction historically, although in recent history the Arya Samaj has made a concerted effort at Shuddhi, which involved an attempt to convert persons back to Hinduism.[21]

Several ideologies are at work here, along with a psychological fear. Ideologically, those Hindus who hold that all religions are essentially the same see no point to people changing faiths. In the Constituent Assembly, Tajamul Husain, a Muslim, agreed that people should have the right freely to profess and practice religion. But, since in his view religion was a personal matter between an individual and his Creator, and since each individual will achieve salvation within his or her own religion, there is no point to propagation. And, since India is a secular state, the state should have nothing to do with religion. "I submit, Sir, that this is a secular State, and a secular State should not have anything to do with religion. So I would request you to leave me alone, to practice and profess my religion privately."[22]

Although Lokanath Misra, a Hindu, did not feel propagation should be ruled out, he was not in favor of placing it as a fundamental right that would encourage it. He voiced a frequently expressed fear that propagation will swell the numbers of other religions at the expense of "Hinduism" and thereby pave the way for the annihilation of Hindu culture and the Hindu way of life.[23] It is important to note that in each of these arguments, it is assumed that propagation will lead to conversions from one religion to another.

If Husain and Misra favored outlawing or limiting propagation, there were others who argued that it should be protected. Pandit Lakshmi Kanta Maitra argued that in a secular state there should be no discrimination on the basis of religion. Furthermore, we live in an irreligious age, and if we are to restore religious values it is important to be able to propagate them. He continues:

> Propagation does not necessarily mean seeking converts by force of arms, by the sword or by coercion. But why should obstacles stand in the way if by exposition, illustration and persuasion you could convey your own religious faith to others? I do not see any harm in it.[24]

L. Krishnaswami Bharati argued that all religions are one and the same if understood properly. Since it is only the same God under different names, there can be no harm to propagation.[25] K. M. Munshi argued that whatever advantages the Christian community might have had under the British, there will be no such advantage under a secular state in which everyone is treated equally regardless of their religion. He saw it as unlikely that any community could gain a political advantage through propagation.

> In the present set-up that we are now creating under this Constitution, this is a secular state. There is no particular advantage to a member of one community over another, nor is there any political advantage by increasing one's fold. In those circumstances the word "propagate" cannot possibly have dangerous implications, which some of the members think that it has.[26]

When it became apparent that the right to propagate would stand, several attempts were made to limit it by making it impossible to convert someone under eighteen years of age or through coercion or undue influence. None of these proposals made it into the Constitution. And, since independence, attempts to pass a national law that would restrict propagation and conversion have all failed.

Three states, however, have passed bills that have placed restrictions on the propagation of religion. The Orissa Freedom of Religion Act (1967) sees the attempt to convert as involving "an act to undermine another's faith."[27] According to this act, the attempt to convert often involves force, fraud, and material inducements. The result is "various maladjustments in social life" which give rise to "problems of law and order."[28] In the light of such circumstances, to place certain constrictions on propagation to convert is not a restriction on freedom of religion. Rather it is seen as a protection of religious freedom for those whose faith is being undermined. Particularly vulnerable were minors, women, and members of a scheduled caste, and penalties were more severe for persons who violated the provisions of the bill in their regard.

The Madhya Pradesh Dharma Swatantrya Adhiniyam (1968)(a state-level Hindu organization) questioned the sincerity of many conversions and again in the interest of public order, conversions by "force or allurement or by fraudulent means" were prohibited.[29] This bill required the registration of conversions with the District Magistrate.

The Arunachal Pradesh Freedom of Indigenous Faith Bill (1978), or simply the Freedom of Religion Act, as it was renamed, focuses on "indigenous faiths, including such named 'communities' as 'Buddhism,' 'Vaishnavism,' and nature worship."[30] Prohibited were shows of force or threats that were interpreted to include the "threat of divine displeasure or social excommunication."[31] This act also required the registration of conversions. These restrictions and their intention is seen by Neufeldt as follows:

> Conversion from indigenous faith is not only to be discouraged, but, as far as possible, prevented. Indigenous faith and nationalism are in some respects seen as synonymous. While conversions from indigenous faith are not welcome, no such attitude to conversions back to indigenous faith is expressed. The content of sermons, exhortations, or religious literature can be deemed to be unlawful if these include references to divine displeasure. Presumably this would apply only to sermons, exhortations, and literature in the context of non-indigenous faith. . . . Presumably it could be used in the other direction.[32]

These state bills did not go without challenge. Rev. Stanislaus of Raipur challenged the Madhya Pradesh Act by refusing to register conversions. The High Court upheld the act by stating that freedom of religion must be guaranteed to all, even those who are subject to conversions by "force, fraud, or allurement." When the Orissa Freedom of Religion Act was challenged in the

High Court of Orissa, the decision went in the opposite direction on grounds that the definition of "inducement" was too broad and that only Parliament had the power to enact such legislation.

The Supreme Court heard both of these cases together and ruled in favor of the acts. A distinction was made between the right to propagate and the right to convert. The former was allowed while the latter was seen as not part of the fundamental rights. Referring to Article 25(1), Chief Justice Ray, writing for the court, held:

> What the Article grants is not the right to convert another person to one's own religion, but to transmit or spread one's religion by an exposition of its tenets. It has to be remembered that Article 25(1) guarantees "freedom of conscience" to every citizen, and not merely to the followers of one particular religion and that, in turn, postulates that there is no fundamental right to convert another person to one's own religion because if a person purposely undertakes the conversion of another person to his religion, as distinguished from his effort to transmit or spread the tenets of his religion, that would impinge on the "freedom of conscience" guaranteed to all the citizens of the country alike.[33]

This distinction between conversion and propagating simply for "the edification of others" was previously stated in *Ratilal v. State of Bombay*[34] which was appealed to as a precedent. Whatever else might be said about these bills and their treatment by the Supreme Court, it is at least the case that they present another constriction placed on the realm of religion as constitutionally understood.

Even though the Supreme Court presumably spoke definitively in 1977, the issue continues to generate controversy. A recent issue of *India Abroad* reported that an eighty-eight-year-old priest and a fifty-year-old nun had been sentenced and incarcerated for violating the Madhya Pradesh Bill by failing to register religious conversions. Father L. Bridget and Sister Vridhi Ekka failed to report the conversion of ninety-four Oraon tribespeople in 1988. They were sentenced to six months in jail and a fine of 500 rupees. They were granted bail and given thirty days to appeal. The news report states:

> After examining the converted tribespeople, the judge said on January 22 that the accused missionaries had not coerced or lured their followers, but they could not escape punishment because they did not inform the district chief of the change of religion within seven days as required under the law.[35]

Hindu Sentiment and Constriction on Religion

In secular states, where attention to "religion" is presumed to be a private matter, "religion" still enters the public arena, particularly if there is a strong cultural and religious dimension that defines the majority community. Since some of India's literary classics such as the *Mahabharata* and the *Ramayana* are also religious classics, it is difficult to exclude them from the public arena. Nevertheless, if they are read over *All India Radio* or if serial episodes of *Ramayana* appear on Sunday mornings on *Doordarshan*, they may excite the Hindu public while raising questions in the minds of the Muslim minority as Hindu themes appear to receive public support. When prime ministers of a secular state engage in *bhumi puja* (a form of deity worship) to open a new bridge or branch of the law faculty of Delhi University, or when *Saraswati puja* (worship of the goddess of wisdom) is performed in public schools, one need not be surprised when minorities raise questions of legitimacy.

In none of these instances, however, do we have a case in which a religious sentiment of the majority community results in legal activity that restricts the lives of those not sharing the sentiment. One instance where this does occur, however, is cow slaughter. It does not need to be labored that most Hindus venerate the cow. Even Hindus, who eat fish or mutton, seldom eat beef. Gandhi would only use leather from the carcasses of fallen cattle. So strong is this feeling that there have been moves to establish *gosodans* or old-age cow farms where cows who have exhausted their usefulness can live out their lives until they die a natural death.

During the Constituent Assembly, there was even an attempt to place an anticow slaughter article among the list of Fundamental Rights. Since, in a secular state, religious sentiments are not to be part of constitutional and legal deliberations, frequently the argument took the form of an economic argument. It would be argued that India needed cows for milk, draught, and dung and that to kill them would be to deplete an important dimension of India's rural economy. Nevertheless, alongside the economic arguments, the religious sentiment appeared. Hindu society has included the cow in its fold according to Shri R. V. Dhulekar who spoke at the Constituent Assembly.

> I can declare from this platform that there are thousands of persons who will not run at a man to kill that man for their mother or wife or children, but they will run at a man if that man does not want to protect the cow or wants to kill her.[36]

Professor Shibban Lal Saksena recognized both the economic argument and the religious sentiment and sought to forge a union of the two:

I personally feel that cow protection, if it has become part of the religion of the Hindus, it is because of its economic and other aspects. I believe that the Hindu religion is based mostly on the principles which have been found useful to the people of this country in the course of centuries.[37]

Although an article protecting the *cow* from slaughter did not find its way into the Fundamental Rights of The Constitution of India, an article to that effect was placed among the Directive Principles. Article 48 reads as follows:

The state shall endeavor to organise agriculture and animal husbandry on modern and scientific lines and shall, in particular, takes steps for preserving and improving the breeds, and prohibiting the slaughter, of cows and calves and other milch and draught cattle.

The Supreme Court case, which became a norm for all subsequent decisions was *M. H. Quareshi v. State of Bihar.*[38] This case involved a number of petitions against bills enacted on the state level, particularly the Bihar Act (1955–1956) and the Madhya Pradesh Act (1951). The petitioners were Muslim butchers who held that they were being deprived of their livelihood. Moreover, there was a religious practice that was thereby prohibited:

As a result of the total ban imposed by the impugned section the petitioners would not even be allowed to make the said sacrifice which is a practice and custom in their religion, enjoined upon them by the Holy Quran, and practised by all Muslims from time immemorial and recognized as such in India.[39]

The court responded that the requirement to sacrifice found in the *Qur'an* did not necessitate the slaughter of a cow, even though that had been the custom. Since sheep or camels could be substituted, the sacrifice could still be performed. After a lengthy discussion of the state of India's cows, and the admission that "there exists a surplus of useless and inefficient animals,"[40] the court still ruled that a total ban on the slaughter of cows was constitutional.

(i) that a total ban on the slaughter of cows of all ages and calves of cows and calves of she-buffaloes, male and female, is quite reasonable and valid and is in consonance with the directive principles laid down in Article 48 (ii) that a total ban on the slaughter of she-buffaloes or breeding bulls or working bullocks (cattle as well as buffaloes) so long as they are useful as milch or draught cattle is also reasonable and valid and (iii) that a total ban on the slaughter of she-buffaloes, bulls and bullocks (cattle or buffalo) after they cease to be capable of yielding milk or of breeding or working as draught animals cannot be supported as reasonable in the interest of the general public.[41]

Along with this case, there were others of less significance in terms of legal precedent and which stopped at the State High Court level.[42] Although religious sentiments seem to have been disregarded in High Court and Supreme Court decisions, some of these High Court cases contain the admission of widespread religious sentiment against cow slaughter. This accounts for the willingness of citizens to report infractions of these laws and ordinances as well as the tendency of local magistrates to set unreasonable penalties for such infractions. The following case illustrates the intrusion of religious sentiment.

In May, 1956, the police investigated a report that a cow was being slaughtered at the house of Phulu of the village of Saipur. Arriving at noon, they found three men including Phulu in the inner courtyard cutting the carcass of a cow into large pieces, while the other three men were cutting the large pieces into smaller ones. Phulu was arrested while the others fled. It was established that the slaughter took place between 4:30 and 6:30 A.M. and that the cow was not diseased. Those who fled were apprehended and they were given eighteen-month sentences. The appeal before the Sessions Judge of Budaund upheld the conviction. The High Court to which this case eventually came emphasized that at both lower levels no reason was given for what was considered an extreme sentence. And this was not an isolated instance. "This court is getting concerned at the punishment which subordinate courts have been thoughtlessly inflicting on persons found guilty of a breach of the Cow Slaughter Act, and has been reducing the imprisonment to the period already undergone."[43] The court then laid down some principles to be followed in sentencing and concluded that "one's political, sentimental or religious preconceptions should be strictly disregarded."[44]

The Supreme Court has determined that the anticow slaughter laws are in keeping with Article 48. There is no religious sentiment in this statement. But not only has religious sentiment entered into numerous local decisions, but it was also influential in placing Article 48 in the Constitution in the first place. Nevertheless, the court is not entirely out of it. As I put it elsewhere,

When the Court determined that to ignore the test of usefulness in the case of the slaughter of buffaloes is unconstitutional while the test of usefulness is irrelevant in the case of cows, that sentiment was surely taken into account. The Court did argue that given the need for bullocks for draught, uneconomical cows needed protection. But what economic argument could be given for protecting from slaughter a cow that gives no milk, is past breeding age, and is of no value for draught? The fact that they continue to produce dung would not have been sufficient to save the buffalo. Only religious sentiment can account for this ruling.[45]

Independent India, then, in an effort to expand freedom of religion to all of its residents, has constricted the realm of "religion" and has also constricted that redefined realm, requiring Hindus to reconfigure their religious practices in a variety of ways. It has also, in deference to the religious sentiment of Hindus, constricted certain freedoms for non-Hindus. No law forbids Hindus to slaughter the cow. But by denying that right to everyone, certain states have limited the practices of those for whom there exists no such religious sentiment.

To the extent that one person's freedom places limits on the freedom of another, freedom is never complete. The Indian state has had to make certain choices. By opting for a modern human Rights oriented Constitution, it has required religious persons both inside and outside the Hindu community to reconfigure their practices and attitudes.

What is the extent of this reconfiguration and has it had an impact on the way people actually live their lives and make their daily decisions? Or, is it merely an interesting moment in the history of Indian law? There is no simple answer to these questions. For those situations that have come before the courts, the judicial decisions have had to be implemented even though this has often been accepted grudgingly. Temples have been opened to all classes of Hindus, and public facilities are broadly available to all. This is not to say that a *spirit of* equality and castlessness permeates the thinking of most Indians. The Constitution of India envisages a nation in which caste, gender, and religion are irrelevant to citizenship. But Muslims are still governed by Islamic law and a uniform civil code has yet to be enacted. Even the suggestion that such a code be implemented is unacceptable to most Muslims. Hindus have been no more eager to have their law secularized, but on the level of law it has been done. To the extent to which that law rules a land or a life, reconfiguration has taken place. However, it is not unique to India to observe that law often floats in an ideal realm somewhat above the daily decisions of life. The courts in India have an incredible backlog of cases. In the minds of many, law is a way that the rich use to harass the poor or wear them down until their meager resources are dissipated.

The question is not whether India is a secular state or not. That designation itself is susceptible to a wide range of definitions. But has India implemented the principles of its Constitution? In some areas it has, but there are many areas in which it has not. The lines dividing Muslims and Hindus has hardly diminished and the reservations of seats for backward groups has continued to grow. The Constitution and the courts have never seen secularity as a model devoid of religion. But whether Hindus and Muslims have received equal treatment at the hands of the Constitution, Parliament, and the courts is a matter of dispute and is basic to understanding the political uncertainty that engulfs India today.

Notes

1. " 'Secular State' and the Indian Constitution," in Robert D. Baird, *Essays in the History of Religions* (New York: Peter Lang Publishing, 1992), pp. 141–69.

2. Articles 25 and 26 of the Constitution read as follows:

25.(1)Subject to public order, morality and health and to the other provisions of this part, all persons are equally entitled to freedom of conscience and the right freely to profess, practise and propagate religion.
(2)Nothing in this article shall affect the operation of any existing law or prevent the state from making any law—
(a) regulating or restricting any economic, financial, political or other secular activity which may be associated with religious practise;
(b) providing for social welfare and reform or the throwing open of Hindu religious institutions of a public character to all classes and sections of Hindus.

Explanation I—The wearing and carrying of *kirpans* shall be deemed to be included in the profession of Sikh religion.

Explanation II—In subclause (b) of clause (2), the reference to Hindus shall be construed as including a reference to persons professing the Sikh, Jaina, or Buddhist religion, and the reference to Hindu religious institutions shall be construed accordingly.

26. Subject to public order, morality, and health, every religious denomination or any section thereof shall have the right—
(a) to establish and maintain institutions for religious and charitable purposes;
(b) to manage its own affairs in matters of religion;
(c) to own and acquire movable and immovable property; and
(d) to administer such property in accordance with law.

3. See my "On Defining 'Hinduism' as a Religious and Legal Category," in Robert D. Baird (ed.), *Religion and Law in Independent India* (New Delhi: Manohar, 1993), pp. 41–58.

4. See "Uniform Civil Code and the Secularization of Law," in Robert D. Baird, *Essays in the History of Religions* (New York: Peter Lang Publishing, 1991), pp. 171–200; and John H. Mansfield, "The Personal Laws or a Uniform Civil Code?" in Robert D. Baird (ed.), *Religion and Law in Independent India,* pp. 139–77.

5. *Panachand Gandhi* v. *State of Bombay* (1954), 7 S.C.J. 487.

6. *The Supreme Court Journal*, vol. XXVI, 1954, 348.

7. *Digyadarshan R.R. Varu v. State of A.P.*, [1970] A.I.R. 181 (S.C.).

8. *Sardar Sarup Singh v. State of Punjab* (1959), 22 S.C.J. 1123.

9. *Bira Kishore v. State of Orissa* [1964] A.I.R. 1501 (S.C.).

10. *Seshammal and Others v. State of Tamil Nadu, Supreme Court Cases* (1972), 2 S.C.J., 11ff.

11. See my "Uniform Civil Code and the Secularization of Law," in *Essays in the History of Religions,* pp. 171–200.

12. Report of the Hindu Law Committee (Government of India Press, 1955).

13. There were four bills passed: Hindu Marriage Bill, Hindu Succession Bill, Hindu Minority and Guardianship Bill, and Hindu Adoptions and Maintenance Bill.

14. *Why Hindu Code Bill Is Detestable* (Calcutta and Allahabad: Shastra Dharma Prachar Sabha, n.d.), p. 41.

15. Article 25(2)(b).

16. (1958), 21 S.C.J. 382.

17. Ibid., p. 390.

18. [1904] I.L.R., 31 (Madras).

19. (1958), 21 S.C.J. 390.

20. Ibid., p. 396.

21. The mid-twentieth century has seen the emergence of the International Society for Krishna Consciousness (ISKCON), which has placed a strong emphasis on proselytizing.

22. *Constituent Assembly Debates,* 7, 818.

23. Ibid., p. 824.

24. Ibid., p. 833.

25. *Constituent Assembly Debates*, 7, 834.

26. Ibid., p. 837.

27. Lalit Mohan Suri (ed.), *The Current Indian Statutes* (Chandigarh, 1968), p. 5.

28. Ibid.

29. *The Yearly Digest of Indian and Select English Cases* (Madras, 1977), 2092.

30. Bojendra Nath Banerjee, *Religious Conversions in India* (New Delhi: Harnam Publications, 1982), p. 262.

31. Ibid.

32. Ronald W. Neufeldt, "To Convert or Not to Convert: Legal and Political Dimensions of Conversion in Independent India," in Robert D. Baird (ed.), *Religion and Law in Independent India* (New Delhi: Manohar, 1993), pp. 323–24.

33. *Rev. Stanislaus v. M.P.*, [1977] A.I.R. 911 (S.C.).

34. [1954] A.I.R. 391 (S.C.).

35. *India Abroad*, February 2, 1996, p. 46.

36. *Constituent Assembly Debates*, vol. VII, 577.

37. Ibid., p. 574.

38. 1958 21 S.C.J. 975.

39. Ibid., p. 986.

40. Ibid., p. 998.

41. Ibid., p. 1006.

42. *Dulla v. The State*, [1958] A.I.R. 198 (Allahabad); *Parasram Ji v. Imtiaz*, [1962] A.I.R. 22 (Allahabad); *Gadadhar v. State of West Bengal*, [1963] A.I.R. 565 (Calcutta); *Bafati v. State*, [1964] A.I.R. 106 (Allahabad); *Abdul Ameed v. Chitradurga Municipality*, [1965] A.I.R. 281 (Mysore); *Kitab Ali v. Santi Ranjan*, [1965] A.I.R. 22 (Tripura); *Babu v. Municipal Board, Kheri*, [1976] A.I.R. 326 (Allahabad).

43. *Dulla v. The State*, [1958] A.I.R. 198 (Allahabad).

44. Ibid., p. 204.

45. "Cow Slaughter and the New 'Great Tradition,' " in Robert D. Baird, *Essays in the History of Religions* (New York: Peter Lang Publishing, 1991), pp. 219–20.

Chapter 13

Religion and Public Education in Canada after the Charter

Elizabeth J. Shilton

Introduction[1]

Modern liberal-democratic states have sought in a variety of ways to facilitate the free exercise of religious practices and the free expression of religious beliefs. Typically these goals have been embodied in constitutional guarantees of freedom of religion, guarantees designed to keep the state strictly out of the business of regulating the nexus between religion and its citizens. The constitution of the United States, for example, guarantees the free exercise of religion, and provides additional constitutional insurance of state neutrality by prohibiting the "establishment" of religion.[2] The "establishment clause" is characterized as erecting an impermeable "wall of separation between church and state."[3] American constitutional guarantees have been invoked historically and frequently to invalidate governmental efforts to provide any measure of support for religion in the public education system.

The founders of the Canadian state adopted a very different constitutional model with respect to religion and public education. Far from constituting a "wall," Canada's founding constitutional approach to religion and education has been described with considerable accuracy as a "bridge" between church and state in matters of public education.[4] The most important span of that "bridge" is section 93 of the Constitution Act, 1867.[5] In empowering the provinces to make laws governing education, section 93 both guarantees rights with respect to denominational schools existing at the time of

Confederation,[6] and contemplates that provinces may make additional laws governing religion and education. In contrast to the American model, therefore, the Canadian constitution not only permits, but *mandates* a measure of state support for religious schools.

For more than a century since Confederation, religion and public education have maintained close contact in Canada. In several Canadian provinces, publicly funded denominational school systems, insulated by section 93 from legislative encroachment, exist side-by-side with a nondenominational public school system.[7] Several provinces provide a measure of financial support to religious schools, usually as part of a system of subsidies to private or independent schools, covering a spectrum from assistance for the purchase of authorized texts[8] to the payment of up to 75 percent of the standard per-pupil operating grant.[9]

At least until the advent of the charter, most provincial education acts also contemplated a role for religion in the public school system. For example, while the laws of both Manitoba and British Columbia require public schools to be secular and/or nonsectarian, religious "exercises" were permitted in Manitoba and required in British Columbia until quite recently.[10] Alberta's legislation allows the establishment of alternative school programs based on religion and culture;[11] the Edmonton school board has recently taken the step of establishing a nondenominational Christian public school under the school board's umbrella.

From Confederation to 1982, section 93 was the only significant constitutional fetter on governments legislating in the area of religion and education.[12] In 1982, however, the Canadian Charter of Rights and Freedoms came into force, guaranteeing freedom of conscience and religion and equality rights.[13] These individual rights have grafted somewhat unevenly upon an educational system in which religion has historically had a significant and constitutionally protected presence. In this chapter, I propose to explore the scope of these new charter rights against the constitutional backdrop provided by section 93.

The jurisprudence examining the role of freedom of religion and other charter rights in education is still at an early stage of its development.[14] To date, decisions have been strongly influenced by the American view that constitutional guarantees mandate publicly funded schools that are religion-free. I suggest, however, that a "wall of separation" may not be the appropriate metaphor for Canadian constitutional law as it monitors the relationship between religion and public education. No such metaphor can take adequate account of section 93, which I will argue contains significant untapped potential as a source of jurisdiction in the provinces to address the claims of religious groups to public funding for religious-based education.

Section 93 and the Original Constitutional Compromise[15]

Section 93 has been described as part of "the basic compact of Confederation," operating "to moderate religious conflicts which threatened the birth of the Union."[16] Section 93 has a number of distinct components. Section 93 (1) guarantees existing rights relating to denominational schools. In Ontario these were the schools of the Roman Catholic minority.[17] In Quebec, both Protestants and Catholics enjoyed pre-Confederation denominational rights.[18] Section 93 (2) explicitly harmonizes the scope of the constitutional guarantee as between Ontario and Quebec, extending to dissentient school boards in Quebec all the rights of denominational schools in Ontario. Section 93 (3) and (4) provide for a form of federal supervision of provincial jurisdiction over education for the protection of the denominational rights of religious minorities.

In restricting section 93 guarantees to existing denominational systems, the constitution entrenched denominational education only for "minority" religions.[19] Why were constitutional protections limited in this way? The answer lies almost certainly in the judgment of the founders that only religious minorities *required* constitutional guarantees for their schools in order to promote and preserve their religious faith through education. In 1867, Canada was overwhelmingly a Christian country; approximately 99.26 percent of the population was Christian. Roman Catholics comprised approximately 42 percent of the total population, albeit with a significant majority in Quebec.[20] The original constitutional compromise simply prevented religious majorities in each province from using their democratic power over the school system to impose their religious beliefs on children raised in other faiths.

The historical evidence is overwhelming that the founders fully embraced the notion that religion should play an important role in education. Public education was to be founded on Christianity and Christian principles.[21] Of Ontario, William Westfall writes:

> Egerton Ryerson, to whom is ascribed such praise for creating the system of public education, never questioned the necessity of religious instruction in his schools. Indeed, he hoped that the creation of a system of public education would expand the place of religion in the classroom by removing special privileges and creating "a common patriotic ground of comprehensiveness and avowed Christian principles. . . . [He] tied the study of practical subjects to the study of the Bible."[22]

Early Ontario education legislation reflects this foundational commitment to Christian religious principles.[23] Likewise in pre-Confederation Quebec the public (or "common") schools were "de facto," if not "de jure" denominational:

> the 1861 [Quebec] law does not prohibit denominational instruction in common schools. Nor does it prevent a school being given a denominational character. Indeed, it is for this reason that the educational system in general has a bi-denominational character in 1861, with on the one hand the majority schools, using the opportunity open to them under the Act of giving a school a denominational character, and on the other dissentient schools . . . the purpose of which was to be denominational in character.[24]

In both provinces, the "common" schools were simply the schools of the "other" denomination.

The Advent of the Charter: Religion and the Public Schools in Ontario

The Bill 30 Reference

That the "nondenominational" public education system would be *secular* was never part of the founding compromise. Subsequent developments in Canadian history have, however, shaken that founding compromise to its core. By the 1980s, it was clear that the constitutional understandings that had generated section 93 no longer reflected a social consensus. It was no longer the case that the principles of majoritarian democracy would protect Protestant hegemony in Ontario, or Roman Catholic hegemony in Quebec. While the majority of Canadians still claim a Christian heritage, most do not still subscribe to a personal faith. Immigration and other pressures on Canadian demographics have given shape and voice to substantial non-Christian religious groups. And last but not least, the charter has changed many of the rules about the relative rights of majorities and minorities in our society, endowing with a new and potentially powerful set of tools religious minority groups and others whose needs had not been well served by the founding constitutional arrangements.

The first case to test the relationship between section 93 and the charter was Ontario's Bill 30 Reference. Bill 30 involved a 1984 initiative by the Ontario government to augment its financial assistance to Roman Catholic separate schools. For many years, the province had provided funding in separate schools only to grade 10; it now proposed to fund separate schools to the end of secondary school. The primary argument advanced in favor of Bill 30 was that it rectified an historic constitutional injustice; champions of the bill maintained that limiting public support for denominational schools to grade 10 was an encroachment on an entrenched pre-Confederation right to public funding for a denominational "basic education."[25] Bill 30 forcefully focused the attention of both non-Catholic religious groups and proponents of secularism in education on the lack of symmetry between the treatment of Roman Catholics and other religions. Vigorous, vocal and well-financed lobbies against Bill 30 were mounted, and opponents of the bill argued that it contravened the charter. To resolve the constitutional doubts, the government launched a reference before the Ontario Court of Appeal.

Section 93 was unquestionably intended to survive the charter. Section 29 of the charter, anticipating a clash, explicitly provided as follows:

> Nothing in this Charter abrogates or derogates from any rights or privileges guaranteed by or under the Constitution of Canada in respect of denominational, separate or dissentient schools.

It is not therefore surprising that both the Ontario Court of Appeal and the Supreme Court of Canada upheld the legislation against charter challenge.[26] What is surprising is the basis on which they did so.

The courts refused to take the safe route mapped out for them by constitutional scholars who had predicted that they would seek to harmonize section 93 with charter rights by narrowly confining the "rights or privileges" encompassed within section 29 to those guaranteed under section 93 (1). They did not ground their decision on a finding that Roman Catholics in Ontario had a pre-Confederation right to a fully funded school system, although in fact a majority in the Supreme Court of Canada so found. Instead, they subscribed to two very broad holdings: (1) section 93 endows provinces with plenary power to legislate denominational rights and privileges, subject to section 93 (1) guarantees, and (2) any exercise of provincial legislative power in the area of denominational schools is immune from charter review, regardless of whether it involves section 93 (1) entrenched rights, or more contingent post-Confederation rights.[27]

The court emphasized that post-Confederation denominational rights and privileges are not "guaranteed" under section 93 in the same sense as pre-Confederation rights: "what . . . the province gives, the province can take away."[28] But in either the giving or the taking, the province is immune from review under the charter:

> The province is master in its own house when it legislates under its plenary power in relation to denominational, separate or dissentient

schools. This was the agreement at Confederation and, in my view, it was not displaced by the enactment of the Constitution Act, 1982.[29]

In the court's view, section 93 clearly contemplated that there would be unequal educational rights, enjoyed by some groups and not by others. To subject to charter review a power clearly intended to be used to make distinctions among groups would, on the court's view, be effectively to nullify that power.[30] While the charter is supreme over ordinary law, it was not intended to reign supreme over other parts of the constitution.

Section 93 emerged from its first clash with the charter not only unscathed, but with new vitality. Not only are rights under section 93 (1) not to be "read down" to accord with newer notions of equality and religious freedom, but in addition provinces are recognized as having power to enhance those denominational rights or create new ones without hindrance from the charter.

Religious Practices and Religious Instruction

The Bill 30 Reference affirmed that the provinces retain all their pre-charter power to pass laws in relation to denominational schools. Subsequent cases have made it clear, however, that their pre-charter power to deal with other aspects of religion and education have been significantly curtailed. Indeed charter guarantees of freedom of religion have made substantial inroads on important aspects of the founding compromise. In particular, the charter has demolished the Ryersonian vision of common schooling grounded on Christian principles.

In early charter cases, mostly outside the context of education,[31] the Supreme Court of Canada had recognized certain principles for the application of the "freedom of religion" guarantees under the charter. Freedom of religion was acknowledged as "the unimpeded freedom to hold, profess and manifest religious beliefs."[32] Both positive and negative aspects of the freedom were identified and protected: freedom to manifest and practice religion, and freedom from coercion to do so. These positive and negative freedoms necessarily included freedom from conformity: "[T]he practices of a majoritarian religion cannot be imposed on religious minorities." In the cases discussed in this part, the courts were faced with the task of applying these principles to the problem of religious practices and religious education in the public school system.

In *Re Zylberberg et al. and Director of Education of Sudbury Board of Education*[33] (hereinafter "*Zylberberg*") and *Re Corporation of the Canadian Civil Liberties Association and the Minister of Education* (hereinafter "*Elgin County*"),[34] two groups of parents challenged regulations under the Ontario

Education Act mandating religious opening and closing exercises and religious education in the public schools. While Ontario's Education Act[35] is permissive with respect to the offering of religious instruction and devotional exercises in the schools, the implementing regulation[36] clearly made devotional opening and closing exercises compulsory, and also required two periods a week of religious education.

The Ontario Court of Appeal readily came to the conclusion that the regulation, particularly in light of its history, was intended to promote indoctrination in the Christian religion. The court concluded that "teaching students Christian doctrine as if it were the exclusive means through which to develop moral thinking and behavior amounts to religious coercion in the classroom. It creates a direct burden on religious minorities and non-believers who do not adhere to majoritarian beliefs."[37]

Those defending the constitutionality of the regulation argued that without a requirement to take part in religious practices, there was no burden on the protected freedom.[38] The cases thus ultimately turned on the constitutional efficacy of the statutory right to claim exemption from participation in religious exercises and religious education. The constitutional impact of the exemption is discussed at length in the *Zylberberg* decision. The majority of the court found the exemption inadequate to save the regulation: "The peer pressure and the class-room norms to which children are acutely sensitive, in our opinion, are real and pervasive and operate to compel members of religious minorities to conform with religious practices."[39] The court characterized the obligation to request an exemption as an obligation to make a religious statement: far from mitigating the infringement, the exemption system itself penalized and stigmatized those who do not wish to participate in the practices of the dominant religion.[40] The court found a "chilling effect" on the free exercise of religion.[41]

In *Zylberberg*, the court found that the religious exercises at issue were constitutionally flawed because of their exclusively Christian character. The decision is somewhat ambiguous on the related question of whether exercises religious in nature but not exclusively Christian would have passed muster. The court hinted that a more inclusive and multicultural approach to religious exercises might be acceptable, but stopped short of making an actual finding to that effect.[42] Likewise, in *Elgin County*, the court did not explicitly come to grips with the issue of whether the problem is religion per se, or merely an exclusive focus on the Christian religion.[43] As in the *Zylberberg* case, the court made a clear finding that the purpose of the regulation, and of the Elgin County religious education curricula based on that regulation, was indoctrination in the Christian faith.[44] The more complex issue of whether opportunities for multifaith education within the school curriculum would be equally unconstitutional therefore did not arise.

Challenges similar to those in *Zylberberg* and *Elgin County* have been mounted in other provinces, and have produced similar results in the courts.[45] Consistent with the approach to freedom of religion espoused by the Supreme Court of Canada, it is now relatively settled law that majoritarian religious indoctrination and coercive religious practices are impermissible within the public school system.

The Adler Case[46]

The Ontario government did not appeal the *Zylberberg* and *Elgin County* decisions to the Supreme Court of Canada. Instead, it responded in 1990 by amending the offending regulation, eliminating the requirement for religious opening and closing exercise altogether, and prohibiting any form of doctrinal religious education during the instructional day.[47] Similar changes have followed in the other provinces in which legislation permitting religion in the public schools has been struck down.

But in some provinces the momentum has been in the opposite direction, toward enhancing the role of religion in the schools, even after the charter. For example, Alberta's law facilitating religious schools under the auspices of public school boards is a post-charter phenomenon. In Ontario, as well as in other provinces, governments and local school boards have been under considerable pressure to provide some measure of public support for religious schooling for groups in addition to the constitutionally protected Roman Catholics. As discussed in Part I, many provinces have long provided and continue to provide financial support to religious independent schools.

Outside of the context of section 93, the question of whether it is lawful for provinces to provide financial support for religious schools has, surprisingly, never been directly litigated. The important Ontario case of *Re Adler et al. and The Queen*[48] explores the far more radical possibility that the charter may actually require provinces to do so. The *Adler* case involved two applications, one brought by parents of children in independent Jewish schools, and another by parents of children in independent Christian schools. The issue in both applications, as described by the Court of Appeal, was "whether, by reason of sections 2(a) and 15 of the Canadian Charter of Rights and Freedoms, the Province of Ontario is now mandated through public funding to foster and facilitate religious education for all the diverse religious groups within Ontario."[49] The parent applicants argued that since the dictates of conscience and religion precluded them from educating their children in the public school system, the charter mandated public support for schools to which they *could* send their children: in other words, religious-based independent schools.[50]

The Court of Appeal emphatically rejected the claim that freedom of religion guarantees were violated by the failure of the state to fund independent religious schools. It characterized the Ontario legislation as leaving parents with a variety of choices for educating their children, including home schooling, publicly funded education in either the public or the separate school system, or independent schooling. The court held that because parental choice was not constrained by the legislation,[51] state action was not implicated: "It was their religion, and not the statute, that caused the appellants not to send their children to the publicly funded school system."[52]

The Court of Appeal likewise refused to find that the system of funding violated equality rights on the basis of religion. The applicants had based their discrimination argument on two grounds. First of all, they argued that if section 93 guaranteed Roman Catholic parents access to publicly-funded education for their children, charter equality principles required the extension of the same rights to other religious groups. The Court of Appeal categorically refused to allow the denominational system to be used as a constitutional lever.[53] Section 93, in its view, carved out a constitutional anomaly, which functions both to guarantee rights to the historically constitutionally privileged groups, and to prohibit other groups from claiming constitutional entitlement to similar rights.

Second, the parents argued that funding accorded to a "secular" education system alone was a legal benefit to the nonreligious, and imposed a discriminatory burden on religious parents who required religious education for their children in order to comply with the dictates of their conscience and religion. The court disagreed:

> If the absence of public funding for private religious schools creates a distinction, it is not one based on religion. The difference is between public schools managed and operated by duly elected school boards under the supervision of the Minister of Education and financed by property taxes and government grants, and private schools managed, operated and financed by private institutions.[54]

All five judges found no constitutional flaw in the refusal of the Province of Ontario to fund alternative religious school systems.[55]

The *Adler* case also raised the more circumscribed but equally interesting alternative issue of whether certain health services such as catheterization and physical therapy required by students with developmental disabilities, funded in public and denominational schools, should also be funded for students in independent religious schools. The majority of the court rejected this claim as well, taking the view once again that parents send their children to private schools by choice, and that section 93 immunized the availability of such services in Catholic schools from Charter review. Weiler J., dissenting, characterized the services as health services rather than educational services, and found it discriminatory on the basis of religion to provide health services in Catholic schools but not in other religious schools.

Toward a New Compromise: Where Does the Law Go from Here?

What do we know after these decisions about the role of religion in education? We know that religious coercion and majoritarian religious indoctrination is unconstitutional in nondenominational public schools. We know that religious minorities who did not enjoy the right to denominational schooling in 1867 cannot *require* the provinces to fund religious schools for their children, or even to fund public services within those schools. At the same time, we know that denominational schools themselves survive the Charter. We know that this lack of symmetry in not an inequality in law, but we also know that it is experienced as inequality by those religious groups who are not beneficiaries of section 93. What we do not yet know is whether Canada's constitutional arrangements permit provinces to "fix" this lack of symmetry should they see fit to do so.

It is arguable that the *Zylberberg* and *Elgin County* decisions leave somewhat more room within the public system for religion, and education about religion, than the Ontario government took advantage of in its 1990 amendments, which constitute a virtual "ban" on religion in the public schools. If the evil specifically at issue in the decisions was the imposition of Christianity in the schools, the province might have chosen a remedy less drastic than banishing religion altogether. In *Zylberberg*, for example, the court manifested considerable attraction to the multifaith, multicultural opening exercises adopted by the Toronto school board, exercises which drew on a wide variety of religious sources, both Christian and non-Christian. The court's gravest constitutional concern is properly reserved for the imposition of the doctrines of the majoritarian religion upon the minority. It is not clear that the Charter mandates a wholly secular school system, as opposed simply to one that is genuinely nonsectarian.

It is improbable, however, that there is or ought to be enough flexibility in the Charter to import generally into the public system a religious content that would meet the needs of many religious parents. A "lowest common denominator" approach would clearly be inadequate for parents, like the applicants in *Adler*, who take the view that religion and education go hand in hand, and that the spiritual welfare of their children and the survival of their religion depend on the maintenance of intimate links between the two.[56] Only schooling with a religious component as doctrinal and pervasive as that permitted within the section 93 denominational schools would truly accord with the dictates of their "conscience and religion." Is it constitutionally permissible for provinces to provide such an education at public expense?

The Court of Appeal in *Adler* hints that legislation funding religious schools might be constitutionally dubious.[57] Nevertheless, while rejecting a claim of constitutional entitlement, the court directs the applicants to the politicians:

> It is important to stress that it is not the role of the court to determine whether, as a matter of policy, public funding of private, religious-based independent schools is or is not desirable. That is for the legislature to decide. The sole issue before us is whether the absence of such funding is consistent with the Constitution of Canada.[58]

And there is indeed a serious argument to be made that provinces *have* the power to fund religious schools beyond the confines of section 93 (1) guarantees. The source of that power is the plenary post-Confederation section 93 power to legislate with respect to denominational schools invoked in the Bill 30 Reference.

Canada's highest courts have never been directly confronted with an exercise of section 93 powers to create entirely new post-Confederation religious schools. The Bill 30 Reference itself dealt only with the enhancement of an existing system. The courts have, however, both before and after the charter, interpreted section 93 as conferring a power to create new denominational rights. In 1928 in *Hirsch et al. v. Protestant Board of School Commissioners of Montreal*,[59] a case involving in part access to education for Jewish children, the Privy Council[60] was asked to respond to the question of "whether the provincial legislature can pass legislation to establish separate schools for persons who are neither Catholics nor Protestants." The court responded affirmatively, noting only that such powers could not be exercised in a way that infringed upon the denominational rights of Protestants and Catholics.[61] Again in 1993 in *Reference re: Education Act (Que.)* the Supreme Court of Canada, in approving a major reorganization of educational governance in Quebec along linguistic rather than denominational grounds, quoted *Hirsch* with approval, commenting specifically on "the legislature's power to create some other kind of school system, neutral or for denominations other than Catholics and Protestants."[62] While charter rights were not specifically at issue in that case, the court records no post-charter reservations about affirming the *Hirsch* principle.[63]

Under American constitutional law, state support of religion within the context of public education has been persistently found unconstitutional. It is important to keep in mind, however, that the issue of whether the state can lawfully provide financial support to religious schools is conceptually quite distinct from the question of whether the state can lawfully require children of different religious faiths, or none, to conform to Christian religious practices within nondenominational public schools. It has been argued elsewhere that the issue of tax support for religious education is exclusively a question of "establishment" rather than a question of freedom of religion.[64] In Canada, with a different constitutional tradition and without an establishment clause, it is far from clear that the outcome should be the same.

Our courts have been hesitant to date to justify distinctions between Canadian and American jurisprudential outcomes in religion cases by resort to semantic differences between constitutional guarantees, and in particular to the lack of an establishment clause in the charter.[65] And such distinctions could not safely be pushed too far. Nevertheless, at a minimum, section 93 should operate as an antidote to the facile importation into Canada of those aspects of the American "religion in the schools" jurisprudence that find their conceptual roots in the establishment clause rather than in the "freedom of religion" guarantees. The case law on financial support for religious schools clearly falls into this category.[66]

To argue, as I do, that governments may constitutionally fund religious schools outside the umbrella of section 93 (1) is not, of course, to say that they should. No one could gainsay the many complex policy questions that must be considered before embarking on such a venture. But neither can the political claims of religious minorities to equitable treatment be gainsaid.

The section 93 constitutional compromise is currently under some pressure. Demography and the charter are only two of the forces that threaten. Escalating deficits in all provinces have strained education funding in general, suggesting to some the wisdom of "consolidating" public and denominational school boards. Fiscal pressures were an important impetus behind the recent referendum in Newfoundland, which supported by a relatively narrow margin some significant modifications to the denominational rights protected by their Terms of Union with respect to denominational rights.[67] In addition, to the extent that section 93 takes its vitality from a "basic compact" between Upper and Lower Canada, the threatened secession of Quebec from Confederation may undermine many aspects of "the basic compact," including section 93.

The section 93 compromise, was at its birth a political compromise, and its survival, despite its constitutional entrenchment, will be ultimately a political question. Those with a stake in section 93 would do well to remember that. The likelihood that section 93 will endure beyond the inevitable next round of constitutional amendment might be considerably enhanced if it can operate as a tool to promote equity among religious groups rather than to engender yet deeper perceptions of inequity. I have argued that it offers that potential.

Notes

1. I gratefully acknowledge the assistance of colleagues Paul Cavalluzzo and Bernie Hanson, whose work on section 93 has been a valuable resource for me in this and other work.

2. The First Amendment provides that "Congress shall make no law respecting the establishment of religion, or prohibiting the free exercise thereof."

3. See *Everson v. Board of Education*, 330 U.S. 1 (1947). The metaphor is borrowed from Thomas Jefferson. I do not mean to suggest that the issue of the relationship between church and state, particularly in the area of public education, has been an entirely uncomplicated one in the United States, but the metaphor has endured in the jurisprudence.

4. Mr. Justice Lacourciere, diss. in part in *Re Zylberberg et al. and Director of Education of Sudbury Board of Education* (1988), 52 D.L.R. (4th) 577 (Ont. C.A.) at 610 and passim.

5. Formerly the British North America Act, 1867. Section 93 reads as follows:

In and for each Province the Legislature may exclusively make Laws in relation to Education, subject and according to the following Provisions—
(1) Nothing in any such Law shall prejudicially affect and Right or Privilege with respect to Denominational Schools which any Class of Persons have by Law in the Province at the Union:
(2) All the Powers, Privileges, and Duties at the Union by Law conferred and imposed in Upper Canada on the Separate Schools and School Trustees of the Queen's Roman Catholic Subjects shall be and the same are hereby extended to the Dissentient Schools of the Queen's Protestant and Roman Catholic Subjects in Quebec.
(3) Where in any Province a System of Separate or Dissentient Schools exists by Law at the Union or is thereafter established by the Legislature of the Province, an Appeal shall lie to the Governor General in Council from any Act or Decision of any Provincial Authority affecting any Right or Privilege of the Protestant or Roman Catholic Minority of the Queen's Subjects in relation to Education.
(4) In case any such Provincial Law as from Time to Time seems to the Governor General in Council requisite for the due Execution of the Provisions of this Section is not made, or in case any Decision of the Governor General in Council on any Appeal under this Section is not duly executed by the proper Provincial Authority in that Behalf, then and in every such Case, and as far only as the Circumstances of each Case require, the Parliament of Canada may make remedial Laws for the due Execution of the Provisions of this Section and of any Decision of the Governor General in Council under this Section.

6. Section 93 uses three different terms, *denominational, dissentient,* and *separate.* In this chapter, the term *denominational* refers generally to religious schools

protected under section 93 (1). The term "public schools" refers both in this chapter and in standard usage to nondenominational publicly funded schools.

7. Section 93 itself applies only to the four founding provinces, Ontario, Quebec, Nova Scotia, and New Brunswick; the latter two did not have denominational schools at the time of Confederation. As new provinces joined Confederation, they entered into constitutional terms of agreement that included provisions similar to section 93. Currently, Ontario, Quebec, Saskatchewan, Alberta, and Newfoundland have denominational school systems. In most of these provinces, Roman Catholics alone have protected denominational rights. In Newfoundland, a number of Protestant denominations were also given constitutional protection by the Terms of Union in 1947. There is now no denominational public system in Newfoundland: see p. 223, below. In Quebec, Protestants as a group have denominational rights.

8. In Nova Scotia, Prince Edward Island and Manitoba.

9. Alberta contributes up to 75 percent. Quebec, Manitoba, Saskatchewan, and British Columbia also provide some operating grant funding.

10. See *Re Russow et al. and Attorney-General of British Columbia* (1989), 62 D.L.R. (4th) 98 (B.C.S.C.); *Manitoba Association of Rights and Liberties Inc. et al. v. Government of Manitoba et al.* (1992), 94 D.L.R. (4th) 678 (Man. Q.B.)

11. *School Act*, S.A. 1988, c.S-3.1, sec. 16.

12. The concept of federalism has on occasion been brought into service for the protection of certain "fundamental freedoms": see Irwin Cotler, "Freedom of Assembly, Association, Conscience and Religion," *The Canadian Charter of Rights and Freedoms: Commentary*, W. Tarnopolsky and G. Beaudoin (eds.), (Toronto: Carswell Co., 1982), p. 165.

13. Section 2 of the charter provides that "everyone has the following fundamental freedoms: (a) freedom of conscience and religion." Section 15, which did not come into effect until 1985, provides that "every individual is equal before and under the law and has the right to equal protection and equal benefit of the law without discrimination and, in particular, without discrimination based on race, national or ethnic origin, colour, religion, sex, age, or mental or physical disability."

14. Important cases include *Re An Act to Amend the Education Act* (hereafter the *Bill 30 Reference*), [1987] 1 S.C.R. 1148; *Re Zylberberg et al. and Director of Education of Sudbury Board of Education* (1988), 52 D.L.R. (4th) 577 (Ont. C.A.); *Re Corporation of the Canadian Civil Liberties Association et al. and Minister of Education* (1990), 65 D.L.R. (4th) 1 (Ont. C.A.); *Adler et al. v. the Queen* (1994), 19 O.R. (3d) 1 (Ont. C.A.) aff'd (1996) 140 D.L.R. (4th) 385 (S.C.C.); *Re Bal et al. and Attorney-General of Ontario*, (1994), 21 O.R. (3d) 681 (Gen. Div.); *Re Russow et al. and Attorney-General of British Columbia* (1989), 62 D.L.R. (4th) 98 (B.C.S.C.); *Manitoba Association of Rights and Liberties Inc. et al. v. Government of Manitoba et al.* (1992), 94 D.L.R. (4th) 678 (Man. Q.B.).

15. This section draws on William Westfall, *Two Worlds: The Protestant Culture of Nineteenth-Century Ontario* (Kingston and Montreal: McGill-Queen's University Press, 1989); C. B. Sissons, *Church and State in Canadian Education: A Historical Study* (Toronto: Ryerson Press, 1959); Franklin A. Walker, *Catholic Education and Politics in Upper Canada,* vol. 1 (Toronto: The Catholic Education Foundation of Ontario, 1955); Egerton Ryerson, *Report on a System of Public Elementary Instruction (1846),* reprinted in J. George Hodgins (ed.), *Documentary History of Education in Upper Canada,* vol. 6 (Toronto, 1894–1910)

16 See *Re An Act to Amend the Education Act* (hereafter the *Bill 30 Reference*), [1987] 1 S.C.R. 1148 at 1174, per Wilson J. quoting Duff C. J.; see also *Reference re Education Act (Quebec)* (1993), 105 D.L.R. (4th) 266 (S.C.C.) at 277: "Section 93 has been unanimously recognized as the expression of a desire for political compromise."

17. Ontario provided a very limited right to establish Protestant separate school boards in any municipality in which the teacher was Roman Catholic. This right still exists: see *Education Act,* R.S.O. 1990, c.E.2, secs. 158–169. There is only one such board in Ontario, in Penetanguishene.

18. The pre-Confederation system in Ontario is thoroughly reviewed in the *Bill 30 Reference*; for a similarly detailed history of the pre-Confederation situation in Quebec, see *Quebec Association of Protestant School Boards et al. v. Attorney-General of Quebec* (1993), 105 D.L.R. (4th) 266 (S.C.C.).

19. Montreal and Quebec City were anomalous. In those urban centers, two pre-Confederation denominational systems coexisted: a Protestant system and a Catholic system, with no "common" system.

20. See M. H. Ogilvie, "What Is a Church Established by Law?" (1990), 28 *Osgoode Hall Law Journal* 179, pp. 193–94; Gordon Bale, "Reference re Funding for Roman Catholic High Schools," 11 *Supreme Court Law Review* (1989): 399, p. 404.

21. For many years, the *Ontario Education Act* required teachers "to inculcate by precept and example respect for religion and the principles of Christian morality." The section, still extant, now reads "Judaeo-Christian morality." This amendment was a late one, however: *Education Act,* S.O. 1974, c. 109, sec. 229 (1)(c); now *Education Act,* R.S.O. 1990, c. E.2, sec. 264(1)(c).

22. Westfall, p. 6.

23. The history of the commitment to Christian religious principles in Ontario education legislation is extensively reviewed in the *Zylberberg* and *Elgin County* decisions.

24. *Reference Re Education Act (Que.),* supra, note 16 at 279–80.

25. The Privy Council in 1928 had decided otherwise in *Tiny Separate School Trustees v. The King* [1928] A.C. 363, but both the history and the legal reasoning in that case have been severely criticized over the years, and the result was never accepted by the Catholic community.

26. *Bill 30 Reference* (1986), 53 O.R. (2d) 513 (C.A.); aff'd [1987] 1 S.C.R. 1148.

27. All the judges in the Supreme Court of Canada were prepared to make this finding even without resort to section 29; they were not prepared to hold that guarantees in other parts of the constitution were subject to the charter.

28. *Bill 30 Reference,* supra note 14, per Wilson J., p. 1198.

29. Ibid., per Wilson J., p. 1198.

30. Ibid., per Wilson J., pp. 1198–99; per Estey J., p. 1206.

31. The exception is *Jones v. The Queen* (1986), 31 D.L.R. (4th) 568, in which the Supreme Court of Canada rejected the claim of an Alberta father that certain aspects of education regulation in the province violated his freedom of religion.

32. The principles are the distillation by the Ontario Court of Appeal of the Supreme Court of Canada jurisprudence, as discussed in *Zylberberg,* supra note 4, pp. 588–89.

33. Supra note 4.

34. Supra note 14.

35. R.S.O. 1990, c. E.2, sec. 51 (formerly sec. 50).

36. R.R.O. 1980, Reg. 262 (*Education Act*), sec. 28.

37. *Elgin County,* supra note 14, p. 24.

38. *Zylberberg,* supra note 4, p. 590.

39. Ibid., p. 591.

40. Ibid., p. 592.

41. Ibid., p. 595. The court found that section 1 of the charter (the "reasonable limits" provision) could not be relied on to justify the infringement because the regulation had not only a religious impact, but also an unconstitutional religious purpose (pp. 596–97).

42. Ibid., p. 599.

43. *Elgin County,* supra note 14, p. 4.

44. Ibid., p. 40.

45. See *Re Russow et al. and Attorney-General of British Columbia* (1989), 62 D.L.R. (4th) 98 (B.C.S.C.); *Manitoba Association of Rights and Liberties Inc. et al. v. Government of Manitoba et al.* (1992), 94 D.L.R. (4th) 678 (Man. Q.B.).

46. This section discusses the judgment of the Ontario Court of Appeal. Since the Symposium, the Supreme Court of Canada (L'Heureux-Dube dissenting, McLachlin J. dissenting in part) has affirmed the decision of the Ontario Court of Appeal: see *Adler et al. v. The Queen* (1996) 140 D.L.R. (4th) 385. A majority of judges found

section 96 "a comprehensive code thereby excluding a different or broader obligation regarding denominational schools" (p. 407, per Iacobucci J.).

47. R.R.O. 1990, Reg. 298, secs. 28–29. The conservative Ontario government has passed a resolution in the house calling for a reintroduction of some form of religion in the public schools; no changes to the regulations have yet followed.

48. Supra note 14.

49. *Adler,* supra note 14 in the Court of Appeal, p. 6.

50. Ibid., pp. 7–8.

51. Ibid., p. 12.

52. Ibid., pp. 12, 25.

53. Ibid., p. 23.

54. Ibid., p. 23.

55. See also *Re Bal et al. and Attorney-General of Ontario et al.* (1994), 21 O.R. (3d) 681 (Gen Div.).

56. The judge at first instance in *Adler* accepted expert evidence that "the Jewish community's survival as an identifiable and practising religious community depends upon broad access for Jewish children to Jewish day schools": see *Adler,* supra note 14, p. 8.

57. *Adler,* supra note 14, pp. 18–19.

58. Ibid., pp. 6–7.

59. [1928] 1 D.L.R. 1041.

60. Until 1949, the Judicial Committee of the Privy Council sat on appeal from decisions of the Supreme Court of Canada.

61. *Hirsch,* supra note 59, pp. 1052–53.

62. (1993), 105 D.L.R. (4th) 266, p. 293.

63. Further support for the argument is found in *Adler v. The Queen,* supra, decided since the symposium, in which a majority of the Supreme Court of Canada explicitly sanctioned, albeit obiter, the use of the plenary provincial power under section 93 to fund other religious schools: "The province could, if it so chose, pass legislation extending funding to denominational schools other than Roman Catholic schools without infringing the rights guaranteed to the Roman Catholic Separate schools under section 93 (1)" (p. 407, per Iacobucci J.).

64. See, for example, Irwin Cotler, "Freedom of Assembly, Association, Conscience, and Religion," *The Charter of Rights and Freedoms: Commentary,* pp. 186–87, 201; this suggestion has been mooted in the cases at note 65, below.

65. See, for example, *R. v. Big M Drug Mart* (1985), 18 D.L.R. (4th) 321 (S.C.C.) per Dickson J. at 355–57; *Zylberberg,* supra note 15, at 594–95, and also per Lacourciere J. diss. in part at 604–14; *Adler,* supra note 14 at 18–19; see also *Jones v. The Queen* (1986), 31 D.L.R. (4th) 569 (S.C.C.), per Wilson J. at 576–77.

66. See also Richard S. Kay, "The Canadian Constitution and the Dangers of Establishment" (1992), 42 *DePaul Law Review* 361.

67. The constitutional amendment that was the subject of the referendum eliminated denominational school boards altogether, while retaining a right to denominational schools where numbers warrant. This amendment was finally ratified by the federal Parliament on December 4, 1996, not without considerable controversy about the appropriateness of abandoning minority rights on the basis of a simple majority vote. The senate refused to ratify, but under Canadian constitutional law a senate vote can delay but not ultimately defeat a constitutional amendment. The amendment became law on May 2, 1997. When the amendment proved unworkable because of a successful court challenge (see *Hogan* v. *Newfoundland* (1997), 149 D.L.R. (4th) 468 (Nfld, S.C.) a new amendment was put through abolishing denominational rights completely.

Chapter 14

The Cultural and Religious Heritage: Perspectives on the Muslim Experience

Azim A. Nanji

A Changing Religious Landscape

The religious and cultural landscape of North America and Europe has undergone dramatic changes in the second half of the twentieth century. Where non-Christian or non-Jewish groups might have been a mere exotic presence once, there are now established communities of Buddhists, Hindus, Muslims, Sikhs, Zoroastrians, and others who have become part of a more complex multifaith, multicultural society in both the "old" and the "new" worlds of the west.

This chapter examines the Muslim presence in North America and seeks to explore different levels of encounter within its dominant cultural and institutional patterns. The conversation of encounter over religious, cultural, and legal issues that has emerged since the development of greater pluralism in Europe and North America in the late twentieth century, often overshadows the alternative histories of encounter already present in the founding period of European discovery and settlement across the whole range of the Old and New Worlds. It is ironic that the year 1492, which marks the beginning of the voyages of Christopher Columbus to the Americas, was also the year of the Spanish conquest of Granada, marking the end of seven centuries of influence and rule by Muslims of the Iberian peninsula. The expulsion of Jews and Muslims from Spain that followed, destroyed what some scholars have regarded as a significant attempt in the medieval world, to create a pluralistic society. Bernard Lewis, in a recent study,[1] notes that Islamic Civilization, was universal in nature, in that it comprised peoples of different races and cultures from three different continents. With the rise in European influence and domination in subsequent centuries, the Muslim world experienced a decline in influence and was subjected to a period of conquest and colonization by Europe. Its heritage of pluralism and diversity, mediated through the instrumentality of the state and a legal system (based on the *Sharia*, but complemented by the incorporation of traditional, indigenous customs known as *urf* or *adat* and by state prescriptions such as the *qanun* of the Ottoman Empire) suffered erosion and marginalization. Moreover, the confluence of Muslim traditions with those of the west and other cultures, that had given Islamic civilization its cosmopolitan character, lost its dynamism and creative impulse, to be overtaken in time by notions of the nation-state, derived from secular, European, and other modern influences. Such a heritage, in differing states of balance and tension, marks most contemporary Muslim societies and states.

Muslims who are now residents of Europe and North America reflect this complex and mutated inheritance of history, culture and influences. While they may generally share a commitment to the defining role of Islam in their lives, their understanding, practice, and capacity to adapt such a heritage to new living conditions varies considerably.

Their experience, however, serves as a case study to illustrate how new and different religious and cultural heritages have to reimagine and rethink their inheritance in different and sometimes hostile legal and national contexts. Such a process also forces the host society to articulate responses to new patterns of life against the background of its own history of dealing with freedom of religion, an articulation that is by no means totally circumscribed or engraved indelibly in past experience. We are therefore compelled to ask not only how we might understand this new diversity, but also to question assumed notions of pluralism, that must be redefined to include indigenous groups excluded from past discourse and strangers from other shores.

This comparative perspective takes on added importance in the current geopolitical context, where diversity is not simply more visible through the media and in legal and religious dialogue, but also because perceptions of diversity have been contaminated by a climate of "culture wars" in which debate and dialogue have been replaced very often by confrontation and violence. The role of law, as an overarching central mediating institution, is crucial in understanding the difficult issues and in adjudicating and negotiating difference, a role in civil society that sometimes the state and institutionalized religion, have failed to play adequately.

If one considers also the often ambiguous role of the media in representing the cultures and religions of "immigrants" and minorities, then we can begin to grasp better how a climate of public opinion is often shaped, driving politicians to focus on narrow and parochial interests in addressing the role of the state. Some of the earlier chapters have highlighted how the "law" and its instruments defended freedom of religion in the same way they had protected freedom of expression. It is ironic therefore that current wisdom among media specialists suggests that there exists a "chasm of misunderstanding and ignorance" between the practitioners of journalism and religion.[2] In the case of Islam, this chasm is even wider given the context of events in the Middle East and the transfer of religious conflicts to Europe and America, reviving some of the older stereotypes and prejudices associated with the Middle Ages. Muslim immigrants, like others in the past, notably Jews, have had to carry a double burden—the surviving prejudice of history and the existing pejorative image attached to their faith and culture.

Although it is difficult, at this point, to provide accurate figures, it has been suggested that anywhere from 3 to 5 million people in North America identify themselves as Muslims. We know that the early European explorers of the New World were accompanied by those of "Moorish" background, whose heritage had been shaped by Islam. Certainly, thousands of Muslims of African origin were brought to the Americas in the eighteenth and nineteenth centuries against their will as slaves. Studies have shown that among emigrants from the Ottoman Empires from 1865 to 1920, at least 80,000 Muslims of Syrian and Lebanese origin came to America. The bulk of the migration from Asia, Africa, and eastern Europe is more recent and accelerated by the changes in immigration laws that allowed large-scale migration from the Third World. Accurate statistics are difficult to come by, so it is difficult to verify the estimates that we have for the immigrant Muslim population in the New World and African-American Muslims who have sought to recover a Muslim identity from the past.[3]

The purpose of this chapter is to illustrate, through our examination of three issues, how immigrant Muslims have interacted with mainstream society. The issues involve interrelated elements: first establishing and creating community spaces for gathering and prayer; second, addressing the normative values embodied in family life and tradition, within an alternative and primarily secular context of law and rights; and third realizing the importance of education as a tool for furthering identity and opportunity within competing and yet assimilative national models.

Making Space

The first theme involves "making space." In one sense a host culture or society makes space for others in order that they might become part of it; in another sense the new arrivals "make space" more literally as they create the markers that embody the places in which they will express their heritage of faith and culture. In the case of Muslims, in whose history architecture has been such a powerful symbol to manifest their presence and power, the "making space" has taken the form of building mosques or congregational centers in which religious, social, and cultural identity can be expressed.

Extending further our trope of the environment, we note that there are two ways in which we construct communities. We may conserve or rehabilitate place as well as tradition or we may design and innovate new structures within which to re-vision a heritage. Mosques and other places of gathering also become extensions of ethnic and family identity, meeting places where relationships can be grounded, maintained, and nurtured. Buildings and spaces include and exclude, enclose and disclose. They are markers of identity and permeability for us as well as the other. They also help define relationships to those with whom the larger local or national space is shared.

My first example concerns a plan to build, in the early 1980s, a religious and cultural center for the Muslims of central Oklahoma in the city of Edmond.[4] More than 1,000 persons signed a petition opposed to such a center, citing their fear of allowing a terrorist network to be established that could threaten the American way of life! Their fears had been fueled by reports of such terrorists having been responsible for hijacking of airlines. Leaders of the Muslim community, headed by a noted Oklahoma heart specialist, Dr. Nazih Zuhdi, stunned by the opposition, decided not to go through with the deal. An editorial in the *Oklahoma Observer* had these pertinent remarks to make after the event:

> Reaction to the proposed mosque might have been predicted in some rural backwater in Oklahoma, but Edmond is one of the highest per capita income communities in Oklahoma. The mosque was to be located near Central State University. Edmond boasts one of the highest literacy rates in Oklahoma . . . The community's religious and political hierarchy stepped gently because of Dr. Zuhdi's national reputation as a heart surgeon. Who knows when one of them may need his quick fingers and famous skill? They referred to him as a "good man"—it's his religion that stinks! The thought of having those oily-skinned folks driving in from all over to pollute the pristine atmosphere of the WASPs was just too much. The holy war was brief—Edmond is safe. But for what?

The second example concerns the establishment of the Ismaili Center and Jamatkhana in Burnaby, British Columbia, completed in 1985. As Don Mowatt, the CBC producer recollected the events in a program broadcast much later,[5] the center had been born in a climate of racial and cultural suspicion. It had been initially opposed by neighbors who feared intrusion of strange customs and rites. He traced how in time the building, with its striking architectural character and sensitivity to regional characteristics, came to be perceived as a common treasure. Ironically, the architect, Bruno Freschi, was a Canadian, who had sought to create a contemporary building that would respect and reinterpret the architectural and cultural values of a Muslim community in a space far removed in time and geography from the origins of their religious and cultural tradition and yet affirming a commitment to enlarge the cultural vocabulary of their new home. Here was a case where another narrative could be added to the master narrative, without cultural values being totally assimilated.

The third example offers a more dramatic choice, where a decision to re-create an exclusive environment was made by an American Muslim community. Such a task was initiated by a group of Muslims in the semiarid and mountainous region of northern New Mexico near the town of Abiquiu. The site was called *Dar-al-Islam.*

The plans for the mosque, which were soon completed, called for the building to be constructed of material indigenous to New Mexico, adobe and brick. The technique of building with adobe had been introduced into America hundreds of years earlier by the Spanish, who, in turn, had probably acquired it during the period of Muslim rule in Spain that lasted for more than 800 years. A great deal of the original technique had fallen by the wayside, however, and no one in New Mexico was capable of constructing the exquisite vaulting domes that were such an integral part of traditional designs. So a working seminar for masons, attended by adobe specialists from all over America, was organized. Hasan Fathy, the famous Muslim architect from Egypt (who died in 1993), attended and brought with him two Egyptian masons to teach the ancient techniques.

The following year, construction started on the mosque. Already, several of those who had attended the seminar had become Muslims and were working full-time on the project. Within a year of very hectic work, the mosque was completed, and a grand opening was held that was attended by architects and builders from all over the United States. While *Dar-al-Islam* was conceived as a complete religious and cultural environment, in which Muslim values could be embodied and preserved, the experience of those living there over the years has not been entirely consistent with the original vision. The space and its role have undergone change as has the direction of its programs of education, employment, and cultural life.

These examples illustrate the range of cultural and legal issues involved in creating new spaces and also suggest the differing options Muslims have chosen to exercise in America. The initial obstacles stem from a persistent racial and cultural prejudice common to both Canada and the United States.

At the local level such prejudice often manifests itself in the use of restrictions and covenants to block or limit the construction and establishment of mosques or similar structures. Often this has meant that Muslim communities have had to move away from preferable locations to zones where such local legal rules are not applicable. The case of Oklahoma is further compounded by hysteria generated by media attention following an international airline hijacking in the Middle East. The New Mexico model consciously sought to establish a remote community, whose character would be self-enclosed and self-sufficient. In general, since the 1980s, most Muslim communities have had great success in building mosques and centers. In North America there are now several hundred such buildings that offer Muslims space for gathering and prayer. Many of these may be spaces converted to congregational use.

The creation of mosques and religious and cultural centers in North America and Europe, has involved for Muslims, an exercise in negotiation and encounter with local, municipal regulations governing the building of religious spaces. That has proven easier where local law and policies have been complemented by benign national legal strategies encouraging and even subsidizing these developments. In the case of Edmond and Burnaby, the permits for occupying and building on specific sites were discussed and negotiated in the context of local councils and municipal law. In Edmond, the city council denied permission to build, while in Burnaby, the permit was eventually granted, through negotiation. By contrast with these examples of outright opposition or grudging concession, Holland offers an excellent example of a liberal, western legal tradition seeking to accommodate the entry of Muslims and other religious groups by facilitating the creation of mosques. While the Dutch constitution articulates a separation between church and state and institutes the principle of nondiscrimination among various religious communities, successive national governments have recognized the need to subsidize space and even social and cultural activities among Muslims. The practice eventually ended in the mid-1980s, and the government has encouraged municipalities to facilitate the foundation and maintenance of mosques. The extent of the practice varies across Holland, but it is noteworthy that where local non-Muslim groups have voiced objections, their focus tends to be on issues such as "noise" (the prayer-call for instance): on the whole municipalities in Holland have been forced to develop policies to enable and assist Muslims in creating new environments that incorporate the practice of their faith as well as the sustaining of social and cultural activity around the mosque.[6]

Local legal and municipal frameworks probably offer the most significant opportunity for Muslims and others to build community consensus and relations in the long run. It is success at this level, building on the tradition of the public square, encouraged by national strategies and policies for forging multicultural and multifaith understanding that will engender positive change and a spirit of accommodation. Already, favorable legal conditions and tax regulations, have engendered and built on a spirit of Muslim philanthropy and giving, to enable these communities to support mosques and centers in North America and Europe. Muslims are contributing to the creation of a shared architectural heritage as they construct visible signs of their presence in the local landscape.

Family Life and Values

The present Muslim population in North America and Europe has its roots in many different parts of the world, from Albania to Zanzibar. They are not a single homogeneous unit. This geographic, ethnic, national, and cultural diversity is reflected in the variety of traditions that constitute the family among Muslims in the west.[7]

Family life in Islam assumes the necessity for and regulation of marriage. Disparaging popular images of Muslim women hidden under folds of clothing and shuttered away in exotic harems have created the unfortunate stereotype of the oppressed Muslim woman in popular western consciousness. In reality, the regulations of the Quran sought to define rights as well as obligations for men and women in marriage, assuming a degree of choice: this is true of rights of divorce and inheritance, opportunities for participation in the public sphere, and safeguards for a distinctive feminine identity in matters of dress and behavior. As among other religious traditions, notably "fundamentalist" understandings of Christianity and Judaism, some in Islam have interpreted these principles in a very conservative manner to assure a separate and subsidiary role for women in public life. In the overall context of Muslim history and society, however, the status and role of women is contextualized within the larger view of the integrity and vitality of the family as the cornerstone of social relationships.[8]

The Quran, within the context of the social circumstances of the times, permitted a man to have a maximum of four wives at one time, thus regulating a system that had allowed for unlimited cohabitation. At the same time, it encouraged the view that equity might only be truly possible within a monogamous household. The Quran recognized the possibility of breakdown in marriage and allowed for divorce after reasonable attempts had been made to reconcile the parties. Marriage was to be accompanied by the signing of a legally binding contract, with the husband specifying the amount of settlement to be made to the wife in the event of divorce. Divorced persons, widows, and widowers were also encouraged to remarry.

Another area of family life touched on in the Quran is that of inheritance. The Quran prohibited Arab custom whereby a son could inherit his stepmother as part of his father's legacy and then convert the wife's property and gifts into his own. It defined a share of the inheritance for both male and female children, granting, in the context of social roles of the time, the male child twice as much as the female. The widow is granted one-eighth, if there are also children involved; if not, she receives one-fourth.

Some Muslim modernists have argued that such regulations based on ethnic and rural frameworks offer alternatives that can be adapted when society undergoes urbanization and that the inheritance shares should change accordingly.[9] A particular concern was also expressed for orphans, needy children, and the disadvantaged within the family and society, for whom particular care was to be exercised and special funds set aside for their use. Compassion and care was thus given institutionalized shape through philanthropic activity. The Quranic teaching on sharing one's wealth and giving charity, through *zakat* and *khums*, for example, provided the basis for institutionalizing through the state or through private endowments and community initiatives, mechanisms that allowed such giving to be specifically directed, by individuals or community leaders, to those most in need.

The legal articulation of the Muslim concept of the family provided individuals with identity and status, and protected them through rights and obligations. The extension of the kinship relationship through marriage created a wider network of contacts. The emphasis on the cultural notions of privacy, intimacy, and seclusion in the sphere of life affecting women, however, gave rise to distinct categories of relationship with those within the kinship sphere and those without. For instance, for Muslims from South Asia, this came to be expressed in terms of two dialectically opposed categories, our (*apna*) and those outside (*ghayr*), which in turn denoted the personal and family spheres as against the impersonal, public sphere.[10] Muslim society, in general, thus developed a patrilocal household that was extended through endogamy and was characterized by strong ties of descent. On the whole, this cultural heritage of social grouping and family values characterized the value system of immigrant Muslims. It provided for a strong sense of personal identity within the private, family network, with its element of mutual support and kinship solidarity, reinforced by a strong Islamic emphasis on the centrality of the bonds of the family.

The first major area of change for Muslim families in the west involved the loss of what was perceived as a traditional cultural environment. Coherence in Muslim family life, it was believed, came from having the security of a well-defined framework of values and institutions to support it. Since the inherited legal rules embodied in the *Sharia* could not be fully applied in

North America, and the cultural network of family or kinship ties did not exist in the same way to reinforce it, tradition might guide how families lived, but these traditions were not anchored within the law and in a shared social setting. In fact, the legal status of individuals within the new system in the west was of a completely different order, assuming individual rights rather than one's status within the family or social unit. In addition, there was a major transition involved in adapting to a highly postindustrialized, market economy, that kept shifting through successive recessions and periods of growth. Polygamy was prohibited and in many cases, marriages had to be notarized by civil authorities.

It can be said that the most significant impact of this cultural dissociation has been on the lives of Muslim women.[9] As in their home countries in modern times, many had to choose, of necessity and as an extension of their new roles, to work outside the home. The wearing of traditional forms of dress, ways of relating to others, both men and women, outside the family, and the degree of displacement of the dominant role of the husband in the household were all issues that came to the fore. Women have thus borne the greater brunt of the stresses created by migration and settlement. The overall expectation of the traditional role of the Muslim woman is not very different from that of many other ethnic and religious groups; as a mother, she is the anchor of the family; as a wife, her role is to complement and enhance the image of her family and husband; and as a homemaker, she is the one on whom the bulk of responsibility falls for the organization and maintenance of the household. This traditional role expectation still constitutes a norm in most Muslim families, but clearly some fundamental changes have taken place in the lives of Muslim women in America. The most important is the transition of women from the sphere of work in the private space within the house to the realm of public space in the workplace. This has meant that the essentially separate worlds of Muslim men and women prevalent in the urban, public sphere in their home cultures, have now become fused. One corollary of this is that Muslim women also tend to participate more actively in the life of prayer and worship in the mosque, whereas in the past they may have prayed almost exclusively at home. Most Muslim womens' social lives, however, still revolve around networks linked to the mosque and the local community. Marriage, however, is entirely monogamous in its North American setting, and increasingly becoming a matter of personal choice rather than simply of family arrangements.

The strains that mark intergenerational conflict are as much in evidence among Muslims as among other tradition-oriented American groups. Some Muslims perceive their children to have imitated aspects of unacceptable social behavior, such as dating, drinking, drugs, and so forth. They also worry about the likelihood of intermarriage. Again, Muslim girls, who, according to traditional Muslim law, are forbidden to marry outside the faith, represent a vulnerable area of stress in such families. In general, as the new generation grows up, the intergenerational gap in perception of North American versus the past home-country system of values tends to grow wider.[11]

It is unlikely that existing codes of family life in North America can be significantly altered to take account of the diverse family traditions of Muslims or for that matter, other incoming religious groups. However, as in Europe, certain efforts can be made to promote reunification of families, greater sensitivity to religious and cultural values in family and social work counseling, and appropriate flexibility in affording rights to individuals within traditional family structures and codes based on foreign law. At the same time, vulnerable groups such as women and children, need greater protection and empowerment during periods of transition. As in Europe, issues related to the recognition of marriages in the home country, divorce, and custody rights related to children, are likely to arise and the court system can only benefit and be an enabler in contributing to changing needs and perceptions, through greater understanding and openness.

Among Muslims in Canada and the United States, as indeed in the world, given their diversity, these strategies can by no means be homogeneous. At the heart of all their responses, one can discern a hope shared by more and more North Americans, that of establishing a balance among all the elements of the world they live in: a greater emphasis on human values in an increasingly programmable information-oriented society; a need for ethical underpinning in the face of a secularization of the means of moral decision making, and an aspiration for the enhancement of the quality of individual and social life and the environment. Erik Erikson's insights have shown us that families across generations strive to create conditions for what he called the "maintenance of the world."[12] The study of American life, *Habits of the Heart* points to the necessity of moral tradition and "communities of memory" as vital to the eventual transformation of our social ecology.[13] Better mutual understanding can help engender a common pursuit of how different groups and faiths can build on their heritage of ethics to combat the negative consequences of change.

Education

Education in democratic societies is often viewed as one of the most significant forces of integration and assimilation into mainstream values. It provides the means to participate in a nation's political and economic life, while conversely creating attitudes and promoting values that might be viewed as undermining inherited traditional and religious ones. For most immigrant groups, such as Muslims, it may not be possible to create their own private system of education, hence a major part of the socialization into the host society will occur through the public educational system.

The attitudes and assumptions of many teachers and fellow students are likely to be shaped by the same popular assumptions held in general by other groups in society. Many schools have felt the need to develop teacher education programs that address the needs of religious and ethnic minorities, and to make their curricula reflect diversity. While this concern is shared by teachers and parents in general, there has of late been growing resistance to what is perceived as undue emphasis on the needs of minority cultures and the steady erosion of established, dominant euro-American values, grounded in the classical and Judeo-Christian traditions. Given the differing histories of education and differing attitudes toward the integration of religion in publicly funded schools in Canada, Europe, and the United States, it is unlikely that uniform Muslim approaches to the issue can be developed. There is case law on religious belief and its relevance to public education in all three regions that places constraints on the ability of Muslim parents to educate their children as they wish with support from the State.

Though there is a long history in Canada of support for religious education, whether Roman Catholic or Protestant, within the publicly funded school system, based in the British North America Act of 1867,[14] recent rulings suggest that the courts, in protecting the rights granted to all Canadians according to the Charter of Rights and Freedoms are now committed to a more secularized form of public school education. A recent Canadian example from Ontario, traced more fully in the chapter by Elizabeth Shilton,[15] illustrates how the courts have responded where parents of non-Christian children challenged existing practices of opening and closing exercises that reflected a Christian pattern of religious belief. These practices were found to offend the freedom of religion and conscience clause in the charter, section 2(a). There is also recent authority to the effect that religious minorities, other than those specially favored by section 93, have no claim to state support for the religious education of their children. Only in provinces that provide funds for denominational schools more generally is access to public education for a religious community such as Muslims, possible.

As a consequence, Canadian Muslim parents have the choice of creating private schools for their children, which may or may not be supported across Canada by public funds. Within the public school system, they may object to religious teaching that they might regard as indoctrination of another faith but cannot demand to have their children be educated in their own religious tradition.

On the whole, Canadian Muslims have different views on how they wish their children to receive Islamic-oriented education. Given the diversity of Muslims, there is, of course, no consensus.

England, by contrast, offers a different kind of illustration. In some school districts in cities such as Bradford, with a large majority of Muslim students, attempts by Muslim groups to seek control over the curriculum and administration of such schools have been rejected by the courts. In the early 1980s some Muslim parents in Bradford had applied locally for the establishment of five schools. Rejection at the level of the borough council caused the parents to take the issue to the minister of education and eventually for review before the High Court. The arguments against allowing such control were based on the view that it would promote social segregation and erosion of the quality of education. In 1993, after further appeals and judicial consideration, the minister of education rejected the application.[16] While a segregated mode of education based on ethnic or religious identity could still easily develop in Britain, there is another answer. Much could be gained at a national level by creating balanced curricula that attempt a proper educational perspective in integrating cultural and religious plurality. The School of Oriental and African Studies of the University of London is already showing how this can be done at the level of tertiary education.

In the United States, under the "nonestablishment" clause of The First Amendment, public schools cannot endorse or include instruction that would promote or privilege the views of any religion. By the same token religious groups cannot secure federal or state funding for educational costs that are seen as promoting their religion. Only if the money is made available for purposes classifiable as secular or otherwise viewed as not involving support of religion (e.g., transportation, medical or therapeutic services, or communication services to physically challenged students) has expenditure by the state been upheld. Public schools may be able to offer courses on religion and culture as part of the curriculum, provided that such courses are nondirective and do not privilege or promote any religion or religious practice. Muslim parents, like others, can legitimately object to having their children subjected to the claims or practices of another faith tradition, but cannot demand that their children be educated in the Muslim tradition, unless it be in their own privately funded schools.

In recent years, the language of "culture wars" has dominated debate in America about such issues as the proper role of religion in society and public education. Observers such as Stephen Carter have tried to demonstrate the marginalization of religion in public discourse about culture and values.[17] Other vigorous proponents of American values, such as William Bennett, former Secretary of Education, have written of the "de-valuing of America," arguing that religion has been shunned in public education. He maintains that "American culture and American greatness—perhaps more accurately American goodness—draw strength and direction from the Judeo-Christian tradition."[18] Muslim leaders, educators, and intellectuals are just entering the debate. An important role in building common purpose through higher education, is evident in the changing curriculum and work of some law schools.

One Muslim scholar of education in the United States, has suggested that Muslims might best approach their situation by seeking to "preserve Islamic identity in an integrative manner within the pluralistic western society."[19] The challenge is likely to take time to resolve, but with cultural empathy and educational initiatives, knowledge about Muslims and their civilizations and cultures can become part of the mainstream curricula in the humanities and social sciences, without privileging any one faith tradition. At Harvard and at Emory University, for example, we are witnessing a gradual integration of materials and case studies involving Muslim societies and legal systems.

Concluding Remarks

It would be appropriate in summing up a discussion of the specific issues addressed in the chapter, to offer some cautionary remarks on methodology in the humanities and social sciences as they deal with questions of law, religion, and the state. In an essay, as far back as 1982, Mary Douglas, the noted anthropologist, remarked that "events have taken religious studies by surprise."[20] As examples, she cited that fact that scholars were unable to foretell the so-called resurgence of Islam, the recent revival of traditional religious forms, and the renewal of right-wing political values based on fundamentalist interpretation of scripture in the United States and elsewhere in the world. In 1996, the issues seem hardly to have changed. Religious studies scholars were taken unawares, Dr. Douglas contends, because of the rigid structure of their assumptions and the fact that their eyes were glued to those conditions of modern life identified by Max Weber as antipathetic to religion. Surely if, in the social sciences and the humanities, as indeed in the study of law, we are to begin to make better sense of the relationship between religion and society, then we may need to discard some of these methodological assumptions that have caused us to focus unduly on secularization as a normative and even desirable process. Academic institutions and intellectuals, as well as the news media, can play a very constructive role in the public debate over these issues, by recognizing and incorporating the new complexity in the teaching and preparation of those who will have a role to play in politics, law, education, and the media. The peril of a failure to do so, is to extend further the gaps in cultural understanding that endanger the building of a democratic, civil society.

Notes

1. Bernard Lewis, *The Middle East: 2000 Years of History* (London: Weidenfeld and Nicolson, 1995), pp. 269–70.

2. John Dart and Jimmy Allen (eds.), *Bridging the Gap: Religion and the News Media* (Nashville, TN: The Freedom Forum, 1995), p. 3.

3. Farid H. Numan, *The Muslim Population of the United States: "A Brief Statement"* (Washington, D.C.: The American Muslim Council, 1992).

4. The incident is described in Azim Nanji, "The Muslim Family in North America: Continuity and Change," Hariette, P. McAdoo (ed.), *Family Ethnicity: Strength in Diversity* (Newberry Park, CA: Sage Publications, 1993), pp. 230–31.

5. Don Mowatt, *A New Space for Islam*, CBC Radio. (Vancouver BC, March 1993).

6. For Abiqui, see Nanji, pp. 238–39; and for Holland, see W. A. R. Shaded and P. S. Van Koningsveld, "Islam in the Netherlands: Constitutional Law and Islamic Organizations," *Journal of Muslim Minority Affairs*, 16:1 (1996): pp. 111–28.

7. Among recent studies on Muslims in North America and their background, see Yvonne Haddad (ed.), *The Muslims of America* (New York: Oxford University Press, 1991) and with Jane I. Smith (ed.), *Muslim Communities in North America* (Albany: State University of New York, 1994). Also, Fred Denny, "Islam in the Americas" and Lawrence Mamiya, "African American Muslims" in Azim Nanji (ed.), *The Muslim Almanac: A Reference Work on the History, Faith, Cultures, and Peoples of Islam* (Detroit: Gale, 1996), pp. 141–48 and 148–57.

8. For the role of women in Islam, in general, see Leila Ahmed, *Women and Gender in Islam* (New Haven: Yale University Press, 1992).

9. Fazlur Rahman, *Major Themes in the Quran* (Minneapolis: Bibliotheca Islamica, 1980), pp. 49–51.

10. Regula Qureshi and Salm Qureshi in Earle Waugh (ed.), *The Muslim Community in North America* (Edmonton: University of Alberta Press, 1983), p. 134.

11. See the section on "Muslim Women: Gender in Socio-Religious Context," Earle Waugh et al. (eds.), *Muslim Families in North America* (Edmonton: University of Alberta Press, 1991), pp. 256–325. Also, Fariyal Ross Sheriff, "Islamic Identity, Family and Community," *Muslim Families in North America,* pp. 101–17.

12. M. Berman-Gibson, "Eric Erikson and the 'Ethics of Survival,'" *Harvard Magazine* (1984): p. 59.

13. Robert Bellah, *Habits of the Heart: Individualism and Commitment in American Life* (Berkeley: University of California Press, 1985).

14. Constitutional Act, 1867 (U.K.), 30 and 31 Vict., c. 3.

15. A number of cases are cited by Elizabeth Shilton in her contribution to this collection of essays, see ch. 13.

16. Jorgen S. Nielsen, *Muslims in Western Europe* (Edinburgh: Edinburgh University Press, 1995), pp. 53–59.

17. Stephen Carter, *The Culture of Disbelief: How American Law and Politics Trivialize Religious Devotion* (New York: Basic Books, 1993).

18. William Bennett, *The De-Valuing of America* (New York: Summit Books, 1992), p. 208. It would be salutary also to keep in mind as these debates unfold, the general thesis of Edward Said's work *Orientalism* (New York: Pantheon Books, 1978), of the intellectual shortcomings and pitfalls of reified cultural constructions of others and of self.

19. Nimat Hafez Barzangi, "Islamic Education in the United States and Canada: Conception and Practice of the Islamic Belief System," *The Muslims of America*, p. 172.

20. Mary Douglas, "Effects of Modernization on Religious Changes." *Daedalus* 3:4. (Winter, 1982): p. 1.

About the Authors

Robert D. Baird is professor of the history of religions and director of the School of Religion at the University of Iowa.

Justin A. I. Champion is lecturer in history at Royal Holloway College in the University of London.

Elizabeth B. Clark was associate professor of law at Boston University School of Law.

Irwin Cotler is professor of law at McGill University.

Harold Coward is professor of history and director of the Centre for Studies in Religion and Society at the University of Victoria.

Cornelia Hughes Dayton is associate professor of history at the University of Connecticut.

Alvin Esau is professor of law at the University of Manitoba, and executive director of that university's Legal Research Institute.

Martin Fitzpatrick is a senior lecturer in history at the University of Wales, Aberystwyth.

James (Sákéj) Youngblood Henderson is director of the Native Law Centre at the University of Saskatchewan.

Azim A. Nanji is professor and chair of the Department of Religion at the University of Florida.

John McLaren is Lansdowne Professor of Law at the University of Victoria.

Phyllis M. Senese is assistant professor of history at the University of Victoria.

Elizabeth J. Shilton practices education, constitutional, and labor law with the Toronto firm of Cavalluzzo Hayes Shilton McIntyre & Cornish.

Carol Weisbrod is Ellen Ash Peters Professor of Law at the University of Connecticut School of Law.

Index

A

Aboriginal religion and spirituality, 5, 9; Aboriginal languages, 175–79; Aboriginal Shield (Charter of Rights and Freedoms), 171–73, 180–83; *American Indian Religious Freedom Act*, 174–75; ecology, 173–74, 175, 178–79; *Guerin v. The Queen*, 175; Míkmaq rites and 1610 Concordat, 182–83; pluralism and, 182. *See also* Christianity; Canadian Charter of Rights and Freedoms

Alcott, Louise May, 65

American Jewish Congress, 82–84

anti-semitism: Britain, modern, 158–59, 163–64; Colonies and modern North America, 159–61, 164; Christian missionizing and, 163–64; Christian roots of, 154–55; Dreyfus *affaire*, 162; France, modern, 159–60, 161–63; and hate speech, 154–55, 159; Holocaust, 165; *The Protocols of the Elders of Zion*, 161; Reformation and Enlightenment, 156–60, 161; Roman Empire and Middle Ages, 155–56. *See also*, Jews

anti-slavery movement, New England, 7, 63–65, 67–70; and Fugitive Slave Law (1850), 64

Audland, John, 13–14

Aylmer, G. A., 17

B

Baptists, 6, 14, 30–40

Bayle, Pierre, 2–3, 48–49

Beere, Richard, 164

Benwet, William, 235

Berlin, Isiah, 46

Bharati, L. Krishnaswami, 196

Bodyansky, Alexander, 123

Braddick, M., 17

Brigham Young (film), 147

Buergenthal, Thomas, 79

Butler, Bishop, 3, 53–55

C

Canada: British North America Act (BNA), 10, 85–86, 87, 218n.5, 234; culture, 5, 9–10, 88–89, 122, 170–71; denominational schools and the Constitution (section 93), 85–86,